FREEDOM
MANIFESTO

FREEDOM MANIFESTO

WHY
FREE MARKETS
ARE MORAL
AND
BIG GOVERNMENT
ISN'T

STEVE FORBES
and ELIZABETH AMES

CROWN
BUSINESS
NEW YORK

Published in the United States by Crown Business, an imprint of the
Crown Publishing Group, a division of Random House, Inc., New York.
www.crownpublishing.com

CROWN BUSINESS is a trademark and CROWN and the Rising Sun
colophon are registered trademarks of Random House, Inc.

Crown Business books are available at special discounts for bulk
purchases for sales promotions or corporate use. Special editions, including
personalized covers, excerpts of existing books, or books with corporate
logos, can be created in large quantities for special needs.
For more information, contact Premium Sales at (212) 572-2232 or
e-mail specialmarkets@randomhouse.com.

Library of Congress Cataloging-in-Publication Data
is available upon request.

ISBN 978-0-307-95157-1
eISBN 978-0-307-95159-5

Printed in the United States of America

Book design by Lauren Dong
Jacket design by Michael Nagin
Jacket photograph © Win Initiative/Getty Images

1 3 5 7 9 10 8 6 4 2

First Edition

*To those visionary individuals who understand
the moral foundations of free markets and
courageously fight for them*

Contents

Contents

FREEDOM
MANIFESTO

Introduction

A BATTLE FOR THE SOUL
OF AMERICA

OUR GOAL in this book is to turn conventional wisdom on its head and explain why the free markets of democratic capitalism occupy the moral high ground—why economic freedom is the best way to a moral society based on our culture's Judeo-Christian values, rooted in the Golden Rule and the Ten Commandments.

The nation has reached a turning point. In the media, in the classroom, and at the dinner table, debates are raging over health care, energy, entitlements, education—the future of America. They all come down to a single question: What kind of society do we want to be?

To put it another way: What best serves the *public* good—free markets or Big Government?

Until recently, most Americans would have answered "Big Government." Since the 1930s, the perception that President Franklin D. Roosevelt's social welfare programs and massive intervention in the economy rescued the nation from the Great Depression has fostered the belief that Big Government is a prerequisite for a humane society. Calls for more government are almost always couched in morality rhetoric. Big Government is synonymous with "compassion," the *only* way to protect against the destructiveness of markets, the way to provide genuine security and a safety net for the less fortunate.

Free, unfettered markets, in contrast, have been viewed as cold, amoral, and uncaring—the primary cause of most economic and social ills. Commerce gets blamed even when the cause of the problems is government.

We saw this during the financial crisis and recession. The collapse of the housing market was the end result of decades of well-intentioned but ultimately misguided Big Government policies and decisions. But in the emotional aftermath, the private sector was largely seen as the culprit. The epidemic of home foreclosures that preceded the crisis was blamed on "predatory lending." The 2008 stock market crash was entirely the fault of "greedy" Wall Street shortsellers who had driven bank stocks into a death spiral. Meanwhile, free market solutions—such as breaking up and privatizing Fannie Mae and Freddie Mac, the government-created mortgage giants that had helped to fuel the lending mania—were never seriously considered by either policymakers or media commentators.

Even its supporters can have a hard time articulating why free enterprise is moral. During a panel discussion in 2010 at Freedom Fest, an annual gathering of libertarians, a young man raised his hand and said that he had no problem explaining the economic benefits of free markets. Far more difficult, he admitted, "was making the moral argument." Despite being passionate enough to attend a conference on economic freedom, he was hard-pressed to articulate the moral virtues of America's economic system—one that has created the wealthiest society in history and attracted millions of immigrants seeking to realize their dreams in the land of opportunity. During the GOP presidential primaries, contenders like Mitt

Romney and Newt Gingrich were reluctant to defend—and wholeheartedly embrace—the moral virtues of capitalism.

This fundamental belief in Big Government as an unassailable moral force has helped drive government on all levels to a size unprecedented in our history—from less than 10 percent of GDP in 1929 to over 35 percent today.[1] Big Government's "fairness" argument has been used as the rationale for Obama administration regulations and bureaucracies that have increased control over vast swaths of the economy, from banking to health care. It has given us the greatest-ever government spending since World War II—spending that, in the words of Forbes.com columnist Peter Ferrara, has "added as much to the national debt as all prior presidents, from George Washington to George Bush, *combined*!"[2]

None of this has brought about a full economic recovery or led to a more humane, or for that matter, a more contented society. Indeed, the nation is, in the view of many, more polarized than ever before. Instead, something else is occurring.

U.S. polls show a new uneasiness with government. A 2011 Gallup poll found that a "historic" 81 percent of Americans—majorities of both Democrats and Republicans—were dissatisfied with the way the nation was being governed. But even more significant, according to the polling organization, "49% of Americans believe the federal government has become so large and powerful that it poses an immediate threat to the rights and freedoms of ordinary citizens. In 2003, less than a third (30%) believed this."[3]

A growing number of economists, historians, and commentators—along with everyday citizens—are questioning Depression-era orthodoxies. They're recognizing that overly large and bureaucratic government is anything but a force for compassion.

It's not the cure but the cause of critical problems plaguing the economy and society. A consensus is emerging: The only way to a truly fair and moral society is through economic freedom—free people and free markets.

This book will explain what is driving this shift in attitudes, the growing perception that *free markets are moral and Big Government isn't.*

IRONICALLY, THIS disillusionment with Big Government comes during an administration that has sought to embody the ideal of "compassionate government" more aggressively than any other in recent memory. Swept to office by an anxious electorate after the stock market crash of 2008, Barack Obama was heralded as a new FDR. A now famous cover of *Time* magazine depicted him in Roosevelt's iconic pose: chin jutting outward, with hat and spectacles, cigarette in its holder. The president immediately set about engineering his spectacular expansion of government—as *Time* called it, his "New New Deal."[4] He resorted to political payoffs to ram through a reluctant Congress the Patient Protection and Affordable Care Act (a.k.a. "Obamacare"). At this writing, the Supreme Court has yet to rule on this unpopular law. But if allowed to stand, in part or in full, its 2,700 pages of rules and regulations give government new and unprecedented powers over health insurers and providers, and the medical treatment of individuals.

Obamacare was followed shortly afterward by the Dodd-Frank Wall Street Reform and Protection Act, 2,300 pages of regulations and new bureaucracies for the already heavily regulated financial industry. The president approved more significant federal rules—those with an impact over $100 million—than his previous three predecessors.[5]

Four years later, this ambitious program has failed to achieve its goals of fairness and compassion. Instead, the nation's Misery Index, which equals the unemployment rate plus the inflation rate, increased to the highest level in three decades.[6] Among Americans today, people of varying backgrounds and beliefs, there is the growing conviction that *something isn't working.*

Something isn't working. Instead of making health care more affordable, the administration's highly controversial health care reform caused premiums to soar.[7]

Big Government energy initiatives have not made energy—green or otherwise—more available. Fuel prices are higher than ever.

Dodd-Frank legislation aimed at preventing events like the financial crisis of 2008 did not prevent investor losses at MF Global. Credit has become harder than ever to obtain for small businesses. Meanwhile, from Detroit to Washington to Wall Street, instances of cronyism—bailouts, political favors, and exception making—seem to be everywhere.

Something isn't working. Time and time again, Big Government fails to solve problems and deliver on its promise of fairness.

Is it fair, for example, that taxpaying citizens, struggling to stay afloat in a difficult economy, are forced to pay higher prices for gasoline, electricity, and food because of politically driven Big Government policies—from bans on energy production and development to monetary policies that dilute the value of the dollar? Or that they have to pay for lavish salaries and pensions for government workers who retire in their fifties?

Is it fair that politically appointed bureaucrats in an unaccountable federal agency can attempt to stop the airline manufacturer Boeing from opening a new plant that would create desperately needed jobs in South Carolina? Why? Because unions in the company's home state were unhappy that the plant was not located there.

Is it fair that the only solution advocates of Big Government seem to take seriously is more government and more taxation for "millionaires and billionaires"? This, despite the fact that past administrations—Democrat as well as Republican—have demonstrated that opening up the economy through deregulation and meaningful, across-the-board cuts in tax rates (and not targeted gimmicks) is the best way to increase prosperity and job creation. Taxes from "the 1 percent" will barely make a dent in the federal government's $15 trillion national deficit—one that has *doubled* in seven years.[8]

Wall Street Journal columnist Steve Moore asks, "Is it fair that the richest 10% of Americans *shoulder a higher share of their country's income-tax burden than do the richest 10% in every other industrialized nation, including socialist Sweden.*"[9] (Our italics).

Is it fair that nearly half the population today does not pay federal income taxes?

Is it fair for Big Government to grow so big that the total national debt vastly exceeds the annual income of all of the American people *and* the profits of American businesses?

Even supporters of Big Government see an ominous portent in the sovereign debt crises and chronic double-digit jobless levels shaking overextended European welfare states like Greece, France, Italy, and Spain. Media images of riots and desperate bureaucrats have prompted nearly everyone to wonder: Was the welfare state, with its cradle-to-grave security and income redistribution, supposed to lead to *this*? And many people are asking, *Is the United States next*?

Dissatisfaction with Big Government is only part of this new awakening. There is also a new appreciation of *the morality of enterprise*. The technology revolution of the past three decades has given rise to a generation of entrepreneurs who have captured the public imagination in a way once reserved for great artists and rock stars. Witness the global outpouring that followed the passing of Apple founder Steve Jobs in 2011. Jobs's premature death at the age of fifty-five from pancreatic cancer was a cultural touchstone event like the loss of John Lennon or John Kennedy. People of all backgrounds, beliefs, and nationalities wrote about what Jobs meant to them and what they learned from him, posting their feelings on Facebook, via Twitter, and in e-mails, many writing on iPads, iPhones, and MacBooks.

More than 6.3 million people clicked on YouTube to watch his famous 2005 speech to graduating students at Stanford University, entranced by his now legendary story of personal empowerment: how he was adopted by parents of modest means because his biological parents had not wanted him; how he dropped out of college and later launched Apple, only to be fired from the company that he cofounded; finally, how he was able to overcome his setback and to eventually return to Apple to create the inventions that were his life's defining achievements. Even Occupy Wall Street demonstrators took time out from protesting to post tributes. Walter Isaacson's monumental biography of Jobs, published days after his death, sold nearly 380,000 *in its very first week.*

This tidal wave of sentiment reflected more than simple gratitude for the products that Jobs had created. It was also an instinctive and universal recognition of the *moral dimension* of

Jobs's achievement. Like few other individuals, Steve Jobs embodied and articulated the moral essence of human enterprise: the ability of an individual to create innovations that help others. He did so by pursuing his passions and developing his extraordinary powers of creativity to the fullest.

At the same time people were mourning the death of this great entrepreneur, President Obama was demanding more taxpayer dollars be spent to "create jobs"—after trillions of dollars in "stimulus" had dismally failed in reviving the economy. Yet Apple's founder had created, directly and indirectly, millions of jobs in the United States and around the world *without taking a dime of taxpayer money.*

Jobs and his partner, Steve Wozniak, built Apple with capital from investors and investment bankers who eventually took their company public—the kind of people now being assailed as "greedy" by Occupy Wall Street protesters and many advocates for bigger government.

There has also been a downside to these achievements. In some sectors of the economy, jobs were destroyed. The iPod and iTunes that allowed people to buy music online devastated music retailers. The graphic arts and music editing capabilities of Mac software also displaced people in the printing and audio industries. Jobs himself was no angel. Famed for his petulant personality, he could be unsparing with employees and ruthless with those who crossed him. His life was by no means a perfect picture.

But the value Jobs and his company generated far outweighed the negatives. Opportunities and wealth were created for millions of people—Apple employees, the company's shareholders, and the people who sold Apple products or used them in their own businesses. *No government program could produce the moral benefit that Jobs delivered to society.*

It is worth noting that among those reflecting on Steve Jobs's death was Sami Moubayed, a university professor in Syria, the birthplace of Jobs's biological father. Moubayed wrote that, while young Syrians were excited about their connection to the visionary entrepreneur, they realized that "had he worked in Syria, he would probably not have achieved any of his innovations."[10] That's because Syria does not provide, in Moubayed's words, "the eco-system and supporting environment." The socialist nation has tight controls on banks and economic policies that were ostensibly imposed to address "class disparities."[11] What they did was create poverty: mean wages are around $2.61 an hour.

The United States isn't Syria. But decades of proliferating Big Government bureaucracy and regulation in this country are today undermining a moral society by destroying economic and personal freedom. Government was supposed to know best for us. But today there are increasing instances of Big Government bureaucracies and regulations violating moral principles. We have seen this with the health care law that resulted in the administration forcing policies on the Catholic Church that people of all faiths saw as a violation of religious liberty. But that is far from the only example. Big Government domination of health care has led to a new ethic of "parsimonious care" that observers feel conflicts with the age-old beliefs of the medical profession, by placing cost over the patient's best interest.[12] Others are dismayed by the growing abuse of eminent domain laws—local governments forcing individuals to sell homes and businesses, clearing the way for commercial projects that benefit municipalities. Big Government's myopic bureaucracies can sometimes forget they're in the business of helping people— such as when the City of New York announced it would no longer accept food donations from churches and synagogues because it could not monitor their fiber, fat, and salt contents.[13] More and more Americans are coming to see Big Government as being guilty of the sins that statists ascribe to the private sector. Its ever-expanding bureaucracies and policies are driven by selfishness, greed, and the hunger for political power.

Questions are also being raised about the true legacy of FDR. Economists and historians, including Amity Shlaes, Burton Folsom, John Cochrane, and Robert Higgs, have all persuasively made the case that FDR's incessant interventionism, in fact, prolonged the Great Depression. The taxes needed for FDR's Keynesian spending and job creation programs sucked capital out of the economy. FDR's price controls and production quotas also created uncertainty that inhibited businesses from hiring. All this delayed recovery until after World War II.

People are also better informed than ever before about current events, better able to see through Big Government morality rhetoric. Until the late 1970s, there were only three major networks. Radio was a local medium. Today there are countless news outlets such as cable, national talk radio, and, of course, the Internet. They're providing a forum for nontraditional perspectives, including a new appreciation of the moral foundations of free enterprise and free markets.

THIS BOOK is intended to give voice to these perceptions. The interests of a humane and compassionate society are best served through economic freedom. Throughout history, free markets of democratic capitalism have done more than any other system to raise standards of living and promote prosperity, improving lives and leading to what the philosophers call "human flourishing."

Free markets enable people to channel their creative energies into meeting the wants and needs of others, improving living standards and making life better by turning scarcity into abundance. Open markets have helped the poor and everyone else by unleashing unprecedented creativity, generating wealth, and raising living standards. Promoting the values of trust and cooperation, generosity, and democracy, economic freedom has been a more powerful force for individual rights, self-determination—and morality—than any government bureaucracy.

The question that arises in any discussion of the morality of free market capitalism is, If markets are moral, how can you get people like Bernard Madoff (or any other scammer you wish to substitute)? There are unquestionably greedy people to be found in free markets. There are bad people in all societies. But democratic capitalism is the most moral system because it does the best job of channeling our energies into activities that benefit all of us.

Politicians and activists portray Big Government as essential to safeguarding the common good. There is no question we need government to protect our rights and assure the rule of law. But overly large and politicized government ends up undermining a moral society. Instead of empowering people, Big Government programs, from welfare subsidies to corporate bailouts, promote dependency and undermine personal responsibility, encouraging both people and companies to make bad decisions. Overbearing regulations and excessive taxation hold people back from starting and growing businesses. They inhibit economic activity and wealth creation, keeping individuals and society from advancing. Intrusive rules—from insurance regulations to trans-fat bans—restrict enterprise, limit individual choice, and encourage abuses of power.

In this highly politicized, bureaucratic world, there is frequently little and often no connection between effort and reward. Politically driven regulations and programs—from corporate subsidies to antitrust laws—favor the interests of the powerful and keep newcomers from rising up. People and companies advance by currying political favor or gaming the system. Instead of promoting cooperation, Big Government tends to polarize society, as various interest groups, young and old, rich and poor, jockey for favors. Instead of encouraging human flourishing and abundance, this politicized, controlled environment leads to rigidity and scarcity. Economies and markets dominated by government are characterized by stagnation and moral malaise—fewer products and services, less innovation, lower standards of living, as well as distrust, unfairness, and corruption.

WE HAVE *almost* been here before. Similar questions about Big Government were raised in the 1970s. The expansion of government under not only Jimmy Carter but also Richard Nixon resulted in a decade of "stagflation." The resulting disillusionment with government helped bring about a renaissance in free market economics that challenged the statist orthodoxies of FDR. In 1980, Milton and Rose Friedman published the book *Free to Choose.* An instant bestseller and later an immensely popular TV series, it provided the intellectual foundation for a movement that reached its height in the years following Ronald Reagan's election. Reagan's economic program liberated the economy. Inflation was conquered, tax rates were slashed, and suffocating regulations were lifted. This not only turned around the U.S. economy but also set off a wave of global prosperity. Nations ranging from India to Sweden followed Reagan's lead and liberalized their own economies. The resulting three decades of growth came to a halt only with the current financial crisis and subsequent recession—traumas that were, as we show later, government created.

Reagan's success should have demolished the moral credibility of Big Government paternalism. But it's difficult to overcome old prejudices. As the saying goes, old beliefs die hard. And bad ideas have a particular tenacity. Since ancient times free markets have been seen as valuing profits over people. Socrates asserted that "the more men value money the less they value virtue." The Apostle Paul declared, "The love of money is the root of all evil." Trade is too often perceived not as an exchange but as a transaction that is "zero-sum"—where one person takes something at the expense of the other.

In the media, universities, movies, TV shows, and literature, corporations and business executives have long been portrayed as greedy exploiters. Free markets are characterized as Darwinian free-for-alls in which the very strongest survive and everyone else loses. Even those who appreciate the ability of commerce to provide material prosperity insist Big Government is essential to prevent the inherent coldness and ruthlessness of markets from destroying civil society.

The belief in government's moral preeminence remains deeply embedded in the nation's DNA. Statist rhetoric—or some would say their *guilt trip*—is good at putting people on the defensive. Those who defend free markets and free enterprise solutions are called uncaring and heartless. The decision to support or oppose a new Big Government regulation is usually portrayed by Big Government advocates as a choice between selfishness and compassion. *You mean you don't want people to be able to get health care?*

It's hard to advocate pro-market policies when those who publicly do so in the media are so often demonized. As *Wall Street Journal* columnist William McGurn quipped, believers in Big Government can appear "to see no practical difference between those who oppose higher taxes and those who would chop off a woman's fingertips for wearing nail polish."[14]

Supporters of free enterprise commonly hear questions like, How is it moral for people to lose their retirement money in plunging financial markets? What about Wall Street greed and sky-high compensation? Why is there growing income disparity? Such questions are usually triggered by a corporate downsizing, a downbeat employment statistic, a scandal or crisis, such as in health care. Events like these are usually covered by a media hostile to markets.

The media had a field day when investment banker Greg Smith published a *New York Times* essay, "Why I Am Leaving Goldman Sachs." He accused his former employer of being profit-hungry and foisting investment products on clients that did not meet their needs.[15]

In the torrent of coverage that followed, no one asked what caused Smith to suddenly leave Goldman after twelve years or whether Goldman clients agreed with his assessment. After all, if things were as bad as Smith alleged, then why wasn't there a mass exodus of clients, which include some of the world's biggest corporations and institutional investors?

Peter Cohan observed on Forbes.com, "The question is why does Goldman have any clients at all?" One possible reason, he speculates, is that "the benefits of working with Goldman exceed its costs."[16]

Unfortunately, the overwhelming focus on greed typifies today's media environment of short takes, where the incident or statistic of the moment that supposedly illustrates greed gets the most attention. Inconvenient details, like the reality of the situation, always get short shrift. Blaming subprime mortgage foreclosures—or the high cost of health insurance or gasoline— on rapacious companies is far more easily understood than an explanation of what actually happens when bad government policies distort a market.

Finally, there is a natural tendency of people to look to place blame when something goes wrong. George Mason University economics professor Bryan Caplan found that people often have a pessimistic bias when it comes to assessing the economy, seeing problems as more dire than they really are.[17]

Thus, the progress of free markets in raising living standards usually goes unreported. Higher airfares get headlines. Lower airfares do not. The accent is so heavily on the negative that it's hard to appreciate the positive bigger picture—if it ever gets mentioned.

Reporters, even those in favor of free markets, also tend to use words like *reform* when discussing legislation. We tend to think of reform as improvement. But many Big Government laws called reform are anything but. People would think differently about the morality of Big Government "reform" if there were greater truth in labeling. For example, what if Obamacare had been named something like "Government Control of Health Care Law"? Remember, many of its most fervent supporters, including then speaker Nancy Pelosi, never even read the bill. What would they have thought if they'd known—as we're still learning now—the law was to result in 159 new bureaucracies, countless regulations, an array of new taxes, and more than 16,000 IRS agents enforcing the mandatory buying of health insurance? Or if they had known that certain provisions of the law would eviscerate private insurers? It's doubtful they would have been quite so passionate in defending the "morality" of the law.

EACH CHAPTER in this book contrasts the virtues of free markets with the moral failings of excessive government. For instance, when it comes to health care—or any market—the real questions that should be asked are, *Do you want an innovative, free market focused on meeting the needs of individual consumers? Or do you want a lumbering, rigid, bureaucratic system that first and foremost meets its own political needs—namely those of politicians and government unions?*

That is the focus of chapter 1, "FedEx *or* the Post Office?," which illuminates a central distinction: *Free markets meet people's needs, while Big Government meets its own needs.* Its foremost need is to expand its bureaucracy and its power. This was observed decades ago by behavioral scientist C. Northcote Parkinson in the book *Parkinson's Law.* It's no accident that, while the nation struggled during the recession, Washington, D.C., kept growing. Its economy racked up an Asia-level growth rate of 6.9 percent between 2007 and 2010—compared with 1.1 percent in other major cities.[18] The insatiable appetite for growth is behind many programs and policies sold to voters as moral necessities—including the administration's controversial $787 billion in economic stimulus, which was supposed to spur the economy by creating jobs. Most of the money went to fund existing jobs in state and local governments.

Chapter 2 poses the question "Freedom *or* Big Brother?" The decision between free markets and Big Government is one between choice and coercion. America's Big Government may not be Big Brother. However, people who support Big Government laws would have second thoughts if they realized the potential for abuse.

People concerned by the supposed power of big corporations like Walmart ignore the real threat to liberty from the micromanaging rules, regulations, and bureacracies that are the by-product of too much government. These responses go well beyond eminent domain and Obamacare. For example, unaccountable Big Government agencies like the EPA and the Department of Agriculture regularly send armed agents to the workplaces and homes of individuals accused of regulatory violations. Chapter 2 also discusses the destructive way governments engage in coercion by manipulating the value of its money.

The tendency toward such abuses is why economist Friedrich Hayek warned in the 1930s that too much government can take people down "the road to serfdom"—or tyranny. In contrast, government-dominated nations that liberalize their economies see a flowering of political freedoms. Economic freedom is ultimately personal freedom.

Big Government not only tramples rights, it suppresses the creativity of people and companies by imposing controls and rigidity. Freedom allows you to experiment, to depart from traditional methods of doing things—to fail as well as succeed. Because economic freedom enables individuals to channel their self-interest and creative energies into constructive enterprises, free markets produce innovation and abundance. Markets and societies dominated by government controls are characterized by stagnation and often scarcity.

Ask people in Canada, whose single-payer government insurance system is what U.S. supporters of government health care want for this country. Canadians are denied cutting-edge treatments available in the United States—because their government does not want to pay for them. According to the Fraser Institute, the Canadian free market think tank, the average wait time to see a specialist is nineteen weeks—twice as long as two decades ago.[19] Several years ago, a man sued the Quebec government after he had to wait a year for a hip replacement. Dr. Brian Day, former president of the Canadian Medical Association, said, "This is a country in which dogs can get a hip replacement in under a week and in which humans can wait two to three years."[20] Meanwhile in Europe, where government health care originated, fewer new drugs and treatments are developed because a government-run system keeps companies from making the profits needed to fund research and development.

This is the focus of chapter 3, "Silicon Valley *or* Detroit?" Government interference is a major reason why the auto industry stagnated and lost its creative edge, while *the lack of interference* is a key reason why Silicon Valley became a creative powerhouse. Occupy Wall Streeters who protest profits might think differently if they realized that such gains are the source of investment capital that give our country its creative edge.

Chapter 4 asks the symbolic question, "Paychecks *or* Food Stamps?" Which is better for people and society?

The choice between economic freedom and paternalistic government is a choice between empowerment and dependence. By artificially propping up both individuals and companies, Big Government policies and subsidies keep people from advancing by corrupting judgment and undermining productiveness and enterprise—creating stagnation.

Supporters of Big Government insist that welfare and entitlement programs are the only way to provide compassion. But is it truly compassionate to create passivity and destroy human initiative? Free markets empower people and organizations to compete, to learn from missteps, and to adapt—to move ahead.

Chapter 5—"Apple *or* Solyndra?"—compares the meritocracy of open markets to government-dominated economies corrupted by what we call Big Government "few-dalism." Too many Big Government solutions promoted in the name of "fairness"—whether in health care or job creation—are really about favoritism. Instead of people and companies getting ahead based on how well they serve the market, a politically favored few are the winners. Critics of free markets have a legitimate complaint when they decry crony capitalism. But Big Government, the dispenser of favors, is the dominant partner in these relationships. The difference between a free society and one dominated by Big Government cronyism is illustrated by the contrast between the United States and Argentina. Both began as frontier societies. But because of its statist policies and Big Government cronyism, Argentina never prospered like the United States and has lurched from one economic crisis to the next.

Our final chapter explores the moral implications of the stark philosophical divide separating free market supporters and statists. Democratic capitalism's free markets are based on moral optimism, the historical conviction that humankind's ingenuity will solve today's problems and create new products and services that lead to a better future. Investing requires belief in progress. Trade is based on trust, the positive expectation that people will live up to agreements and make good on their promises. Big Government, in contrast, is founded on a more pessimistic view of people and the future. Chapter 6 poses the question "The Spirit of Reagan *or* Obama?" because the differences are reflected in the language and point of view of these two presidents.

EVERYONE WANTS a fair and moral society. But is the best way to get there through a politically driven government bureaucracy or through the democracy of the marketplace, where everyone votes with his or her dollars? More to the point, are government bureaucrats beholden to political interests really the ones to decide what is fair and moral?

Calls for more government intervention to end poverty and injustice ignore the fact that previous government regulations and programs failed to solve those problems. And in many cases they helped to cause them. Americans are a humane and charitable people. There are unquestionable real problems in sectors like health care and elsewhere in our society. Resisting demands for a government program that will supposedly help others can be difficult. But the heart-tugging rhetoric deflects attention from the fact that the proposed solution is usually more bureaucracy. Liberals advocating "compassion" and "human rights" might think again if they realized that what they're really fighting for is more rules, regulations, and red tape that restrict our freedoms. Government bureaucracies have a poor record of respecting the rights of individuals. And bureaucracy deals in strictures—more and more rules.

The discussion in this book is about how America sees itself as a nation. Is America still committed to the Founding Fathers' vision of economic and personal freedom—the fundamental right to "life, liberty and the pursuit of happiness"? Or are we to become a European-style welfare state? The chapters that follow present the real alternatives to be considered in this debate. Our national identity and our future are at stake.

1

FEDEX *or* THE POST OFFICE?

Free Markets Meet People's Needs; Big Government Meets Its Own Needs

*Free markets are about meeting the needs and wants of people.
Adam Smith described the fundamental free market transaction
using his iconic metaphor of the butcher and baker. Both sell you
dinner in order to make a living.[1] Buyer and seller are motivated
by self-interest. But this self-interest is not selfishness. Each party
meets the needs of the other. In a sense, the reciprocal transaction
that takes place in a voluntary market is the economic expression of
the Golden Rule: Do unto others as you would have them do unto
you. Each side seeks to meet the other's needs by giving something of
equal value.*

*A free market, Smith explained, consists of millions of these mu-
tually beneficial exchanges. They form an "Invisible Hand" that
spontaneously creates and allocates resources in a way that provides
the most benefit to the greatest number of people, given real-world
conditions of supply and demand.*

*Free market critics insist that markets are driven by "greed." But
selfish, greedy people and companies won't last in the marketplace
unless they provide a product or service people want. The quest of
individuals and companies to find solutions for people's needs occurs, furthermore, when profits are far from assured. Entrepreneurs*

will launch a venture with the knowledge that, if it fails, they may never see a dime of profit.

This motivation of individuals and companies to solve problems and meet needs—what John Maynard Keynes called "animal spirits"[2]—is the heart and soul of free enterprise. When government doesn't interfere, people in free markets will always mobilize to meet a demand. Many times, entrepreneurs will try to anticipate it. As Steve Jobs put it to biographer Walter Isaacson, "Our task is to read things that are not yet on the page."[3] This entrepreneurial impulse is why free markets have been historically successful at generating the innovations and wealth that have raised living standards and allowed society to advance.

Big Government, in contrast, is not accountable to a market. Unlike private sector companies that have to compete for customers, government does not have to get results or please people to stay in business. Executives or entrepreneurs must constantly answer to customers, investors, and shareholders. But government officials only face voters at election time.

Big Government's foremost concern, therefore, is with its own bureaucratic interests. This is clearly apparent whenever government delivers services. The classic illustration is the comparison between FedEx and the Postal Service. Ask the question, "FedEx or the post office?" and even those who otherwise support Big Government know what you're talking about. Mention the post office, and just about anyone will think of long lines and sluggish service. FedEx, meanwhile, has become a symbol of efficiency and reliability. Over the years, both FedEx and the Postal Service have had to raise prices.[4] But FedEx has responded to change and competition by consistently and dramatically expanding its services, offering more options to meet customer needs—like cheaper ground shipping, and also printing. The Postal Service, with some limited exceptions, *has continually charged* more *to deliver* less. *Mail today takes longer than ever to arrive and twice-a-day delivery has long been a thing of the past.*

That is the story of Big Government in most of what it manages. The selfish need for more political power and "turf"—in other words, bureaucracy—means that Big Government takes ever more from taxpayers while delivering less. This bureaucratic inefficiency means that Big Government is usually behind the curve when providing services. An excellent example is Medicare, which won't cover prescriptions for certain new drugs and procedures for the elderly that are already in widespread use in the marketplace and covered by private insurance.

This is the very opposite of what takes place in the private sector, where people must deliver more to achieve the self-interested goal of profit. The private sector would never get away with financing a pension system the way Big Government has financed Social Security, now on the brink of insolvency.

Big Government's emphasis on politics over people is also the reason why it inevitably fails in its attempts to direct markets. Instead of encouraging the creation and allocation of resources in a way that satisfies people and raises the standard of living, politically driven Big Government imposes controls that kill jobs and growth. Instead of lifting society with an Invisible Hand, Big Government, the larger it gets, becomes a not-so-Invisible Deadweight dragging down an economy.

BOTTOM LINE: DO YOU WANT THE BUREAUCRACY THAT GAVE YOU THE POST OFFICE TO DIRECT YOUR MEDICAL TREATMENT AND RUN CRITICAL INDUSTRIES?

BIG GOVERNMENT'S ENDLESS
QUEST FOR *MORE*

Even Big Government politicians like the president, from time to time, will concede that economic freedom and limited government best serve the needs of people. After the political rebuke to his party delivered by the 2010 midterm congressional elections, the president and his supporters briefly and miraculously acknowledged a central free market principle when they consented to extend the Bush tax rates. Raising taxes, they said, was harmful for people in a recession struggling to put food on the table. At other times President Obama has admitted, though some believe not altogether seriously, the need to "streamline" government to free up the economy.

We prefer to think these epiphanies were not simply responses to political pressure, but rare admissions of a commonsense principle that transcends politics: Generating the prosperity that meets society's needs and helps people get ahead is best accomplished with pro-market policies like reasonable taxation and regulation. People will more easily build job-creating businesses if you remove the restrictions and bureaucratic red tape. And it's easier to build wealth—not only for yourself, but for others—if government simply lets you keep more of what you earn and not punish success.

Yet such moments of clarity are few and far between. Far more often, liberal politicians and activists will revert to form, insisting that more government is the only moral solution to any real or perceived inequity. In good times and bad, the problem is nearly always described as an "emergency"—whether it may be a health care crisis, a housing crisis, an obesity crisis, or a jobs crisis.

Those who suggest otherwise are commonly branded as "heartless." When New Jersey governor Chris Christie first took office in 2010, he had to cut out-of-control state spending—or else not make the March payroll.[5] He was reviled as "Adolf Christie" and his budget was called "an assault on the poor" and antieducation. You would have thought that Christie was shutting down the entire social services bureaucracy. In fact, New Jersey spends more on education per student than every state in the union except for New York and Washington, D.C.

Wisconsin governor Scott Walker similarly sought to restore fiscal sanity to his state, which had a multibillion-dollar deficit largely driven by high employee costs. His reward for acting like any responsible CEO? Heated union demonstrations and a recall election, which fortunately he survived.

Remember the reaction to Congressman Paul Ryan's proposed Republican budget that would have simply cut back government spending to what it was before the economic crisis and the Obama spending binge? Ryan's plan included ways to prevent Medicare and Social Security—whose out-of-control costs both Republicans and Democrats agree are unsustainable—from financially imploding.[6] Opponents ran advertising showing a Ryan look-alike pushing an elderly woman in a wheelchair over a cliff.

Christie, Ryan, and Walker have all been portrayed as extreme. Yet they were simply trying to do what millions of people in households and companies in the private sector do when costs and spending get out of control: look for ways to cut back. This kind of fiscal belt-tightening can be painful. However, it takes place every day in the private sector. And reasonable people, Democrats as well as Republicans, usually consider such actions to be practical, necessary, and, above all, responsible.

So why do Big Government advocates—publicly, anyway—characterize the same behavior as immoral?

The answer illuminates a fundamental truth about Big Government. What today's budget and policy debates are really about is not a health care "crisis"—or some other crisis—but Big Government's quintessential quest to get bigger. It places this need first and foremost above the needs of people.

THE HISTORIAN C. Northcote Parkinson cast a sharp light on this central trait of bureaucracy in his 1950s management classic *Parkinson's Law*. Studying the British navy in the early twentieth century, he made an ironic discovery: after World War I, the number of seaman and shipyard workers, as well as warships, decreased dramatically. But the bureaucracy that oversaw them actually *expanded*.

Parkinson noted wryly that there is "little or no relationship between the work to be done and the size of the staff to which it may be assigned."[7]

> Politicians and taxpayers have assumed (with occasional phases of doubt) that a rising total in the number of civil servants must reflect a growing volume of work to be done. . . . The fact is that the number of the officials and the quantity of the work are not related to each other at all.[8]

Parkinson could have been talking about our ever-expanding Big Government with its countless redundant agencies and programs. In 2011, the Government Accountability

Office tallied up the result of decades of rampant, unchecked growth of federal agencies. As reported in the *Washington Post,* the GAO found that there were

> . . . more than 100 programs dealing with surface transportation issues, 82 monitoring teacher quality, 80 for economic development, 47 for job training, 20 offices or programs devoted to homelessness and 17 different grant programs for disaster preparedness. Another 15 agencies or offices handle food safety, and five are working to ensure the federal government uses less gasoline.[9]

The existence of all these bureaucracies doesn't mean that Big Government is doing a more thorough job of helping or protecting people. That GAO report, in fact, suggests the reverse. It cites the example of the 2010 nationwide recall of more than five hundred million salmonella-tainted eggs. That disaster was partly due to the fact that a total of *four* agencies were responsible for the safety of eggs.[10] So many people were responsible that ultimately no one was. Basic efficiency and common sense, you might say, fell between the cracks.

Parkinson's law isn't just a characteristic of government bureaucracies. But, in the private sector, companies that grow too large and inefficent won't survive. Apple, GE, Cisco, and Bank of America are among the many that have laid off people when they overexpanded or when times got tough. There's no such discipline in the world of Big Government. That's because there's no market feedback—that is, profits or losses—to signal whether the needs of people are successfully met.

Without this vital information, there is, in effect, no such thing as failure. Inept agencies aren't shut down. They only get bigger. Thomas DiLorenzo, a professor of economics at Loyola University, explains in "The Futility of Bureaucracy" that "the worse any government bureaucracy performs, as a rule, the *more* money it gets":

> The NASA budget rose after it exploded a space shuttle; the worse the government schools become, the more money they get; the war on drugs is a more abysmal failure each year, which guarantees that we spend more and more money on it; the list is endless. This is exactly the opposite of what occurs in the free market, where success in pleasing consumers is rewarded financially and failure punished.[11]

Big Government politicians continue to insist that the answer to just about every problem is more spending and more bureaucracy. But Big Government already consumes four out of ten dollars people earn. If we continue on our current path, this percentage is set to increase to 50 percent or more by 2035, if not sooner. Total government spending in the United States (federal, state, and local) in 2011 now accounts for some 41 percent of the economy's total gross domestic product (GDP)—the highest level ever except for World War II. Compare this with 1900, when government spending as a portion of GDP was not even 7 percent.[12]

What are the American people getting for our government's most recent expenditure of tax dollars? A government leviathan bigger and less productive than C. N. Parkinson's worst nightmare: Obamacare, the administration's 2010 health care "reform," is expected to result in the hiring of more than sixteen thousand IRS agents to enforce the law. That's in addition to imposing twenty-seven hundred pages of new regulations and creating more than 150 new bureaucracies. The administration's Dodd-Frank legislation creates still more bureaucracies and imposes some four hundred new rules on the financial services industry, one of the most heavily regulated sectors of the economy. And we're only warming up. Government salaries are exploding. *USA Today* reported that in the U.S. Department of Transportation *only one* person made $170,000 or more at the start of the recession. Some *1,690 employees* made more than that eighteen months later.[13] The budget of the agriculture department now exceeds the net incomes of the nation's farmers.

It's easy to understand what author William Voegeli meant when he lamented that the liberal appetite for more government lacks "a limiting principle."[14] Unfortunately, this impulse is not limited exclusively to liberals. Richard Nixon created such regulatory agencies as the EPA and the Consumer Product Safety Commission and then vastly expanded their powers. President George W. Bush pushed through the Medicare prescription drug program, a new entitlement, in 2003.

In this Big Government era of Parkinson's law run rampant, there's no end to the demand for more economy-destroying taxes to fund programs that never seem to have enough money to do their jobs. And they talk about private sector "greed."

BIG GOVERNMENT: THE ANTI-WALMART

You might call Big Government the anti-Walmart. Unlike shoppers at that retail chain, who get more value for "everyday low prices," citizens paying for Big Government and receiving its services, over time get *less* while paying more.

Like C. Northcote Parkinson, Dr. Max Gammon was a student of organizational behavior. In the 1960s, the British physician wrote of the tendency of ever-growing bureaucracies to produce diminishing returns. It's worth noting that his observations were based on the bureaucracies of British socialized medicine.

Gammon wrote that bureaucracies "act rather like 'black holes,' in the economic universe, simultaneously sucking in resources, and shrinking in terms of 'emitted production.'" Hence Gammon's law: *an increase in expenditure by a bureaucracy produces a fall in production.*[15]

The Securities and Exchange Commission provides a perfect example of Gammon's law. Responsible for overseeing the financial industry, the agency's regulations govern everything from accounting practices to what corporations reveal in their financial statements and annual reports. Congress more than doubled SEC funding after the Enron scandal of 2001. Yet this regulatory behemoth with its thirty-seven hundred employees failed to spot Bernard Madoff's historic Ponzi fraud. Despite his exceptionally high profile in the securities industry as the one-time chairman of the NASDAQ Exchange, Madoff was able to steal billions of dollars from investors over decades through fake stock trades. The SEC didn't act even after Harry Markopolos, an expert in securities fraud, repeatedly contacted the agency with evidence that included an exhaustive report pointing out dozens of red flags.

In the private sector, a mistake of this magnitude would mean that the responsible people would lose their jobs. Or a company might lose business. But the SEC and its allies in Congress only pushed for more funding.[16] So it goes in the upside-down universe of Big Government.

WHEN IT COMES TO THE NEEDS OF BIG GOVERNMENT, PEOPLE BE DAMNED

The takeover of the Detroit automakers is a classic illustration of how Big Government puts politics before people. The Obama administration insisted that the seizing of GM and Chrysler and their subsequent restructuring were needed to "save jobs" by preventing the automakers from falling into bankruptcy. However, many large employers—including all the major airlines—have been able to keep operating during a bankruptcy restructuring. This "solution" was really to benefit the United Auto Workers (UAW), a powerful union and a key administration supporter.

Big Government essentially handed over Chrysler to the UAW, which got 55 percent of the company's stock. Fiat and the governments of the United States and Canada got the remaining equity. Bondholders who invested in the automaker were shafted. They lost far more of their investment than would have happened in a bankruptcy court. This was a political solution, pure and simple.

In its takeover of GM, the government invested some $50 billion in taxpayers' money, owning more than 60 percent of the company. The UAW got some 17.5 percent of GM stock *plus* $6.5 billion in preferred stock and another $2.5 billion to fund retiree health care costs—three to four times as much as the bondholders that loaned money to the old GM.[17]

Few people remember that the administration's effort to restructure the auto companies and "save" jobs also resulted in the closing of more than twenty-six hundred GM and Chrysler dealerships employing as many as a hundred thousand people.

Given scant coverage by the largely pro-administration media, the forced shutdown of private businesses by the federal government was a shameful episode in our history. Some auto dealers had been in business for generations and were prominent in their communities.

Administration supporters claimed the move was needed to reduce the cost burden on automakers of large dealership networks that were no longer needed in the face of shrinking demand for domestic cars. Dealerships should obviously close down if the market doesn't support them. But a dealer's customers—or a bankruptcy court—and not the government, should decide who best meets their needs in selling cars.

Over the years, Detroit made mistakes. But decades of politically selfish decisions by both Democrat and Republican administrations helped create the conditions that brought the automakers to the verge of bankruptcy. Ever-escalating Corporate Average Fuel Economy (CAFE) standards boosting the cost of auto manufacturing made it harder for domestic carmakers to compete. The problem wasn't the efficiency rules, per se. Detroit would have been able to meet these standards with its foreign manufactured cars. But a rule imposed to please unions requires that the cars used to meet U.S. CAFE standards contain at least 75 percent domestic parts. To comply, Detroit has been forced to rely on union labor whose costs have been inflated by lavish pensions and health care packages, thus depriving the industry of needed profits.

Big Government advocates and union activists say they're in the business of saving jobs. Their rules have had just the opposite effect and helped destroy them: GM once employed 395,000 blue-collar workers. Today it employs around 40,000.[18]

There's no better example of Big Government selfishness and greed than the battle over the administration's health care legisation. Polls had consistently showed it to be unpopular. And supporters originally did not have the votes to pass the bill in Congress. But politicians were more concerned with pleasing a narrow political base than with the desires of most Americans. To get votes they wouldn't have gotten otherwise, Obamacare proponents promised states like Louisiana and Nebraska hundreds of millions of dollars in extra Medicaid funds, the so-called "Louisiana Purchase" and the "Cornhusker Kickback." They rammed the bill through Congress, forcing it on a majority that didn't want it. Polls continue to show that a wide majority oppose the law.

Imagine if Steve Jobs had tried to ram the unsuccessful Newton—the handheld personal device that didn't fully work and didn't meet the needs of users—down the throats of consumers who weren't buying it. Apple would be out of business.

Bureaucratic self-interest is also the reason that New York City has further constricted its already narrow, congested streets with 250 miles of costly bike lanes used by very few people. Bike riding is a great pastime with many health benefits. And one can understand how well-meaning bureaucrats want to encourage it. But the plain truth is that bike lanes don't meet the needs of most New Yorkers. The city's streets, designed in the age of horse-drawn carriages, can barely accommodate cars. If anything, the need is for more space for autos, not less.

Not surprisingly, drivers hate the bike lanes. Merchants hate them because they make it harder for trucks to park and make deliveries.[19] And only a fraction of New Yorkers are brave enough to risk their lives riding between buses and trucks in treacherous city traffic. Taking all this into account, one could certainly argue that there are better ways to spend millions of taxpayer dollars than on bike lanes only a tiny number of people use—and most people don't want. Smaller-scale attempts to install lanes in the 1970s and 1980s met with such fierce opposition that the lanes were removed.[20]

So why did New York's Big Government ignore the needs of its majority, not to mention common sense and past history? Because New York City bike riders today are an influential constituency with the ear of the city transportation commissioner. Thus they're more politically powerful than merchants or people who drive. That may be starting to change. The lanes are facing a growing backlash from people finally fed up with an impractical Big Government "solution" designed to assuage a small, highly vocal minority.

SELFISH BIG GOVERNMENT IS BAD
FOR YOUR HEALTH

Big Government's bureaucratic focus on its own internal needs is a major reason why it should not have power over decisions concerning your health care. It's bad enough when politically motivated policies result in annoying bike lanes or even auto bailouts that stiff taxpayers and make a mockery of the rule of law. But under Obamacare, selfish, politicized bureaucracies will increasingly influence your doctor's decisions. This has dangerous and destructive consequences for each and every American.

The need for government bureaucrats to save money will increasingly supersede your medical needs. This penny-pinching will affect your treatment—regardless if you are government or privately insured.

Liberals laugh at the notion of "death panels." There may not be secretive committees deciding who lives and who dies. But the new bureaucracies of Obamacare amount to health care rationing. As Nancy Pelosi predicted, Americans are finally learning what's in this monstrosity. One controversial provision provides $1 billion for what's known as *comparative effectiveness research* (CER). CER is supposed to inform insurers and doctors which medical treatments get the best results for the least cost. On its face, this sounds benign, but it's actually more ominous: CER is an idea borrowed from Britain's national health care system. The British CER bureaucracy is the National Institute for Health and Clinical Excellence. Known by the ironic acronym of NICE, it generates data that serve as guidelines for health care rationing under the British system.

The United Kingdom has a measure of "quality-adjusted life years" that actually puts a price tag on how much each added year of individual life is worth. Health care policy analyst Michael Tanner of the Cato Institute explains, "To be exact, each year of added life is worth approximately [$44,000]."[21]

If providing a medical procedure to certain patients fails to produce a sufficient return in terms of these "quality adjusted life years," the U.K. government may not provide it. What this means is that, if you are, say, seventy years old and need heart surgery—which many people do at that age—it will be denied to you in our new world of bureaucratized health care because it will fail to meet the comparative effectiveness standard of "benefit." Forget about your individual needs or desires as a patient.

President Obama implied that this kind of rationing to the

elderly was on the horizon when he complained that "the chronically ill and those toward the end of their lives are accounting for potentially 80 percent of the total health care bill out here. . . . There is going to have to be a very difficult democratic conversation that takes place."[22]

Washington State's Health Technology Assessment (HTA) program, which oversees insurance policies provided to employees and Medicaid recipients, illustrates the kind of medical treatment you can expect under comparative effectiveness guidelines. The board recently questioned the necessity of glucose monitoring for children under eighteen, a treatment that for years had been considered standard medical practice. It's even covered by those supposedly "greedy" private insurance companies.[23]

What happened? After public outcry, the HTA eventually decided to continue covering glucose monitoring, although it's limiting coverage of expensive spinal injections for people with chronic back pain.

Then there's the powerful Independent Payment Advisory Board (IPAB) that is supposed to keep down the cost of Medicare by slashing reimbursement rates for drugs it believes are too costly—thereby discouraging doctors from prescribing them. Noted health care analyst Sally Pipes, of the Pacific Research Institute, and many others say this is rationing for seniors.[24]

Big Government advocates respond by saying that, without Obamacare, the private sector would also "ration" health care through the mechanism of price. That's simply not true. Unlike a government bureaucracy, companies in free markets don't respond to rising demand by cutting back on something. If there's a need for more food or clothing or flatscreen televisions, entrepreneurs find a way to meet it. If we had an open market for health care, the solution would not be to cut back on expensive injections to help ease pain for elderly people. Businesses would find new ways to provide *more*—and at less cost. This has happened in tiny slivers of the health care market that are not affected by today's regulations. One example: the availability of flu shots at discounters like Walgreens.

Statists insist that Big Government is needed to fix health care. But today's system evolved in response to *regulation,* not consumer demand. During World War II, employers couldn't raise wages because of wartime wage and price controls. So they started offering health insurance. Federal tax law allowing employers to deduct health care costs institutionalized the practice.

The result? A government-configured industry where corporations are the primary buyers of health insurance. The market is therefore about meeting their needs, not those of consumers.

In a truly open market, individuals, and not companies, would be the buyers of health care. Employees, and not just employers, would receive a tax deduction for buying insurance. Barriers to a national market would be removed.

Those very simple reforms would quickly produce a consumer-driven market. If *you* were the primary buyer of health care, insurers, doctors, and hospitals would have to compete to win your business. Freed from the constraints of state regulations, entrepreneurial problem solvers would meet your needs—just as they have in every other market. You'd get better care and friendlier service. Prices, above all, would come down.

SELFISH BIG GOVERNMENT IS NOT ACCOUNTABLE

So why do government bureaucrats spend taxpayer money on hundreds of miles of expensive bike lanes that most people don't use or on "Bridges to Nowhere"? Why do they pass thousands of pages of costly, life-changing legislation that they haven't even read? The reason is that those who work in government, however noble their intentions, are simply not accountable to the rest of us.

As we pointed out, politicians and officials have to answer to voters mainly at election time. There's no day-to-day feedback from a marketplace to restrain the forces of Parkinson's law. And there's less pressure to care about pleasing Big Government's "customers" and "shareholders"—We the People who are paying for and receiving government services.

In the words of the *Wall Street Journal*'s Daniel Henninger, the taxpaying private sector is perceived as a vague "intellectual abstraction."[25] It's hard for politicians and officials to comprehend that the billions of dollars they heedlessly spend are actually your hard-earned money.

During the debate over the 2011 federal budget, President Obama said one way he would reduce the federal deficit was through a "debt failsafe trigger," bureaucratic jargon for automatic tax increases that would kick in without anyone having to vote on them.[26] These automatic hikes would be the "gift" that would keep on taking from people's pockets even after his administration left office. Congress nixed the idea.

Automatic *spending* increases, however, are all too common.

When New York governor Andrew Cuomo first took office in 2011, the *New York Post* reported that he found to his dismay "a projected 13 percent spending increase driven largely by a series of automatic spending increases buried into law by generations of lobbyists and complicit legislators."[27] Spending on areas like education and Medicaid had to increase no matter what—even if a down economy was generating lower taxpayer revenues.

Where is all the money going? To those ever-expanding bureaucracies and lavish employee benefits. To cite just one example, public sector benefits for New York City workers have grown twice as fast as those in the private sector over the last decade. Firefighters and police officers can retire at half pay after only twenty years on the job, even though they may be only in their forties. The pensions are exempt from state taxes and are topped off by an annual bonus and health insurance. The state must foot this bill year after year, at taxpayers' expense.[28]

The situation is much the same in the federal government. Analyses of data from the U.S. Department of Commerce's Bureau of Economic Analysis found that federal employees on average earn more than twice the salaries of their private-sector counterparts. From 2000 to 2009, the total compensation of federal employees (including benefits) more than doubled—from $30,415 in 2000 to $61,998.[29]

Daniel Henninger has explained in the *Wall Street Journal* that the needs of government workers began to take precedence over those of their taxpaying "customers" in the 1960s. President John F. Kennedy signed an order allowing federal workers to unionize. The new and quickly growing government unions, Henninger has pointed out, had radically different priorities from private sector unions. Workers in the private sector are "tethered to a real world of profit and loss."[30] They have a stake in helping their companies do well, because they gain through continued employment and more jobs. Public sector unions, however, are insulated from market forces. There's nothing to restrain them from pushing for ever-higher salaries and benefits. And they do—because they can.

This kind of mentality has given us stratospheric worker salaries that have helped push states into fiscal crisis—and it has encouraged rampant corruption. Sick leave scams have cost states hundreds of millions. Other examples include the Long Island Railroad disabilities scandal. For almost a decade, nearly all retiring employees on the commuter rail line received disability benefits. Most of the "retirees" were barely over age fifty. Typical was one "disabled" office worker who had complained of being unable to stand for more than five minutes to qualify for disability payments but was later seen shoveling snow for more than an hour. Then there was the retired worker who received $100,000 in annual disability and pension payments. Despite reporting that he was in too much pain to bend or grip objects, he very frequently played golf and tennis—on the taxpayer's dime.[31]

THE ECONOMIC TOLL OF BIG GOVERNMENT GREED

Unlike the Invisible Hand of the free market that generates prosperity by meeting the needs of society, Big Government's red tape and bureaucratic meddling act is an Invisible Deadweight that drags down a nation's economy.

This isn't just true of nations like impoverished communist

North Korea or the now defunct Soviet Union with its chronic shortages. The Invisible Deadweight of Big Government is also responsible for the sluggish economies of European social democracies. British journalist and politician Daniel Hannan reminds us that, in the decades after World War II and up until the mid-1970s, Western Europe actually *outperformed* the United States. But then those nations turned to socialist policies intended as a "Third Way"—a middle ground between Russian communism and American capitalism. Europe's economic growth has lagged that of the United States ever since.[32]

The countries that now form the European Union had a 36 percent share of world GDP in 1974. That has fallen to 26 percent—and by 2020 it's expected to be only 15 percent. In contrast, the U.S. share for thirty years has remained surprisingly constant. Hannan makes the startling observation that, "if we exclude the United Kingdom, *the EU failed to produce a single net private-sector job between 1980 and 1992*" (our italics).[33]

Meanwhile, the United States surged ahead. From the early 1980s until the financial crisis, U.S. economic growth averaged 3.3 percent, while Western Europe grew at a rate of less than 2 percent a year.[34] That's despite the fact that we have the largest economy in the world, and "big" doesn't usually grow as fast.

Since the financial crisis, the United States has had a taste of European-style stagnation and unemployment. Is this kind of listless economic torpor—where people linger for years without jobs or hope—a moral society or the kind of life Americans want?

PARKINSON'S LAW RUN AMOK:
HOW GREECE HIT THE SKIDS

When Big Government greed and selfishness run rampant, you get Greece, whose obese government has sent the nation into convulsions. Even C. Northcote Parkinson would be horrified by the out-of-control growth of the Greek government, which has corrupted every corner of society. Michael Lewis reported in *Vanity Fair* in 2010 that the cost of Greek public sector salaries had doubled in the past ten years—"and that number doesn't take into account the bribes collected by public officials."

> The average government job pays almost three times the average private-sector job. The national railroad has annual revenues of 100 million euros against an annual wage bill of 400 million, plus 300 million euros in other expenses. The average state railroad employee earns 65,000 euros a year.[35]

Greece's onetime minister of finance has said that, at those salaries, it would be cheaper to put all the country's rail passengers into taxicabs. Greece's public schools fare little better. The country employs four times as many teachers per pupil as highly ranked Finland. Their bloated system, however, is at the bottom of Europe's totem pole. Lewis writes, "Greeks who send their children to public schools simply assume that they will need to hire private tutors to make sure they actually learn something."

Much like Americans, the Greeks have tried to stimulate their sagging economy with pork-laden stimulus spending. Lewis reports that this included "a great number of off-the-books phony job-creation programs." One of them employed some 270 people whose jobs were to digitize the photographs of Greek public lands. The problem was that the political hires had no experience with digital photography.[36]

How did Greek government become such a toxic leviathan? The country's finance minister told *Vanity Fair* that the bureaucracy's Parkinsonian appetite for growth resisted all restraint. Big Government greed caused bureaucrats long ago to forget their moral obligation to taxpayers or society. As Lewis put it, "The party in power simply gins up whatever numbers it likes, for its own purposes."[37]

* * *

THE BASIS OF FREE MARKETS: NOT GREED BUT GIVING

People who become successful often talk about the need to "give back." Think about how misguided this is. Did Thomas Edison need to "give back" for bringing electric light to people's homes? Should Mark Zuckerberg have to give back for revolutionizing the way we communicate online with Facebook? Or for creating wealth and jobs for thousands of people that would not have otherwise existed? And why should a successful car dealer or real estate broker have to apologize? Think of where you'd be without their services.

This is not about the merits of giving to charity (we'll get to that later). What we are disputing, however, is the underlying notion that those who have created wealth in our market system need to somehow atone for "taking" from others.

Free enterprise guru George Gilder put it succinctly in "The

Moral Sources of Capitalism": "Capitalism begins with giving." Trade, by its very nature, is reciprocal. Each side gives to the other. The self-interest in free markets means that it is in your interest to *provide sufficient benefit* to the other person or company so that an exchange will take place. Gilder tells us that the very earliest trading relationships were based on giving, not taking:

> The capitalists of primitive society were tribal leaders who vied with one another in giving great feasts. Similarly, trade began with offerings from one family to another or from one tribe to its neighbor. The gifts, often made in the course of a religious rite, were presented in hopes of an eventual gift in return.[38]

What Gilder was really describing was a form of investing. You put resources to work without knowing for certain what kind of return you will get. This tradition of giving is at the heart of capitalism's customer service ethos. People generally take it for granted when businesses of all kinds post signs and run ads asserting "We're here to serve you." No doubt, some businesses do a better job than others at fulfilling their promises. But the fact remains that service—giving—is fundamental to our market-based culture.

Our free enterprise culture of giving is the real reason why the United States is a philanthropic country. Private philanthropy has dropped a bit with the recession, however, Americans still give around $300 billion to charity each year.[39] According to the Independent Sector, a coalition of nonprofits concerned with charitable giving, nearly 90 percent of American households contribute to charities or religious institutions. The

Hudson Institute, a policy think tank, has reported that before the financial crisis and recession, Americans privately contributed more charitable dollars to the developing world than any other nation.

Big Government liberals have a hard time believing entrepreneurial people in the private sector are driven by anything other than the craven desire for material riches. Antimarket biases have distorted perceptions of exactly what constitutes free market self-interest. However, Milton Friedman explained in *Free to Choose* that free market transactions are not driven by "myopic selfishness." Self-interest involves fulfilling personal goals and desires, such as "the scientist seeking to advance the frontiers of his discipline, the missionary seeking to convert infidels to the true faith, the philanthropist seeking to bring comfort to the needy—all are pursuing their interests, as they see them, as they judge them by their own values."[40]

Money is just one of many factors pushing people to choose a career or focus on an interest. It may not even be the primary reason. Maybe the work appeals to you. Or you like the product you're selling or creating. Or you have something in common with your colleagues in your workplace.

Entrepreneurs are driven by this kind of "self-interest." Most of the time they start businesses not to get rich, but because they are seeking a solution to a problem in their own lives. Insurance broker Lewis Waterman invented the modern fountain pen in the 1800s after his old-fashioned pen leaked during the signing of a major contract. Returning with a replacement pen, Waterman found that a competitor had swooped in to close the deal and Waterman lost the business. He resolved to prevent a repeat of the disaster from ever happening again by inventing a pen that would not leak.[41] Software developer Drew Houston had the idea for the Internet file storage service that became Dropbox when he was an MIT student. He was unable to work during a trip to New York after leaving behind his USB flash drive.[42] Houston came up with an answer—a Web-based service that stores your documents and lets you work on them from any device. The company is today one of the Web's hottest start-ups, with fifty million users and a valuation of $4 billion.[43]

Dropbox and the fountain pen are typical of free market innovations that make life easier, while creating jobs and wealth—not just for their creators but countless others. If that's not "giving," what is?

HOW PROFIT ENABLES MARKETS TO DO GOOD

There is a story about Steve Jobs that illustrates the moral value of profit. Biographer Walter Isaacson writes that Jobs and Apple cofounder and childhood friend Steve Wozniak had very different views of the world. Wozniak, a brilliant engineer, subscribed to the ethos of "Give to help others."[44] Like his fellow hackers, he believed in giving away information and technology. When he developed the Apple I personal computer, he wanted to give it away for free. The visionary Jobs, however, saw the potential of what his friend had created and talked him out of it. He convinced Wozniak that they should start a company and sell his creation. They founded Apple and the rest, as they say, is history.

Was Jobs being selfish and greedy? Some may be tempted

to say yes. Widely known to be hard-nosed and often prickly, Jobs clearly acted in his own self-interest. But the course he took was the moral one. Had Wozniak given away his technology, things would have likely turned out very differently. Wozniak's schematics might have remained on the worktables of his fellow hackers. Or someone else might have developed his technology only not as spectacularly. Instead, Wozniak's invention became a success that generated profits, which soon attracted investors and capital that enabled Apple to grow and develop its now-famous innovations. Jobs's "selfish" drive for a profit literally, as he liked to say, "changed the world." Apple's innovations have revolutionized and transformed not only computing but also the entertainment and media industries, improving the lives of untold millions.

Did Jobs "exploit" Wozniak? Hardly. Today he's worth an estimated $100 million. Jobs's self-interest made Wozniak and others who worked at the company millionaires many times over—in addition to creating wealth for hundreds of thousands of shareholders.

Free market opponents who sneer at "greedy" profits frequently insist that people shouldn't be allowed to make them. However, without the ability of people to make a profit, markets would be unable to fulfill their vital function of providing for society. New companies and ventures would never come into being. Innovations like the iPad and countless others would never be developed. Entrepreneurs like Steve Jobs and others wouldn't be able to "change the world." Profits aren't just critical to the successful operation of markets—they're moral.

Friedrich von Hayek and Milton Friedman explain that prices and profits are actually a system of communication. They indicate what's in demand—and what isn't. When there's a high level of demand for something, prices and profits rise. Producers will rush in to provide services. Falling prices and profits, meanwhile, signify declining demand. Producers respond by scaling back production or improving their product or service. In this way, profits mobilize people to meet the needs of others.

Remember what happened several years ago when Amazon unveiled its e-reader, the Kindle. The online retailer couldn't keep the device in stock. The company's success showed there was money to be made from this emerging market. Others, including Apple with its iPad, soon jumped in with their own offerings. Thanks to profits, demand for the e-readers was quickly filled—not only with more Kindles but with competing offerings.

Then something interesting happened. All these competing products caused prices to drop. The price of the Kindle, originally $400, dropped to less than $80. E-readers became available to students and others with limited budgets who, just a year or two before, could not afford the cutting-edge technology. Technology that only a short time earlier had been considered a "luxury" became widely available. Profits not only helped the market meet demand, they helped produce abundance. They spurred an upsurge of competition that helped bring down prices and make e-readers more affordable. The mechanism of profit is behind what we call in chapter 3 "the Staples principle," the ability of creative markets to increase living standards by bringing advances to more and more people.

As we saw with Steve Jobs and Apple, profits provide the capital for investment and encourage people to take risks by investing in new ideas that may or may not succeed. People decry the "obscene" profits from hedge funds or private equity firms such as KKR and Blackstone. What they don't see is the *value* their investments create—not only for direct investors but also the broader society. Between 1991 and 2006, private equity firms worldwide created more than $430 billion in net value for their investors—which include universities, charitable organizations, and pension plans covering tens of millions of Americans.[45] Those "greedy" profits translated into stronger pension plans for employees, more financial aid and scholarships at public and private colleges, as well as funds for research that will develop cures for diseases.

Another reason why we need profits is that new ventures have very high rates of failure. Profits provide a source of new capital that covers the cost of those failures. They're also vital to maintaining the operations of existing companies. Without profits, companies couldn't replace machinery that becomes obsolete, or worn out. That's why you so often see run-down buildings in third world Big Government nations where people are prevented from making a profit. After expenditures on day-to-day operations, there's no money left for maintenance and new investment. The result is decay.

FREE MARKETS AND THE "ME-CONOMY"

We discussed earlier how Big Government's inward-looking bureaucracy causes it to disregard individual needs and impose rigid, "top-down" solutions on markets like health care. Competitive open markets do the exact opposite. Companies vying for business are constantly developing new and creative ways to deliver what customers want with pinpoint precision.

There's no better illustration of this than the boom in

customization brought about by the rise of the Internet and personal computing. *U.S. News & World Report* has described this growing "Me-conomy," in which people are able to design their own products—from sneakers, shoes, and T-shirts to credit cards.[46] We're even seeing the rise of "3-D printing," inexpensive cutting-edge software that lets people design and create their own furniture, toys, and other three-dimensional objects that they would normally have to buy from someone else.

Business writer and management guru B. Joseph Pine speaks for the movement toward the "mass customizable" economy when he writes that "Every customer is his own market." He declares, "Every customer deserves to have exactly what he wants at a price he's willing to pay, and companies must make that happen in a way that makes them money."[47]

The move toward a customizable economy is really technology amplifying the natural needs-meeting impulse of free markets. Imagine the possibilities if we removed today's Big Government constraints and permitted the same thing to happen in heavily regulated markets like health care. Unfortunately, imagining is all we can do right now.

MEETING SOCIETY'S NEEDS
BY OPENING UP MARKETS

When government interference *is* cut back, and choice and competition are reintroduced to markets, something miraculous happens. You get an explosion of abundance, more affordable goods and services, more choices for more people—and generally more fairness. The market meets people's needs and wants.

That's what happened when the state of Louisiana brought more choice to public education in New Orleans. For years, public schools there had been a disaster. After Hurricane Katrina, the state finally stepped in and implemented market reforms. Charter schools were established, giving students and parents more choice and increasing competition within the system. Principals are able to make their own hiring decisions. The result? Test scores are way up. The number of students meeting grade-level standards has almost doubled. Low-income students from the newly created charter schools outperformed students at other public schools by as much as 20 percent.[48]

In Sweden, a system of independent schools has been credited by political parties of the left and right with dramatically improving academic performance and bringing new innovative approaches to Swedish education.[49]

Another example: air travel. Back in the 1970s, the Civil Aeronautics Board heavily regulated airlines. Air travel was affordable only by people with means, and planes often flew half full. That all changed after the industry was deregulated in 1978. The number of airline passengers has doubled. People don't have to scramble to make connections as often as they once did, because there are more flights. Fares have fallen nearly by half in real terms.[50]

The flight delays and cancellations currently plaguing air travel are not the result of deregulation—but by the fact that airports themselves continue to be government controlled. Slow-moving Big Government bureaucracy has prevented airports from installing modern GPS-based air traffic control technology. Recent regulations that fine carriers for long waits on runways have also increased cancellations. As always, Big

Government rules intended to solve problems end up creating destructive unintended consequences.

A classic illustration of what happens when you cut back Big Government and liberalize markets is the dismantling of the old AT&T—"Ma Bell." Many people today are too young to remember the deregulation of the telephone industry. The breakup of the government-mandated telephone monopoly transformed the nation's phone system into a competitive industry with numerous players. This produced an explosion of new offerings—not only new kinds of hardware, but totally new technologies.

Before deregulation, consumers had a choice of only one or two types of phones in a few colors. Today there are not only cell phones but Internet phones, with features like call waiting, call forwarding, and voice mail. The cost of telephone calls and equipment has also dramatically decreased. Between 1984 and 2003, interstate long-distance rates dropped by some 68 percent. Intrastate rates declined by 56 percent.[51]

A final example: Brokerage commissions for buying and selling stocks were once set by the SEC at a fixed level. The commissions were high and brokers were, in effect, being subsidized by government-mandated rates. But in 1975, government price fixing ended. The industry was freed up. Discount brokers rushed into the market. Many old brokerage firms went out of business while others became more efficient. Today, even small traders can do thousands of trades at pennies a share. Stock trading became cheap and accessible for the first time to millions of people. It contributed to the boom in stock ownership that has helped drive the last three decades of prosperity up until the financial crisis.

Cutting back inward-looking Big Government bureaucracies

has the same liberating effect on nations. Examples are everywhere. Within the past thirty years, free market reforms have brought an unprecedented explosion of global wealth creation and have lifted hundreds of millions of people out of poverty in nations from India, China, Brazil, central and Eastern Europe, as well as Latin America and Africa.

After gaining their independence following the collapse of the Soviet Union, the Baltic states of Estonia, Latvia, and Lithuania had the highest growth rates of any nation in Europe. The three were slammed dramatically during the world economic crisis, but growth is now steadily returning.

The former East Germany has also prospered since reuniting with economically freer West Germany. Disposable income increased from 60 percent of the western level to 78.6 percent in 2007, according to a report by the Munich-based Institute for Economic Research.[52] Unemployment, while still high, has dropped significantly.

When an economy is freed from the arbitrary rules imposed by self-interested Big Government bureaucrats, entrepreneurs inevitably rise up. As we will see in succeeding chapters, they start and expand businesses and invest in innovations—services and products that meet the needs of people in ways that no myopic bureaucrat could ever envision.

2

FREEDOM *or* BIG BROTHER?

Choice Versus Coercion

Freedom is the moral heart of democratic capitalism. As economist Milton Friedman put it, you are "free to choose."[1] You chart your own course according to your needs and desires. You decide what to buy or sell, set prices—or engage in other pursuits—not in response to directives from a government authority, but because you judge these activities to be in your self-interest. You have the right to make your own decisions because you and no one else "owns" yourself. The latitude and choice of free markets is founded in respect for the rights of individuals.

Not only are you "free to choose" in democratic capitalism, you have more to choose from. Open markets mean entrepreneurial newcomers can rise up and create new products. Thus, in sectors where there is the least government interference, you see the greatest array of goods and services.

Through generating material abundance and promoting individual rights, economic freedom fosters a democratic, prosperous society. Big Government, in contrast, achieves its goals through coercion.

We may not think of our democratic government as being coercive. However, all law is ultimately coercion. Free market advocates dating back to Adam Smith have agreed that certain forms of coercion are needed for markets to work. Government must bring the power of the state to bear in order to levy taxes, punish criminals, enforce contracts, and impose laws that benefit society, even if not everyone wants to abide by them. Friedrich von Hayek wrote in a famous passage that government is needed to establish "rules of the road," creating a stable environment where transactions take place according to the rule of law.[2] That means defining and enforcing basic legal parameters of honest conduct and protecting people from fraud.

The problem with Big Government is that it goes too far in using and abusing this power. America's Big Government today has strayed beyond Hayek's rules of the road, becoming a virtual GPS system. Through coercive regulations and taxes, it is increasingly directing people's decisions, imposing constraints on economic and personal freedom. In the marketplace, the workplace, the doctor's office, and even at the dinner table, Big Government is imposing top-down "solutions" that are strangling enterprise and liberty.

Friedrich von Hayek, who witnessed the rise of totalitarian regimes before World War II, famously warned that outwardly benign expansions of government power can take nations down "the road to serfdom."[3] People entranced by central planners promising protection and equality end up surrendering their liberty to tyrants.

Americans have not traveled that far down the road to serfdom—yet. Few people in our democracy see America's Big Government, even at the size it is today, as a totalitarian Big Brother. But something is wrong when government starts telling people what food they're allowed to eat or what lightbulbs they're supposed to buy, or when it forces people to buy health insurance. George

Washington is believed to have said, "Government is not reason; it is not eloquence. It is force. And force, like fire, is a dangerous servant and a fearful master."[4]

BOTTOM LINE: DO YOU REALLY WANT THE STATE TAKING AWAY YOUR CHOICES AND MAKING YOUR DECISIONS?

"YOU ARE NOT FREE"

Just when does government coercion become unreasonable—and immoral? The Founding Fathers grappled with this question. Having fought for their freedom from King George III, they knew firsthand the dangers of an overly powerful ruler and believed that limiting the powers of government was vital to a free republic. James Madison summed up their dilemma eloquently in *The Federalist Papers*: "the great difficulty lies in this: you must first enable the government to control the governed; and in the next place oblige it to control itself."[5]

Americans think of themselves as a free people; compared with most nations we are. But in critical areas of our economy and society, government has crossed the boundary delineated by James Madison. Milton Friedman once listed some of these restrictions on our freedom:

> You are not free to work overtime at terms mutually agreeable to you and your employer, unless the terms conform to rules and regulations laid down by a government official.

> You are not free to set up a bank, go into the taxicab business, or the business of selling electricity or telephone

service, or running a railroad, busline, or airline, without first receiving permission from a government official.[6]

Unfortunately, there's plenty more we can add to Friedman's list. Following are a few examples.

Education. People rarely think of the nation's public school system as coercive. One Ohio mother, Kelley Williams-Bolar, discovered otherwise. Bolar falsified her address in order to get her daughters into a better school district. She wound up spending nine days in jail.[7] Bolar's frustration is shared by many parents fed up with a government education monopoly whose schools have failed their children. They're joining the movement for school choice, pushing for charter schools, vouchers, and other reforms to improve education by introducing competition into the market.

Your health care. You are also not free when it comes to health care, as we discussed in chapter 1.

Starting in 2014, unless Obamacare is repealed, the law's individual mandate will require you to have insurance. Despite the Supreme Court ruling, this remains an outrageous coercion that forces Americans to buy a product they may not need or want. It is an unprecedented infringement on individual rights. Justice Anthony Kennedy echoed the reservations of several colleagues during oral arguments when he commented that the mandate forcing people to buy health insurance "threatens to change the relationship between the government and the individual in a profound way."[8]

Federal judge Roger Vinson, of the Northern District of Florida, after ruling the law unconstitutional, wrote in 2011: "Never before has Congress required that everyone buy a product from a private company (essentially for life) *just for being alive and residing in the United States*" (our italics).[9]

The individual mandate unfortunately is only the beginning of this massive overreach. The 2,700-page law takes Big Government command-and-control of health care to a frightening new level. Noted health care policy analyst and former New York State lieutenant governor Betsy McCaughey is one of few who have read the entire law. She points out that it is the first time government has asserted control over the medical treatment of privately insured patients, and not just those in government programs like Medicaid and Medicare.[10]

McCaughey is especially troubled by Obamacare's invasion of privacy. The law establishes a national electronic database that will hold your medical records and history, regardless of whether you or your doctor want to participate. (Doctors and hospitals that don't will be penalized.) Physicians will be required to enter the details of your medical visit and receive federal guidelines regarding what the government considers to be "cost-effective" and "appropriate care." McCaughey writes on her website, "The result is that doctors will be forced to choose between doing what's best for their patients and avoiding a government penalty."[11]

The database will also make your medical information "accessible to a troubling number of strangers, including government employees and a variety of health-care personnel." People get incensed over "privacy violations" when Internet sites sell their consumer preferences to marketers. Yet—astoundingly—few have raised any objections to Obamacare's national database, a trespass with far greater potential for abuse.

Your money—what you keep. Yes, we need taxes to pay for government. But what you lose to income and payroll levies is only the beginning. You have to pay and pay again. By one tally, Big Government imposes a total of more than fifty taxes on Americans:

Accounts Receivable Tax
Building Permit Tax
Capital Gains Tax
Cigarette Tax
Commercial Driver's License Tax
Corporate Income Tax
Court Fines (indirect taxes)
Dog License Tax
Federal Income Tax
Federal Unemployment Tax (FUTA)
Fishing License Tax
Food License Tax
Fuel Permit Tax
Gasoline Tax
Gift Tax
Hunting License Tax
Inheritance Tax
Inventory Tax IRS Interest Charges (tax on top of tax)
IRS Penalties (tax on top of tax)
Liquor Tax
Local Income Tax
Luxury Taxes
Marriage License Tax
Medicare Tax
Payroll Taxes
Property Tax
Real Estate Tax

Recreational Vehicle Tax
Road Toll Booth Taxes
Road Usage Taxes (Truckers)
Sales Taxes
School Tax
Septic Permit Tax
Service Charge Taxes
Social Security Tax
State Income Tax
State Unemployment Tax (SUTA)
Telephone Federal, State, and Local Surcharge Taxes
Telephone Federal Excise Tax
Telephone Federal Universal Service Fee Tax
Telephone Minimum Usage Surcharge Tax
Telephone Recurring and Nonrecurring Charges Tax
Telephone State and Local Tax
Telephone Usage Charge Tax
Toll Bridge Taxes
Toll Tunnel Taxes
Traffic Fines (indirect taxation)
Trailer Registration Tax
Utility Taxes
Vehicle License Registration Tax
Vehicle Sales Tax
Watercraft Registration Tax
Well Permit Tax
Workers Compensation Tax[12]

While everyone does not pay all of these taxes, we pay many of them. And there are new ones all the time—like the seventeen new taxes under Obamacare, including the individual mandate, which also drives up the cost of insurance. According to the nonpartisan research group the Tax Foundation, the average American works almost four months before reaching "Tax Freedom Day." That's the day you've generated enough income to pay all state, federal, and local taxes. You're no longer essentially an indentured servant of Big Government. Those living in high-tax states like New York and Connecticut, unfortunately, have to add in a few weeks more.

How you're forced to pay some of these taxes is still more coercive. Government, via your employer, reaches into your pocket and takes "withholding" directly from your paycheck. You never even see the money.

We accept the practice of withholding as if it were an ancient decree. In fact, it is a fairly recent development resulting from the expansion of government during World War II. The Current Tax Payment Act of 1943 instituted withholding to increase government cash flow and help pay for the war. Before that, people paid taxes in one lump sum on March 15, a month earlier than they do today.

Libertarians such as Representative Ron Paul, businessman and respected free market advocate Lew Lehrman, former House majority leader Dick Armey, and others criticize the concept of withholding precisely because it numbs people to how much government actually takes out of your income. Big Government can "silently" take from taxpayers who barely feel a thing—and are therefore less likely to object to Washington's demands for tax increases.

As if these levies weren't coercive enough, they're often used for "social engineering"—pressuring people to make decisions serving the interests of politicians. You get tax credits so you'll use "green technologies." Or you may have to pay taxes on cigarettes or sugary sodas. These "sin taxes" can be avoided if you don't buy the products being taxed. They nonetheless can have immoral unintended consequences. Cigarette taxes, for example, have resulted in black markets attracting criminals engaging in activities like smuggling and theft. Whether the "sin" being taxed is cigarettes, alcohol, or even sugary sodas, critics question the morality of the state profiting from products that it seeks to discourage. In the words of free market ethicist Reverend Robert Sirico of the Acton Institute, the levies place the state in "the peculiar and contradictory position of professing to discourage certain behaviors while relying on their continuance as a source of revenue."[13]

Your money—what it's worth. Our system of "fiat" currency, in which the dollar's value fluctuates based on the policies of the Federal Reserve, is also a form of Big Government coercion. In an open market, two parties may voluntarily agree to a transaction at a certain price. But by manipulating the value of currency, government can arbitrarily change the real value of your agreement. This has been the case since Richard Nixon in the early 1970s abandoned the gold standard.

The purpose of money is to make easier transactions between parties. Before money, transactions had to be conducted by the cumbersome process of barter. The invention of a stable currency enabled commerce to expand enormously. Not only trade but also investment became possible. Money is thus a fixed measure of value, such as sixty minutes in an hour or sixteen ounces in a pound. Imagine what life would be like if the number of minutes in an hour changed each day—or if every state had its own currency. Doing anything would be infinitely more complicated and difficult. The same is true when the value of money fluctuates.

For most of our history, the dollar's value was fixed to a defined quantity of gold. Why gold? Because the intrinsic value of gold hardly changes. From the 1930s until 1971, it was set at one thirty-fifth of an ounce of gold and did not fluctuate as it does today. Prices were thus determined solely by market demand—what you and the millions of others in the economy decided things were worth by "voting" with your dollars. These intrinsic market values are today undermined and complicated by the fluctuating dollar.

The Federal Reserve was engaging in this kind of currency coercion following the financial crisis of 2008, when the central bank lowered interest rates and twice injected money into the economy via "quantitative easing," buying financial assets—that is, bonds—from major financial institutions. Big Government advocates prefer today's system with its floating dollar because it allows policymakers to "guide" the economy. Most people are uncomfortable with the highly technical-sounding language of monetary policy. So they rarely question when Big Government "wise men" like Federal Reserve chairman Ben Bernanke and his predecessor Alan Greenspan insist this kind of manipulation is "good" for us. But it is extremely damaging. In the inflationary 1970s, oil soared from $3 a barrel to $40. After Reagan ended the inflation with tight money, oil prices plummeted, bottoming at under $10. From the mid-1980s to the early part of the last decade, oil averaged a little more than $21 a barrel. Look at what has happened since the Fed turned on the money-printing presses again. Oil companies got windfall gains while much of the economy suffered windfall losses.

When government devalues a currency, people instinctively seek to preserve the worth of their money. Artificially high levels of money go into commodities, such as oil and hard assets like housing. The housing bubble could never have happened without the Fed creating too much money.

What you eat. Big Government initiatives at both the state and federal level—from trans-fat bans and antiobesity sin taxes on sugary sodas to prohibitions on school bake sales—are increasingly telling people what they should eat and making it harder for them to eat what they want. In the state of North Carolina, a rare hamburger is illegal.[14] It can't even be medium rare. That's right. If you order a burger, it has to be cooked to a temperature of 155 degrees Fahrenheit. Violators risk a downgrade in the health scores posted in the windows of all food establishments. Perfectly clean restaurants trying to please their customers can end up losing business—or have their licenses revoked. North Carolina isn't the only state waging war on rare burgers and other undercooked food. Massachusetts and other states require restaurants to post health warnings against undercooked eggs and meat. Some establishments, as a consequence, have stopped serving them. In 2012, the food nannies called for a national campaign against sugar, a staple of daily life that has been consumed for hundreds of years, suggesting that it, too, should be regulated.

Is it really the role of government to intrude this deeply into our lives? There's plenty of knowledge about the dangers of obesity or eating undercooked food to be gained from the media, from the Internet, and from your own experiences or those of friends and relatives. No doubt your mother has weighed in as well. Aren't sentient individuals equipped to decide for themselves whether they care to risk enjoying the occasional rare burger, poached egg, or sushi?

Do we really need government food nannies protecting us? The pioneers who settled the American frontier survived without the benefit of warnings from state health departments or information about the number of calories in their venison.

In North Carolina, a state lunch inspector—yes, the state really has them—recently confiscated and discarded a four-year-old's school lunch that was packed by her mother. Why? The meal—a homemade turkey sandwich, banana, chips, and apple juice—violated federal nutrition guidelines. Instead, the child was made to eat the school lunch, which consisted of *chicken nuggets.*[15] Clearly these food fights are less about nutrition than fattening state bureaucracies.

There's no end to the pettiness. In the states of Georgia, Iowa, Wisconsin, and Texas, lemonade stands have been prohibited or shut down by police because they lacked food vendor permits. *National Review* editor Rich Lowry reports that in one Georgia town:

> the chief of police explained why she had to act to protect the public from the unauthorized sale of the unknown substance purporting to be "lemonade": "We were not aware of how the lemonade was made, who made the lemonade, or what the lemonade was made with."[16]

This defies the boundaries of ridiculousness—not to mention reasonable government. In the wise words of Ronald Reagan, "Government exists to protect us from each other. Where government has gone beyond its limits is in deciding to protect us from ourselves." Lowry supplies his own rule of thumb: "When it makes kids cry."

BIG GOVERNMENT'S COERCIVE "CURE" IS OFTEN WORSE THAN THE DISEASE

A story: Decades ago, New York City instituted rent control to bring "fairness" to the housing market by putting an end to the sky-high rents charged by "greedy" landlords. What happened? Price controls made it impossible for property owners to generate the capital to maintain and build new housing. Supply shrank. Desirable apartments became so scarce, New Yorkers often had to pay "key money"—i.e., bribes—to snag an apartment. Controls have since been loosened but not lifted. The average rent in Manhattan is almost $3,500 a month. Finding a new apartment, especially for young people, is notoriously difficult. How is that fair?

This is typical of overly coercive Big Government regulations and taxation. They don't produce "fairness" but unintended consequences that make things worse. Problems don't get solved—and you give up your freedom.

Another example: the much-decried crisis in health care, a mess caused not by free markets but by prior government regulations and mandates. Even today, few people fully appreciate that health care was already among the most heavily regulated sectors of the economy.

Over the past decade, proliferating rules dictating what insurance companies have to cover have driven insurers from many states. Between 1999 and 2009, the cost of the average family policy jumped 131 percent, according to the Kaiser Family Foundation.[17]

Obamacare is only worsening the damage caused by these state regulations. The law's cuts in Medicare have meant more stringent price controls on drugs and medical treatment—and more shifting of unreimbursed costs by insurers to the privately insured.

Americans felt the pain of these disastrous policies almost immediately after the law was passed. Premiums have risen sharply. Some two hundred cancer drugs have been reported in short supply. There are also longer waits for care. Frustrated physicians are abandoning their practices. A shortage of as many as 150,000 doctors is expected by 2025.[18] Taxes on medical device makers will reduce the new innovations that come into the system.

Critics who decry the greed and brutality of capitalism fail to grasp the extent to which markets are influenced by government, with its mammoth powers of taxation and regulation and its ability to direct, and print, trillions of dollars. The most painful recent illustration of the profound damage that can be wreaked by this kind of excessive coercion is the housing bubble and financial crisis. Three decades of "affordable housing" regulation, imposed in the name of "fairness," eventually created the culture of high-risk lending that led to the disaster.

It began in the late 1970s with the Community Reinvestment Act (CRA), a response to charges that loans were being "unfairly" denied to people in low-income areas. To open new bank branches or undergo mergers or acquisitions, banks had to show that they were open to lending to affordable housing buyers in low- and moderate-income neighborhoods. Under the administration of Bill Clinton, the rules got tougher. Banks had to actually make a percentage of loans to low- and moderate-income borrowers to be CRA compliant.

The Federal Reserve's low interest rate monetary policies of the early 2000s, which knocked down the value of the dollar, were intended to boost the economy. But they further stoked the mortgage lending mania. Enter Fannie Mae and Freddie Mac. During the George W. Bush years, the two government-created mortgage leviathans bought hundreds of billions of dollars in subprime loans. International banking regulations also encouraged excess by requiring banks to set aside far less reserves for possible losses on mortgage securities than with business loans.

The loosening of credit standards resulted in millions of unqualified borrowers getting mortgages, producing a tsunami of defaults. The resulting shock waves caused the near collapse of the U.S. financial system, as well as global markets. We have yet to recover.

THE UNINTENDED CONSEQUENCES OF "SAVING" THE PLANET

Contrary to the assertions of partisans, including President Obama, believers in sensible government want clean air and clean water. The problem is that certain environmental regulations can be extremely coercive—and they don't work. Cap-and-trade programs, for example, have resulted mainly in raising the cost of energy by forcing companies to buy and trade emissions permits—a glorified form of taxation. Even environmentalists have acknowledged that these programs have been a failure.[19]

Experts also express doubts that some efficiency regulations are really saving energy. That's because of something known as "the energy rebound effect." People who believe they're saving energy by owning fuel-efficient cars will drive more frequently. Or they'll buy bigger air conditioners because the energy-efficient models don't cool rooms enough. *New York Times* columnist John Tierney writes, "In some cases, the overall result can be what's called 'backfire': more energy use than would have occurred without the improved efficiency."[20]

And what happens when consumers use those pricey energy-saving washing machines? Thanks to energy efficiency rules, today's new washing machines use less hot water than a decade ago. But a *Consumer Reports* study found that, in many cases, they leave clothing "nearly as stained after washing as they were when we put them in."[21] A reasonable response in this situation? Forget about saving energy and put the load through again.

Those "low-flow" toilets intended to save water don't work particularly well, either. Environmentally conscious San Francisco changed its building codes to require them. The move may have saved water, but it also created a far more immediate environmental disaster. Without enough toilet water to flush out sewer pipes, human waste gummed up the sewer system. On hot summer days, residents in some areas complained of a rotten-egg stench. The problem is one reason San Francisco has spent $100 million to upgrade its sewer system. When that failed, the city turned to another solution—bleach. It invested $14 million in a three-year supply to inject into its sewer system—prompting an outcry from environmentalists concerned about "irreversible" damage to the environment, such as the production of poisonous chlorine gas and the release of cancer-causing toxins into San Francisco Bay.[22]

Another potentially toxic coercion: highly controversial Bush administration legislation that may eventually force Americans to give up the incandescent bulbs they've used for 130 years in favor of far more expensive alternatives supposed to save energy. One of those, the compact florescent, previously failed with consumers in a free market because it costs as much as $50 a bulb—and contains mercury. When you break a CFL, as millions inevitably will, it will "[require] something approximating a Superfund cleanup," notes Scripps Howard columnist and *National Review* contributor Deroy Murdock.[23]

These fiascos have caused Sam Kazman of the Competitive Enterprise Institute (CEI), a free market think tank, to call Big Government efficiency regulations "feel-good mantras that politicians invoke." "If the technologies were so good," he says, "they wouldn't need to be imposed on us by law."[24]

TSA-STYLE GOVERNMENT

The TSA may be the reigning symbol of Big Government's tendency toward excessive coercion. The job of screening air travelers was previously handled by private firms under contract to airlines and airports. The Transportation Security Administration (TSA) was established as part of the Department of Homeland Security in the wake of the 9/11 tragedy. Fortunately there has been no repeat of that disaster. However, the agency has been criticized by just about everyone for its invasive security techniques and brusque treatment of passengers.

Every air traveler on the planet loathes the TSA's lengthy pat-downs and millimeter wave scanners that see under people's clothing. There are constant media reports of overly intrusive searches and mistreatment by the agency's security screeners.

Elderly people and individuals with medical devices are routinely harassed. A bladder cancer survivor was soaked in urine after a pat-down broke his urostomy bag. Reason Foundation aviation expert Robert Poole explains that the TSA's infuriating one-size-fits-all screening is symptomatic of its centralized bureaucracy. The agency is not accountable to individual airports, but to Washington. There's no impetus to design security systems that address the genuine risks at individual airports.[25]

Defenders insist this heavy-handedness is necessary to protect Americans. But the TSA's methods have not been wholly successful. There have been some twenty-five thousand security breaches at U.S. airports since 2001, according to a congressional inquiry.

If a private business treated customers the way the TSA handles travelers, it would not long survive in democratic capitalism's customer-centered open market. Many security experts believe there are more effective, less sweepingly intrusive ways to deal with today's very real security threat.

People are enraged at the TSA because—for many—its intrusion is a tipping point. Millimeter wave machines and pat-downs violate personal privacy much the way the Obamacare's medical database will when it makes your intimate medical history available to people who do not need to see it. The TSA's rigid, top-down approach scanning grannies in wheelchairs shows the same lack of common sense as so many other Big Government controls—from trans-fat bans to asset forfeiture. The agency's top-down, strong-arming coercion typifies what is happening as Big Government takes over other parts of the economy, imposing rules that ignore the needs and desires of individuals.

COERCION CREEP:
THE INSIDIOUS SPREAD OF OVERREACH

The bigger government becomes, the more bureaucrats seek to enlarge their power. Parkinson's Law also applies to coercion: The original Constitution of the United States was only four pages and about 4,400 words. Compare that with the 2,700 pages and 500,000-word health care bill that was too long for even its supporters to read—or for that matter the 2,300 pages of the Dodd-Frank "financial reform" law. Legal expert and reformer Philip K. Howard writes that "decades of accumulated law" have given us "more than 100 million words of binding statutes and regulations."[26]

One rule, regulation, or bureaucracy can produce untold and entirely unexpected infringements on fundamental rights. Americans of all faiths were outraged when the Obama administration announced that its health care law would force employers affiliated with the Catholic Church to violate religious beliefs and offer insurance covering contraception.

Cardinal Timothy Dolan, president of the National Conference of Catholic Bishops, voiced the shock that rippled through the Catholic community: "Never before has the federal government forced individuals and organizations to go out into the marketplace and buy a product that violates their conscience. This shouldn't happen in a land where free exercise of religion ranks first in the Bill of Rights."[27]

This strong-arming of the Catholic Church, however, only confirmed the worst fears of Obamacare opponents. Many predicted from the beginning that the coercion of this law would reach beyond health care.

Such overreach is typical of today's gargantuan legislative packages written expressly to give bureaucrats near-limitless authority. The Dodd-Frank Wall Street Reform and Consumer Protection Act, signed into law in 2010, is a masterwork in this respect. Advocates insist Dodd-Frank's so-called reform was needed to keep people from being ripped off by unscrupulous companies, and to prevent recurrence of the financial crisis of 2007–2009. But we already have laws to protect people against fraud. Dodd-Frank does nothing about the massive distortion of the mortgage markets produced by the two government-created leviathans, Fannie Mae and Freddie Mac. Nor does it address the real causes of the crisis.

What the law does is establish bureaucracies like the Financial Stability Oversight Council, charged with "identifying and responding to emerging risks throughout the financial system."[28] Exactly what constitutes a "systemic risk" is never spelled out. It's what the government says it is—which of course can change day to day.

Another Dodd-Frank creation is the Consumer Financial Protection Bureau, whose mission is to protect consumers against "unfair, deceptive or abusive" practices by financial firms. This could mean virtually anything. James Gattuso of the Heritage Foundation points out that "the term 'abusive' is particularly open-ended, having never been previously defined in law."[29]

Vagueness, in fact, *defines* the 2,300-page Dodd-Frank bill. Unfortunately, this is no accident. Regulations open to interpretation give bureaucrats more power, opening the door to politically motivated enforcement, unfairness—and abuse.

Coercion creep also takes place with taxation, as activist Grover Norquist has pointed out. The brutal alternative minimum tax, for example, was supposed to apply only to the rich when it was imposed in 1969. By 2012, it affected some four million households. In 2013, it will affect *twenty-seven million more.* In the coercive world of Big Government, this is called "spreading the wealth." Unfortunately, most people end up a lot poorer.[30]

AGENCIES ACCOUNTABLE TO NO ONE

Like Dodd-Frank, the Obama administration's new health care law establishes a myriad of health care bureaucracies— "councils," "advisory groups," and "task forces"—whose purpose and powers are left mostly undefined.

Many of today's proliferating Big Government rules and regulations are not being made by our elected representatives, as the Constitution intended. They're being imposed by these bureaucracies or by executive branch agencies like the Environmental Protection Agency, the Federal Trade Commission, the Federal Communications Commission. These bureaucracies are basically accountable to no one.

There's no end to the arbitrary rules they impose via bureaucratic diktat. The Federal Code of Regulations had 54,000 pages in 1970. Today it has 165,000 pages. If you wanted the complete set of bound volumes for your library, you'd need 27 feet of shelf space.[31]

Instead of protecting people, laws like Obamacare and Dodd-Frank hurt the economy by creating uncertainty and enormous compliance costs. Each law means thousands of pages of new rules that will be issued for years to come.

ARMED AND DANGEROUS

There is a darker side to this coercion creep. Regulatory violations are increasingly being treated as criminal offenses by Federal bureaucracies that are increasingly resorting to the use of force.

In 2009, armed agents from the Fish and Wildlife Service converged on Gibson Guitar, the Nashville-based century-old maker of musical instruments. The agents seized rosewood and ebony that the government believed was illegally imported. No charges were ever filed against Gibson, which says it obtained the wood legally. This is not an isolated incident. It's not uncommon for agents with guns to conduct raids on business owners who may not be aware they have violated any law.

Some 138,000 officers now work for federal agencies outside traditional law enforcement. The number of investigators is rising dramatically. Criminal prosecutions by agencies other than the Departments of Justice, Treasury, and Homeland Security have increased by some 50 percent since the mid-1990s.[32]

Economist and former Reagan administration official Paul Craig Roberts and his coauthor, ethicist Lawrence Stratton, write that overzealous prosecutors are increasingly bringing criminal charges against individuals who do not meet the traditional test of mens rea, or criminal intent. The two cite numerous cases in their book, *The Tyranny of Good Intentions: How Prosecutors and Law Enforcement Are Trampling the Constitution in the Name of Justice.*[33]

Freedom advocates frequently bring up the tragic case of David McNab, a lobster fisherman whose family had been in the business for generations. Acting on an anonymous fax, the National Marine Fishery Service confiscated his boat and his seventy thousand pounds of lobster. His offense: the spiny lobsters he caught were undersized, violating wildlife and fishing laws. McNab's lobsters had been caught in the Caribbean off Honduras. That was of little consequence to the feds. They charged McNab, two of his customers, and a distributor, under the Lacey Act, the same law used by the feds in the case of Gibson Guitar. It prohibits the taking of any wildlife in any way that violates local, domestic law and regulations—not just in the United States but of any country. The government of Honduras intervened during the trial and said McNab hadn't committed a crime. No matter: he spent eight years in prison. His associates got ten years.[34]

Everyone wants to protect the environment and endangered species. But does that mean we should treat those suspected of violating these laws—sometimes unknowingly—in the same manner as the most violent criminals?

Not only are these smaller federal agencies becoming more aggressive. Another trend alarming civil libertarians is the rise in asset seizures that are ensnaring innocent third parties. Law enforcement has long had the power to seize assets used in the commission of a crime or gained from criminal activities. But these seizures have become disturbingly more aggressive since the 1990s. Some $2.5 billion in cars, boats, and cash were confiscated by the feds in 2010—twice as much as in 2005.[35]

James Lieto had $392,000 in cash seized when a federal investigation confiscated vaults belonging to the armored car firm that transported money for his check cashing business. Lieto, however, was not suspected of any crime. The feds were investigating the owners of the armored car business he happened to use.[36]

After struggling to stay open, he eventually got everything back. But not everyone has been so lucky. Other innocent customers of the armored car company were treated as fraud victims—who often get back about twenty-five cents on the dollar. The *Wall Street Journal* points out that state law enforcement agencies that help the feds on these criminal cases get to keep up to 80 percent of the proceeds. So there is a disincentive to return your money—even if you never did anything wrong. The intent of asset seizures—like those TSA searches—may be to protect the public by enforcing the law. But when government gets too big and bureaucratic, the end result, too often, is TSA-style disregard for individuals.

Lawmakers who enact Big Government controls rarely think about their potential for violating our personal freedoms. Because of the success of our democracy, Americans generally consider Big Government power, in the words of Roberts and Stratton, to be "a force for good [that] must be less and less restrained." The authors warn we should think again: "Self-rule ceases to exist when elected representatives don't make the law. Eventually, power that is unrestrained becomes, in Lenin's words, 'unlimited power, resting directly on force.'"

A BRAIN DEAD SOCIETY

Big Government's excessive coercion may not always mean police state tactics. But it often leads to what author and legal reformer Philip K. Howard has famously called "the death of common sense." Too many rules and regulations prevent people and businesses from independently making decisions. This destruction of personal responsibility and initiative, he says, is "a progressive disease, dragging [down] the rest of society."

It's gotten so bad, Howard says, that the Obama administration was unable to implement parts of its own economic stimulus:

> The stimulus money for weatherproofing homes, for example, couldn't be spent last year because a 1931 law, designed to keep union wages high, requires an army of federal bureaucrats to set wages in 3,000 different localities before anyone can start caulking those windows. No kidding—that's what federal law requires.[37]

Howard writes that the problem is particularly acute in health care, where doctors, in his words, are "immersed in law all day long, preventing them from using their common sense to do what they believe is right."

> Bureaucratic reimbursement formulas drive doctors and hospitals to make treatment decisions based on what bureaucratic guidelines will reimburse—not care that's actually needed. The breakdown of judicial responsibility to keep lawsuits reasonable causes doctors to squander billions in defensive medicine. Universal distrust of justice has chilled the open interaction needed for safe hospitals. Thousands of tragic errors occur because doctors and nurses are reluctant to speak up when they suspect something is amiss—"Are you sure that's the right

dosage?"—because they're not certain, and they don't want to be legally responsible.[38]

Howard proposes that all new laws include sunset provisions that stipulate they expire after ten or fifteen years. People will never learn to take responsibility and think for themselves, he says, if bureaucratic rules, or the threat of them, drive every decision.

Countless rules kill more than common sense. "Jerry B.," an employee of a government office "hamstrung by union rules," believes they also crush the human spirit. He despairs that his colleagues "will never know the joy of being treated as an individual or as a professional." Rigid union rules that practically dictate his every move have not improved work conditions. They've made them worse by destroying any chance for personal initiative. "In short," he writes, "it all robs me of my pride."[39]

BIG GOVERNMENT COERCION *CREATES* CRIMINALS

French economist and political philosopher Frédéric Bastiat wrote in 1848 in *The Law,* "When law and morality contradict each other, the citizen has the cruel alternative of either losing his moral sense or losing his respect for the law."[40] Instead of encouraging morality and the rule of law, Big Government creates criminals and corrupts society.

When Big Government imposes price controls or when products are banned or heavily taxed, you get illegal markets run by criminals. The classic case, of course, is 1920s Prohibition, which spurred the rise of organized crime in the United States. Mob families became rich and powerful running bootlegging rackets. The government's ban on alcohol gave us violent criminals like Al Capone, who took control of a broad range of criminal activities, from extortion to drugs and illegal gambling.

Black markets are a way of life in socialist dictatorships like Venezuela and Cuba, the only places where people can find essentials of daily living.

Democratic socialist Sweden has a black market in rental housing not unlike what existed in New York City at the height of rent control. People seeking a rental apartment in Stockholm end up paying huge sums to landlords to avoid waiting on long lines and to get around the rent control laws. The state of New York has a growing black market for cigarettes—thanks to overly high taxes that have caused a pack of smokes to cost as much as $14.

Some Big Government rules create law breakers because it's hard to avoid violating them. In the state of Texas, for example, every new computer repair technician is required to purchase a private investigator's license. That's right. *A private investigator's license.*[41] An individual must either have a degree in criminal justice or complete a three-year apprenticeship with a licensed private investigator. To make matters worse, you can violate this ridiculous law if you are simply a regular citizen who has a computer repaired by someone who doesn't have a PI license. Violators can be fined up to $4,000 and put in jail for a year.

Will every computer technician in the state of Texas have the resources or the time to comply with this law? And how many people getting their computers repaired violate it unknowingly? Mike Rife, a computer repair technician who sued unsuccessfully on behalf of Texas computer technicians and their customers to get the law repealed, has pointed out that he would have to close his business and do a three-year apprenticeship as a private investigator in order to comply.

Washington, D.C., regulations actually make it illegal to "describe . . . any place or point of interest in the District to any person" on a tour without a license. Violators risk being arrested and thrown in jail for up to three months. Tour guides Tonia Edwards and Bill Main take groups on Segways to historic sites in the nation's capital. Their business is located near the National Archives, home to the Bill of Rights. Edwards and Main are providing an important service, educating people about Washington, D.C.'s, place in our history. The fact that they're working in this tough economy is no small feat. Yet Washington, D.C., considers these entrepreneurs to be lawbreakers.[42]

The two filed a federal First Amendment challenge to the city's tour-guide licensing regulations, contending they are unconstitutional: the government cannot require people to get a license in order to talk.

CUBA'S ROAD TO SERFDOM

Americans concerned about Big Government threats to our freedom can learn much from the story of Cuba. The island nation offers a textbook example of what Hayek was talking about in *The Road to Serfdom*. Since Castro took over in 1959, millions have fled its harsh dictatorship, many swimming or rafting to the United States in shark-infested waters. Yet Cuba's totalitarian regime was initially perceived as having good intentions.

In the beginning, Castro was seen as a champion of the oppressed. His rise to power was viewed as a victory for "fairness."

Government essentially took over the entire economy—imposing wage and price controls, confiscating large private estates, and spending on public works programs to "create jobs." It imposed coercive laws and levies that are the dream of many people today on the American left. The result was a massive redistribution of the nation's wealth to the poorest 40 percent of the population. Lower-income people got jobs with higher salaries (labor contracts were renegotiated) and homes with lower rents. About a million people were "given" jobs during the 1960s. Castro's communist government instituted stiff price controls that drastically drove down the prices of electricity, gas, and public transportation. Rents across the country dropped by 50 percent. Social services like education and health care, even burial services, were provided by the government for "free."[43]

However, this massive coercion in the name of "fairness" ended up killing Cuba's economy and keeping people desperately poor. Many who had supported the revolution turned against their charismatic leader. But Cuba's Big Government, typical of brutal dictatorships, would brook no opposition. Not only have millions fled, experts estimate that at least a hundred thousand have died on account of the regime. Thousands of people have been shot by Castro's firing squads. Many more have been thrown in jail.

Cubans who remain live in grinding poverty with chronic shortages created by Big Government rationing and price controls. The *Washington Post* reported that ordinary citizens are forced daily to "go to the left," violating the law and risking jail by making back-alley deals to buy everything from basic food staples to illegal satellite dishes.

Despite the intention to impose fairness, Cuba's coercive Big

Government ended up forcing only misery on its citizens. In *The Road to Serfdom,* Friedrich Hayek quotes Alexis de Tocqueville on the dangers of coercive "democratic socialism." What the French social observer said in 1848 could have been written today:

> Democracy extends the sphere of individual freedom, socialism restricts it. Democracy attaches all possible value to each man; socialism makes each man a mere agent, a mere number. Democracy and socialism have nothing in common but one word: equality. But notice the difference: while democracy seeks equality in liberty, socialism seeks equality in restraint and servitude.[44]

✻　✻　✻

THE MORAL BASIS OF CHOICE

The quest for liberty is the heart of the American experience. Since the first settlers arrived on these shores, millions of people from all cultures and walks of life have come seeking freedom. Famed historian Frederick Jackson Turner described how the "love of wilderness freedom" and the quest for property that drove Americans west resulted in a new society "productive of individualism" with "[an] antipathy to control, and particularly to any direct control."[45] He wrote that "the most distinctive fact" of life on the frontier "was the freedom of the individual to rise under conditions of social mobility, and whose ambition was the liberty and well-being of the masses."[46] These values, he said, "vitalized all American democracy, and has brought it into sharp contrasts with the democracies of history, and with those modern efforts of Europe to create an artificial democratic order by legislation."[47]

Americans' "antipathy to control" has launched many crusades in the name of liberty, from the abolition of slavery to the later campaign for women's rights. They attest to the desire for freedom that motivates the American people.

Americans of all backgrounds and beliefs instinctively know freedom is better. But why is it moral?

Freedom means self-determination, choosing your own direction based on your needs and interests. It means being able to pursue one's dreams and goals—whether that may be starting or growing a business or achieving happiness—without intrusion or oppression. Freedom implies the sovereignty of the individual and self-ownership: you have a right to make your own decisions because you—and not government—own your self.

George C. Leef, director of research for the John William Pope Center for Higher Education Policy, writes in *The Freeman* that this belief in "self-sovereignty" is a fundamental instinct shared by all people. "No one, not even the most ardent statist, likes having his freedom to choose how to spend his time and money usurped by others. Most people realize that turning decision-making authority over to others is apt to leave them worse off."[48]

Seventeenth-century political philosopher John Locke, whose ideas influenced the Founding Fathers and are reflected in the Declaration of Independence and the Constitution, wrote, "Every man has a property in his own person: This no body has any right to but himself. The labour of his body, and the work of his hands, we may say, are properly his."[49]

The ideal of respect for the individual is deeply rooted in Western Judeo-Christian tradition. Noted historian and Baylor University professor Rodney Stark reminds us that, at one time, it was a radical idea. "Even the Greek philosophers had no concept quite equivalent to our notion of the 'person.'"

> Thus, when Plato was writing the *Republic,* his focus was on the polis, on the city, not on its citizens—indeed, he even denounced private property. In contrast, it is the individual citizen who was the focus of Christian political thought, and this in turn explicitly shaped the views of later European political philosophers such as Hobbes and Locke. This was, quite literally, revolutionary stuff, for the Christian stress on individualism is "an eccentricity among cultures." Freedom is another concept that simply doesn't exist in many, perhaps most, human cultures—there isn't even a word for freedom in most non-European languages.[50]

Statists know freedom and choice are things people want. That's why they'll incorporate the idea of "choice" into Orwellian labels for their Big Government rules; for example, "The Employee Free Choice Act." That law would have allowed unionization of a workplace without the benefit of a secret ballot. Instead of more, it gives workers *fewer* choices.

This gets to the cultural contradiction of liberalism: the very Big Government advocates who purport to champion individual rights, creativity, and free expression routinely support Big Government policies and bureaucracies that crush individualism and choice. This is true not only in the workplace but everywhere else.

HOW FREEDOM PROMOTES GOOD BEHAVIOR

The conventional wisdom is that, without Big Government, open markets would degenerate into reckless free-for-alls. Not true. Even believers in economic freedom can fail to appreciate the self-regulating influence of free market self-interest.

In a voluntary market, people and companies have to treat you well enough so that you'll choose to do business with them. If they don't, you can take your business elsewhere, or seek other employment.

In other words, *the fact that people freely choose to enter into an open market exchange works to encourage cooperation and moral behavior.* It's true that sometimes one side may violate the terms of a voluntary transaction—for example, you buy a car that's a lemon. That's why a free market requires a fair and impartial legal system—to enforce the terms of contracts and mediate disputes.

The competition and openness of free market societies also help to curtail too much power and "greed." Free markets allow newcomers to rise up and challenge major players. The flow of information in an open market society through institutions like a free press provides additional checks and balances.

The self-regulating power of self-interest is demonstrated by historic examples of truly free markets. Some have functioned for years without interference from government. What happened? People did just fine.

William Anderson, economics professor at Frostburg State University and a scholar at the Mises Institute, recounts, "For about a century after the founding of the United States, business activity faced little or no government regulation, especially compared with the situation in modern times."[51]

America in the nineteenth century is not the only example of a self-regulating market. In their book *Money, Markets & Sovereignty,* Benn Steil and Manuel Hinds write that much of today's codified commercial law was not developed by lawmakers but comes from lex mercatoria—"merchant law"—which arose spontaneously in the eleventh and twelfth centuries. The laws of lex mercatoria evolved from the customs and practices of merchants who needed common rules of the road to conduct business beyond their borders. "Even outside the realm of common law systems, commercial practice has throughout history driven the codification of systems of law, and not vice versa."[52]

Lex mercatoria included principles such as requiring that both parties act according to "good faith" and a general standard of "fair dealings," in addition to fundamental property rights. These rules were enforced by a system of merchant courts called Pie Powder courts at merchant fairs along trade routes that were separate from local legal systems.

Bruce L. Benson, economics professor at Florida State University, notes that lex mercatoria is but one illustration of the spontaneous regulation that takes place in free markets. He explains: "Merchant [law] evolves whenever commerce emerges. Practices that facilitated emergence of commerce in medieval Europe were replayed in colonial America, and they are being replayed in Eastern Europe, Eastern Asia, Latin America, and cyberspace."[53]

Like the markets of medieval times, the Internet is today still a largely unregulated market. Yet what Benson calls "markets for trust" have sprung up to aid consumers and businesses attempting to establish trust in first-time transactions. He gives the example of VeriSign, which provides a "trustmark" that Internet businesses can display, assuring customers that their personal data is secure. But that's far from the only example. Benson writes,

> [T]he American Institute of Chartered Public Accountants and the Canadian Institute of Chartered Accountants offer a WebTrust program. This combined group audits on-line business practices regarding privacy, security, and the handling of complaints about quality and performance. . . . Similarly, BBBOnline offers a "Reliability seal" certifying an on-line business as "reliable" and "trustworthy."[54]

Free market critics insist we need Big Government intervention because of disasters like the financial crisis, and the sensational implosion in 2011 of investment firm MF Global Holdings. However, the financial industry is already the most regulated sector of the economy, overseen by bureaucracies such as the Federal Reserve, the Office of the Comptroller of the Currency, the Securities and Exchange Commission, the Commodities Futures Trading Commission, and numerous state agencies. Remember, the MF Global disaster occurred *after* passage of the Dodd-Frank Bill, and earlier, Sarbanes-Oxley, which mandated elaborate new expensive accounting controls ostensibly to prevent Enron-like fraud and promote higher executive accountability. Unfortunately, no amount of government strictures will prevent accidents or bad decisions.

FREEDOM, ETHICS, AND RESPONSIBILITY

Fox News Business network senior correspondent Charles Gasparino has an interesting take on MF Global. He believes Jon Corzine made risky bets on government bonds from Italy and Spain because he believed that those countries, like America's biggest financial institutions, were too big to be allowed to fail. He invested based on the attitude, as Gasparino puts it, that "If you can bail out a massive bank like Citigroup, with nearly $1 trillion in customer deposits, why can't you bail out a country like Italy?"[55]

In other words, Corzine's awareness of the protection and heavy regulation of Big Government, instead of reducing risk, encouraged the investor to be less careful. Had he thought that the governments of Italy and Spain would fail, Gasparino believes, he would not have been so quick to take such enormous risks. The MF Global fiasco, Gasparino suggests, is ultimately an example of the "moral hazard" of too much government that we will discuss in chapter 4.

British economic columnist Tim Harford, author of *Adapt: Why Success Always Starts with Failure,* believes Big Government's coercive interventions in markets *increase* risk *because it stifles the market's natural impulse to self-regulate.* People who think the marketplace is "safe" because of Big Government rules and safeguards—what happens? They take even *greater* risks.

Free markets, in contrast, *demand* that individuals take responsibility. You—and not government—are the primary agent determining your future. You're more inclined to make responsible decisions because you bear the consequences.

Coercive Big Government rules and regulations do not

instill ethics and responsibility. People have to choose to behave morally because of their own convictions or because it is in their self-interest. Overly large, coercive government can keep society from developing a moral compass—and not just because of meddlesome rules. State-run societies frequently limit the influence of religious institutions—or ban them outright.

Free market critics like to blame tainted products and corruption in China on that nation's economic liberalization. But some observers believe the real cause is state hostility to religious institutions, as well as overbearing, corrupt bureaucracies. Economist Qinglian He, former senior editor of the *Shenzhen Legal Daily,* points out that "in contemporary China, where religion was once banned and is still strictly controlled by the state, poor business ethics became rampant as the market economy took root."[56] It's worth noting that Russia—where religion was banned during the days of the Soviet Union—suffers from similar problems of ethics and trust. When the Soviet Union collapsed, Russia became notorious for rampant corruption and violence in the business world. Oligarchs, including former members of the KGB, looted prized industrial assets like oil and gas. While things have improved since then, problems persist.

Adam Smith and countless others have written that free markets can only operate in a society where social and religious institutions help foster agreed-upon moral values. Institutions like schools, churches, and synagogues are critical ethical influences. Not all people consider themselves believers. But values like "do unto others" and other principles based in Judeo-Christian belief are vital guideposts for behavior.

Michael Novak explains that "the roots of commercial society—habits of innovation and invention, the blessedness of hard work, a focus on the future—spring from imperatives in the Jewish and Christian religions."[57] America's Founders recognized, in Novak's words, "the crucial role of religion and morality in curbing commercial instincts, keeping them within bounds and steering them from self-destruction." He quotes Tocqueville, who noted, "There are many things that the law does not prevent citizens from doing that the religion of Americans prevents them from doing."[58]

A common refrain in America during Tocqueville's time was that *a self-governing nation must have self-governing individuals.* Freedom does not imply license. A free society and a free market, then as now, require people who can control their passions—who have the discipline to put aside selfish, present-oriented needs to work toward a better future. In the words of Ben Franklin: "Only a virtuous people are capable of freedom."[59]

ECONOMIC FREEDOM MEANS MORE "COMMON GOOD"

In 2004, Hillary Clinton told a group of well-heeled liberal supporters that the need for revenue for ever-expanding government meant they should reconcile themselves to the prospect of higher taxes. No one likes to hear that. So Clinton put it a different way. She told the group, "We're going to take things away from you on behalf of the common good."[60]

Certainly taking money away from the people in the room is not advancing *their* common good. Taking away money from "rich people" who are the country's job creators has never been shown to help poor people.

The "common good" argument is always used to persuade people to accept more coercive taxes and regulations. Yet it is freedom, not Big Government bureaucracies and restrictions, that has produced the prosperity and democracy that are the real common good.

As we noted earlier, Steve Jobs couldn't have produced his world-changing innovations if he had grown up in socialist Syria, the birthplace of his biological father. In every case, the common good is best served in a democratic capitalist economy where individuals and businesses have the greatest latitude and ability to choose for themselves.

No system has been more effective than democratic capitalism in producing prosperity and lifting people from poverty. In the United States, people are living longer and living standards are higher. Between 2003 and 2007, the growth of the American economy alone exceeded the size of the entire Chinese economy. Free market economic reforms—especially since the fall of the Berlin Wall—have brought an unprecedented explosion of wealth to India, China, Brazil, and nations in central and Eastern Europe as well as in Latin America and Africa.

Noted economic historian Deirdre McCloskey has called this freeing up of the world's economies "the Big Economic Story" of our times. Open markets can be disruptive. But in the end they have vastly improved the common good for the world's population: "The idea of bourgeois dignity and liberty," McCloskey writes, "led to a rise of real income per head in 2010 prices from about *$3 a day* in 1800 worldwide to over $100 [a day] in places that have accepted the Bourgeois Deal and its creative destruction" (our italics).[61]

The greatest poverty and the *least* good are found in the government-run countries in the developing world, where there are endless bureaucratic obstacles to economic activity. To start a business in Zimbabwe, entrepreneurs have to pay the government fees that add up to the equivalent of five times that nation's per capita income. In the United States, by comparison, those fees are nominal.[62]

The common good in emerging nations has immeasurably increased when governments grant people freedoms like the right to own property. Those who distrust landlords and "greedy" developers fail to appreciate the moral dimension of property ownership. Where people have property rights, land and buildings can be used as collateral and become sources of capital. When China sought to liberalize its economy, it began to grant more property rights, allowing people to own their homes. (The land under them, however, is owned by the state, which can confiscate it at any time.)

Edward Younkins, executive director of the Institute for the Study of Capitalism and Morality at Wheeling Jesuit University, points out that property ownership encourages self-determination because it's "based on the natural human desire and right to survive and pursue one's vision of happiness."[63]

That's one reason why economic freedom has been a force for democracy, another social good. In Younkins's words, "Freedom is based on ownership. If it is possible for a man to own assets, it is also possible for him to have freedom of speech, religion, [and] the press."[64] People who have choice in the marketplace eventually seek to have more political choice.

Historian Frederick Jackson Turner made this point in his classic "Turner thesis" about the cultural and political influence of the American frontier. The push for more liberal suffrage provisions in the constitutions of states like Virginia and New York came from people in the states' frontier regions. He wrote in *The Significance of the Frontier in American History,* "The rise of democracy as an effective force in the nation came in with western preponderance under Jackson and William Henry Harrison, and it meant the triumph of the frontier . . ."[65]

Another reason open markets promote democracy, explains Cato Institute author Daniel Griswold, is that "economic freedom and trade provide a counterweight to governmental power."[66] Affluent, educated individuals and corporations with resources to protect are more likely to stand up to authoritarian rulers.

A final benefit: Economic freedom and choice make people happier. Researchers Sebastiano Bavetta and Pietro Navarra of the London School of Economics analyzed data from sixty countries drawn from the World Value Survey database and the Heritage Foundation/Wall Street Journal Index of Economic Freedom. They found that happiness correlates with economic freedom and the perception of autonomy, a feeling of control over one's life.[67]

ECONOMIC FREEDOM IS PERSONAL FREEDOM

Each year hundreds of thousands of people continue to come to the United States fleeing the political and economic suffocation of their country's Big Government. We have become all too accustomed to hearing these stories. It is time to start listening again.

In 1994, Norberto Gonzalez Jr. was among thousands of Cubans picked out of the open sea during the Balsero Rafter Crisis. He was one of thirty-eight thousand Cubans, allowed to leave by dictator Fidel Castro, who attempted to flee to the United States on a makeshift raft flotilla.

It was Gonzalez's second attempt to escape. A failed first

attempt had landed him in a Cuban prison, which strength-ened his resolve. "Food rationing . . . Clothes provided by the government . . . No freedom whatsoever," he said. "That's why I decided to leave. I didn't want to live there any more . . . There was no other way. There was no future."[68]

After winding up for a time in a refugee camp at Guantá-namo Bay, Gonzalez eventually made it to the United States, where he joined the Marines after 9/11. Gonzalez acknowledges that his life has had ups and downs (he was blinded in one eye in the Marines in a freak accident). But he recently told a re-porter that his ordeal had been worth it. "I'd rather be eaten by a shark than die in Cuba."[69]

William and Mary law professor Lan Cao and her family fled communist Vietnam during the 1970s. She points out that the war was not what made people leave: "After the war," she re-calls, "millions of people fled. Not during the war: after the war. These were not refugees fleeing from the violence and danger of war, but millions of people fleeing a totalitarian state in search of freedom."[70]

Democratic capitalism is no utopia. Markets are people, and people aren't perfect. There are excesses and dishonest in-dividuals. And there can be massive scammers like Bernard Madoff. Big Government advocates like to focus on instances of bad behavior. But they get attention precisely because they are exceptions. And, in a free market system with an impartial court system and a free press, wrongdoers are more likely to be exposed—and punished.

There are trade-offs in democratic capitalism. But most people, when asked to choose between freedom and Big Gov-ernment coercion, would choose freedom. Lan Cao puts it this way: "When you look at the history of the world, no one ever flees toward a totalitarian communist system. You don't need a lot of theory to know that people yearn to be free. And an essential part of that freedom is an economic market system that offers options and possibilities for people. Even with all its flaws, people are drawn to a free market system."

3

SILICON VALLEY
or DETROIT?

Creativity and Abundance Versus Rigidity and Scarcity

*"To be moral," says economist and Nobel laureate Edmund Phelps,
"is to foster the betterment of humankind."*[1] *Democratic capitalism
meets this standard better than any other system. Unconstrained by
the restrictive rules and capital-destroying taxation of more heavily
regulated economies, individuals and companies have greater latitude to find new ways to meet the wants and needs of others. The
freedom of open markets enables people to depart from traditional
approaches and try new ideas. Democratic capitalism is an engine
of innovation because it allows millions of entrepreneurial individuals and companies in the marketplace to engage in this process of
exploration, both failing and succeeding. It further promotes creativity by allowing people to make the profits that fund development
of these new ideas and ventures.*

*The new products and services developed in open markets im-
prove our lives and raise living standards* by turning scarcity into
abundance. *Take silicon. Without free markets unleashing human
ingenuity, it would have remained in its natural state as sand on a
beach, rather than being used to power billions of computers.*

*Moral creativity, however, has a price. Innovation, as we've
noted, involves trial and error. Certain ideas and ventures will be
rejected by the market and not succeed. Failure is painful for both*

companies and individuals. But it's vital to the learning process and sets the stage for bigger successes later. Financial Times *columnist and author Tim Harford points out that high tech, the "most successful industry of the last forty years, has been built on failure after failure."[2] Few people today remember that Apple's immensely successful iPhone and iPad were preceded in the 1990s by the Newton, an early handheld device that was widely ridiculed when it hit the market.*

Successful innovation also brings what economist Joseph Schumpeter called "creative destruction." When a new product comes along, jobs tied to old technologies may be lost. The iPod with its iTunes software revolutionized buying music, making it easier and more affordable. But brick-and-mortar music retailers became largely obsolete. This disruption was painful. But society as a whole benefited.

Big Government, in contrast, seeks to suppress the randomness and risk taking needed for innovation. Its job is maintaining order and security. Instead of arising from the collective ingenuity of the marketplace, Big Government solutions come from a handful of bureaucrats. Profit is often controlled or prohibited. Taxes necessary to sustain a Big Government leviathan suck up capital needed for advancement. Instead of fostering innovation, Big Government–controlled economies or markets, like health care, stagnate under rules and bureaucratic rigidity.

The decline of the Detroit automakers illustrates how Big Government stifles innovation in both companies and industries. Government regulations put in place to please politically powerful unions have burdened automakers with rigid work rules, as well as high costs. The auto industry over decades has increasingly struggled to innovate and compete. Compare this government-inflicted sclerosis to the vibrancy of Silicon Valley, where government interference has been limited. Companies and people have been free to experiment and learn from failure. This freedom—to fail as well as succeed—has produced a vibrant creative community whose technology innovations have helped power the U.S. economy.

BOTTOM LINE: DO YOU WANT TO LIVE IN A STAGNANT WORLD OF SHORTAGES AND BUREAUCRACY—OR A DYNAMIC ECONOMY WITH MORE JOBS, PRODUCTS, AND OPPORTUNITIES?

THE TRUE ENGINE OF INNOVATION: FREE MARKETS, NOT GOVERNMENT

President Obama has repeatedly declared that new government initiatives were needed to make the United States more competitive. He's called for a "Sputnik moment," evoking the 1950s launch of the Russian space orbiter that rattled American nerves and led to the U.S. space program. Insisting "we cannot cut back on those investments that have the biggest impact on our economic growth," the president believes that the way to boost innovation and competitiveness is more government—more spending on education and science.[3]

Big Government advocates often talk about innovation as though government can simply switch it on. Government has helped develop certain basic technologies, and there's nothing wrong with supporting some government-funded research. But Big Government is by no means the *engine* of a creative economy.

Big Government did not invent the automobile, the airplane, and most other innovations. Government may have played a critical role in developing computer technology. But entrepreneurs gave us the personal computer. Only a truly free market is capable of the kind of creativity and innovation that brings far-reaching improvements in our way of life.

Take a classic example—the automobile. Developed over decades by a succession of European inventors, Henry Ford finally put the auto within the reach of the consumer at the turn of the twentieth century through developing the technology for the moving assembly line. Ford's innovation reshaped our entire way of living. Allowing people to travel far vaster distances, the automobile led to the rise of suburbs, highways—and a new culture of mobility. It led to convenience stores, gas stations, and drive-through fast-food chains. Totally new kinds of businesses generated hundreds of millions of jobs, many in categories that had never before existed.

Mass-producing the automobile gave us modern life as we know it today, including countless conveniences we take for granted. A single innovation remade society and set off a tidal wave of wealth and job creation.

Government does not possess the collective ingenuity, or the bandwidth, to develop such advances—or to see them to fruition. Think of the details that have to be managed. Remember chapter 1. Do you think the bureaucratic culture that gave us the post office would be capable of coming up with the idea for a drive-through Starbucks, with all the various coffees and varieties of Frappuccino?

Even a large federal bureaucracy of the "best and the brightest" is still a handful of individuals compared with the hundreds of millions of people in open markets. The kind of revolutionary creativity that produced the automobile, modern air travel, the personal computer, and other innovations can only arise, as Friedrich von Hayek so wisely pointed out, from the spontaneous activities of people in open markets. Unlike bureaucrats and politicians in government who must please political constituencies, individuals in the marketplace are motivated by the need to solve real-world problems. They do so based on practical experience—what Hayek called the "special knowledge of circumstances of the fleeting moment not known to others."[4]

This information enables them to meet the needs of the market in ways that are not always easy to anticipate. You see this with even the smallest inventions. Who would have expected the simple microplane rasp, which was invented for woodworking, to end up being widely used by cooks to grate citrus peels and hard cheeses?[5] Another unexpected innovation: a tiny, eraserless pencil from IKEA that has become popular with health care professionals who use it to mark patients before surgery.[6]

And how many of us would have imagined that people would want to get low-cost flu shots at walk-in clinics in big box stores? Or that businesses would spring up providing medical consultations via telephone and e-mail? Yet both arose spontaneously in the tiny slivers of the health care market that are free of restrictions. We would see more of these innovations in health care if we had a truly free, consumer-driven market without today's constraints on entrepreneurial creativity.

Allowing insurance companies to sell across state lines and giving individuals tax deductions for buying insurance would create a larger consumer-driven market. This would spur innovation. Health insurers and care providers would find customer-friendly ways to deliver their services. Visionaries would rise up just as they have in other free markets, transforming health care in ways impossible to foresee today.

HOW FREE MARKETS CREATE ABUNDANCE

Economists miss the point when they say innovation is about improving "efficiency." Free market creativity means producing *abundance.* The distinction is vital when it comes to appreciating why markets are moral. New technologies not only help people work more productively. They produce *more*—more products and services for lower cost. In this way innovation improves living standards and, yes, to use that term statists love, "spreads the wealth."

One of the first thinkers to describe how this occurs was Henry Adams, the Harvard historian and grandson of President John Quincy Adams. In his autobiography, *The Education of Henry Adams,* he reflected on what he called "The Law of Acceleration": the ever-quickening pace of technological advances that spawned inventions like the ocean steamer, the railway, the electric telegraph, and the daguerreotype. Once considered "impossibilities," these advances, Adams observed, led to ever more abundance. Adams gives the example of "the coal-output of the United States [growing] from nothing to three hundred million tons or more" in the course of the nineteenth century.[7]

Adams's intellectual descendant is Gordon Moore, the cofounder of Intel, who observed that the rate of computing power, reflected by the number of transistors on a silicon chip, doubles approximately every eighteen to twenty-four months. This became known as "Moore's law." Because Moore's law is narrowly applied to computing, people practically regard it as a principle of physics. But Moore was talking about the speed at which creativity and innovation take place in the computer industry in a free market.[8]

Moore's law is why the computer you purchase today delivers two times more power per dollar than one bought two years ago. It's why the memory in your iPod that costs only $49 today cost $7,000 twelve years ago. But it's not just how much computing power you can buy for the money. Ever cheaper computing allows a range of new, unexpected applications and conveniences—from handheld cell phones that are actually wireless computing devices to digital tablets to the GPS device in your car to, yes, greeting cards. According to Peter Singer, an analyst at the Brookings Institution, a simple Hallmark musical greeting card now contains more computing power than the entire U.S. Air Force had in 1960.[9]

These examples of ever-accelerating innovation and efficiency at lower and lower cost account for what we call "the Staples principle": *Technologies out of reach for most people today end up at Staples or another big box retailer at cheap prices, if not tomorrow, then in the very near future.*

In 2000, the first computer flash drive from IBM stored eight megabytes and cost fifty dollars. Today you can get a four-gigabyte flash drive that holds five hundred times more for well under $10. Cell phones that started at $4,000 and gave you just thirty minutes of talking time, fully charged, are now available for as little as $30 or less. (Some plans offer them for free.) The first big flatscreen TVs that came out in the 1990s sold for $15,000. Today you can get one for less than $500.

Innumerable examples abound, not just in technology but also in markets like furniture and clothing. The very first commercially successful ballpoint pen, breathlessly advertised as "guaranteed to write for two years without refilling!" cost $12.50 in 1945, the equivalent of more than $150 today. These days you can buy an entire pack of pens for a fraction of that amount.

We take these developments for granted as part of everyday living. Henry Adams, however, grasped their broader implications. In his autobiography he wrote about the dynamo, the electric motor that was his era's icon of technological advancement. It was not just a machine, but "a symbol of infinity"—the limitless possibility created by the human imagination.

CREATIVE MARKETS ADVANCE "THE GREATER GOOD"

Adams found the inspiration for his ideas at the 1900 Paris Exhibition, the famous world's fair celebrating the era's technological achievements, where he experienced what can only be described as a religious epiphany. The historian "began to feel the forty-foot dynamos as a moral force, much as the early Christians felt the Cross." In a more jaded twenty-first century, such enthusiasm may strike some as being somewhat over the top. But Adams was making an important point about the moral value of free market innovation. More than simply generating wealth, the creativity of democratic capitalism has been a powerful force for what advocates of Big Government like to call "the greater good."

Today we have scant appreciation for just how harsh conditions were just two centuries ago. As noted author and theologian Michael Novak has described them:

> Famines ravaged the civilized world on average once a generation. Plagues seized scores of thousands. In the 1780s, four fifths of French families devoted 90 percent of their incomes simply to buying bread—only bread—to stay

alive. Life expectancy in 1795 in France was 27.3 years for women and 23.4 for men. In the year 1800, in the whole of Germany fewer than a thousand people had incomes as high as $1,000 [in today's dollars].

Liberty of religion and speech was rare. In most cultures, absolute rulers reigned simultaneously over political, economy, and moral-cultural matters. In such a world, in most places, traditional Christianity and Judaism lived under severe constraints.[10]

The development of the market economy in Britain and the United States, Novak writes, changed everything. "After five millennia of blundering, human beings finally figured out how wealth may be produced in a sustained, systematic way."[11] Economic freedom gave rise to an era of innovation that dramatically improved living conditions. People were able to look beyond the necessities of survival. They gained a greater "liberty of personal choice" and advantages like "a varied diet, new beverages, new skills, new vocations."

Philosopher Thomas Hobbes's famed description of life as "nasty, brutish and short" has become less true with each generation.

In the bestselling, influential book *The Rational Optimist,* British journalist Matthew Ridley describes in powerful detail how free markets have uplifted mankind:

[T]he vast majority of people [today] are much better fed, much better sheltered, much better entertained, much better protected against disease and much more likely to live to old age than their ancestors have ever been.

Even allowing for the hundreds of millions who still

live in abject poverty, disease and want, this generation of human beings has access to more calories, watts, lumen-hours, square feet, gigabytes, megahertz, light-years, nano-meters, bushels per acre, miles per gallon, food miles, air miles and of course dollars than any what went before. They have more Velcro, vaccines, vitamins, shoes, singers, soap operas, mango slicers, sexual partners, tennis rackets, guided missiles and anything else they could even imagine need-ing. By one estimate, the number of different products that you can buy in New York or London tops ten billion.[12]

Even in poor countries, Ridley tells us, people are living lon-ger. "The average Mexican lives longer now than the average Briton did in 1955. The average Botswanan earns more than the average Finn did in 1955." Food, clothing, fuel, and shelter over decades has grown steadily cheaper:

[S]urprising as it may seem, the average family house prob-ably costs slightly less today than it did in 1900 or even 1700, despite including far more modern conveniences like electricity, telephone and plumbing.[13]

We also get far more for our labor, he notes, than we ever did: "An hour of work today earns you 300 days' worth of read-ing light; an hour of work in 1800 earned you ten minutes." (This achievement may dim considerably if Big Government ends up making consumers buy those expensive bulbs.)

Entrepreneurial creativity has been the foremost force for good that society has ever known. Entrepreneur and free en-terprise evangelist Michael Strong believes that "the creation of new enterprises is the most powerful way to make positive change in the world. If all the energy that is currently invested in zero-sum political conflict was gradually transferred to the committed creation of sustainable enterprises, the cumulative impact on behalf of good would be extraordinary."[14]

THE PROBLEM-SOLVING POWER OF MARKETS

The ability of creative free markets to solve problems, however, remains woefully underappreciated. Many otherwise astute people are steadfastly convinced, for example, that energy and medical care are forever destined to be expensive. They can't imagine that solutions will arise from letting free markets work.

We made this point earlier, but it should be hammered home: *Creativity is an ever-present impulse of open markets.* People will *always* mobilize to solve problems and meet the needs of others when they are not constrained by government. We may not be able to predict exactly how they will do so—and that is precisely the point. Free market innovations can seem serendipitous and unpredictable.

For example, decades ago people subscribed to the flat-earth belief that resources are "fixed." In the 1790s, Reverend Thomas Malthus did elaborate calculations supposedly demonstrating that a growing world population quickly outpaces the available food supply. Malthusian pessimism, not surprisingly, was a hallmark of the economically stagnant 1970s. People feared "overpopulation" would result in shortages of food and other vital resources. The public's concern over this prospect was expressed in the dire *Global 2000 Report to the President,* commissioned by President Carter and released in 1980. It predicted that "if present trends continue," mankind faced a future of overcrowding, deteriorating living standards, and widespread misery:

> Despite greater material output, the world's people will be poorer in many ways than they are today. For hundreds of millions of the desperately poor, the outlook for food and other necessities of life will be no better. For many it will be worse.[15]

The subtext of this doomsday forecast was that *something had to be done* about this unfettered growth—by government, of course.

The late free market advocate Julian Simon was among the first to see through this fallacious thinking. Simon and fellow futurist Herman Kahn countered the Carter-era gloomsaying with their own coedited book, *The Resourceful Earth*:

> If present trends continue, the world in 2000 will be less crowded (though more populated). . . . The world's people will be richer in most ways than they are today. . . . The outlook for food and other necessities of life will be better . . . life for most people on earth will be less precarious economically than it is now.[16]

Three decades later, there are 2.5 billion more people in the world than there were in the late 1970s. The global population has passed seven billion—twelve times more than there were two hundred years ago in Malthus's time. However, the Global 2000 prediction of crushing scarcity never materialized. The last three decades have instead supported Simon and Kahn's prediction of increasing abundance. This progress was not the result of government activism—but the fact that governments around the world *got out of the way.* They liberalized their economies and allowed greater economic freedom.

Greater freedom produced a flowering of ingenuity and enterprise that lifted hundreds of millions of people out of poverty in nations like China, India, Malaysia, Indonesia, as well as the states of the former Soviet Union. Thanks to innovations like genetically modified crops, which increase yields—by making produce more resistant to insects and disease—there is more food than ever before.

Poverty has yet to be eradicated. However, people in developing nations, who just thirty years ago were living at subsistence level, are now able to afford consumer goods like cell phones and automobiles. Indeed, the present-day fear is not that the people of China and India will starve, but that they will economically outpace us.

Writing in the liberal Slate.com, journalist Brian Palmer acknowledges that, these days, "few economists lose sleep over the prospect of absolute exhaustion of any particular resource."[17] He reports that the U.S. Geological Surve once estimated the global reserves of zinc at around seventy-seven million tons. Improved exploration and mining technologies have since enabled people to dig up nearly four times that amount. "Experts" have been similarly surprised by larger-than-predicted supplies of tin, copper, iron ore, and—most significantly—oil. Palmer writes, "In 1970, researchers thought we had only 30 years of oil left. By 1990, the estimate had risen to 40 years . . . [and] few in the industry think all the wells will have run dry by 2050."

Daniel Yergin, a noted industry analyst, has pointed out that people have feared that we've run out of oil five different times in modern history—and it's never happened. In the late 1970s, he recalls, people were scared to death that we'd fall off the "oil mountain."[18] Instead world oil output has increased *30 percent* since then. In fact, thanks to major advances in oil and gas drilling, the United States and the world are experiencing rapid increases in oil and gas supplies.

Doomsday forecasts for the environment have also not held up. It's true that, at first, economic growth can have negative environmental effects in poor countries. But as nations become more affluent, things get better. After a country's per capita income exceeds $8,000, its environment starts getting cleaner. Researchers have been able to chart this trend for pollutants such as sulfur dioxide emissions. Their increase and eventual decrease can be charted on a graph as an upside-down U.[19] The trend is known as the "environmental Kuznets curve," named after the late Wharton economist Simon Kuznets, who charted a similar U-shaped pattern while studying trends of income inequality.

In today's era of 1970s-style gloom and doom, Malthusian thinking has recently been making a comeback. *MarketWatch* columnist Paul Farrell echoed fellow pessimists in 2011 when he warned that the "population bomb" described by biologist Paul Ehrlich more than forty years ago is finally on the verge of exploding. The planet, he claimed, was reaching a "tipping point." World population "could top 15 billion by 2100, all demanding a better lifestyle, all demanding more natural resources, more commodities, starting revolutions to achieve their economic goals."[20]

Big Government advocates, alas, persist in fearing "scarcity," while history shows their concerns are groundless.

THE MORAL POWER OF CELL PHONES

The cell phone is a powerful illustration of how *a single free market innovation* can vastly improve the lives of billions of people. Thirty years ago, only a handful of businesses and individuals could afford one. The pioneering Motorola cell phone cost almost $4,000. Today there are over five billion cell phones in the world. Even the poor have access to them, including three million people in Haiti, the poorest nation in the Western Hemisphere.

Those who get annoyed by incessant texting and overhearing personal conversations in public places should consider the impact these devices have had, especially in the developing world. Cell phones have become a powerful wealth creator by generating job opportunities and boosting productivity. For many people in poor countries, they are a critical link to health care services providing access to doctors. Cell phones have helped farmers increase productivity and profits: they can get information to help set prices for their crops or farm animals without having to travel to market. In Kenya, small-business people who never had access to banking services use phones to make purchases and transfer money.

A United Nations study confirms this: "Mobiles have spawned a wealth of micro-enterprises, offering work to people with little education and few resources. Examples are selling airtime on the streets and refurbishing handsets."[21] A 2005 study by the London Business School found that GDP growth in developing nations is higher when there is greater cell-phone penetration. We think of cell phones as conveniences. But in poor nations they are critical catalysts for wealth creation.[22]

WHAT BILL GATES CAN LEARN FROM INDIA
ABOUT "CREATIVE CAPITALISM"

Several years ago Bill Gates, in a widely discussed speech at the annual World Economic Forum in Davos, declared that free markets did not do enough to help the world's poor. He called for a new "creative capitalism" with philanthropic efforts to help the needy. At the heart of Gates's complaint:

> Capitalism harnesses self-interest in helpful and sustainable ways, but only on behalf of those who can pay. Government aid and philanthropy channel our caring for those who can't pay, but the resources run out before they meet the need. But to provide rapid improvement for the poor we need a system that draws in innovators and businesses in a far better way than we do today.[23]

Yet experience—and outlays of hundreds of billions of dollars—has demonstrated that aid, whether it comes from a handful of companies or governments, has never ended poverty. The only way to bring about the kind of sweeping changes that Gates seeks is through giving people more economic freedom—removing the constraints of government.

To see the real meaning of "creative capitalism," one should embark on a passage to India, which was once one of the most desperately poor countries on earth. As recently as 1985, 90 percent of the population lived on less than a dollar a day. Decades of socialist taxes and regulations had strangled India's economy. Would-be entrepreneurs seeking to escape starvation by selling wares on the street had to get countless permits. Even if you were among the lucky few living above subsistence level, there was little to buy. Those who wanted a car, for example, could choose from only a few models with outdated technology.

In the early 1990s, the country was jolted by a debt crisis into implementing pro-market reforms. The government cut back regulations and opened markets to trade and investment, along with taking other steps like tax reform and privatization. The results were miraculous. Nations around the world mobilized to help India—not with one-time infusions of aid but through trade and investment, generating jobs and much-needed products. Economic growth exploded, with GDP expanding 7 to 9 percent a year.

India's reforms have done what no corporate philanthropy or government aid could ever do. In less than three decades, the country cut its poverty rate in half.[24] Three hundred million Indians have escaped extreme poverty—a number equivalent to the entire population of the United States. While considerable poverty remains, India now has a thriving consumer society. Indians today can go to shopping malls. Food is available like never before. People can now buy high-quality cars. Indeed, one problem today is how to modernize the country's still-inadequate roads to accommodate the increasing number of vehicles.

Corporate philanthropy of the kind that Gates describes would have never brought about such sweeping changes. You don't need "creative capitalism." Capitalism is already creative.

BUT WHAT ABOUT WALL STREET?

People who appreciate the achievements of entrepreneurs like Steve Jobs or Henry Ford can nonetheless have a harder time seeing creativity in finance. This has been especially true since the economic crisis.

Filmmaker Michael Moore expresses the view shared by many—and not only on the far left—that it's okay for people to be rewarded for "making things or inventing things." What he objects to is when "we reward people for making money off money and moving money around and dividing up mortgages a thousand times over, selling it to China."[25]

On the right, former Republican presidential hopeful Newt Gingrich set off a furor among free market supporters when he voiced similar criticisms of primary opponent Mitt Romney's activities at Bain Capital, the investment firm he cofounded and ran during the 1990s. Gingrich asked, "Is capitalism really about the ability of a handful of rich people to manipulate the lives of thousands of other people and walk off with the money, or is that somehow a little bit of a flawed system?"[26]

Others questioned the morality of Romney's tax returns, which revealed that he paid a 15 percent tax rate because his income came from investments. Sparse attention was paid, by Romney's critics or by the media, to the rationale behind the capital gains rate. Critics make it sound as though the gains are a certainty—however, most new ventures fail. The capital gains rate is low because investors like Romney help society by risking money on other people's ventures that may or may not pan out. Not all of Romney's investments succeeded. Those that did generated thousands of jobs and hundreds of millions of dollars for countless investors and shareholders. But to his loud and vociferous critics, Romney was just "moving money around" and had gotten an unfair tax break.

These sentiments are rooted in age-old prejudices. Economist Thomas Sowell has written brilliantly about the long-standing distrust of "middleman minorities" that cuts across cultural boundaries. Middlemen include not only Jews and Asian immigrants in the United States, but groups like the Ibos in Nigeria and the Parsees in India. Prejudices against them, Sowell explains, were never about ethnicity. "Retailing and money-lending," he explains, "have long been regarded by the economically unsophisticated as not 'really' adding anything to the economic well-being of a community."[27] Like Michael Moore, people for hundreds of years have been unable to see how those who "make money off money" are really making anything.

Moore and others could not be more wrong. Private equity and investment capital firms like Bain Capital are a major reason why the United States has created jobs and has grown at a faster rate than the world's other developed economies. Few realize that the venture capital industry originated in this country and remains—with the exception of the U.K.—largely a U.S. phenomenon. In the mid-2000s, before the financial crisis, the United States invested $27 billion in new and emerging companies, compared with just $10 billion in the U.K.[28] Other countries, like Holland and France, invest far less than that—and in Italy, venture capital activity is almost nonexistent. Firms like Bain are the reason that—as we discuss in chapter 5—the entrepreneurial enterprises are able to emerge and become powerhouses of innovation and job and wealth creation.

Among the companies Bain has helped to grow or thrive include Staples, The Weather Channel, Brookstone, Sealy Corporation, and Burger King.

But what about Newt Gingrich's complaint that firms like Bain often destroy jobs? There is job destruction—but the charge is highly misleading. Even without firms like Bain, the economy creates and destroys jobs all the time. As we explained in the beginning of this chapter, creative destruction of some jobs and companies is a necessary consequence of market creativity. According to a recent study by researchers at the University of Chicago, the University of Maryland, and Harvard, venture firms in the long term don't destroy jobs at a higher rate than the rest of the economy. There is more job destruction at first, as they streamline companies to make them better able to compete. But the job creation that takes place later washes out the initial losses. Many companies that would have failed were saved and better positioned to grow.

Daniel Henninger points out in the *Wall Street Journal* that after we emerged from the economic malaise of the 1970s, firms like Bain helped "save America" over the following ten years by shaping up sluggish companies. Henninger reminds us, "Back then it was called the Greed Decade, with asset-stripping barbarians at the gate. Virtually everything about this popular stereotype is wrong. Properly understood, the 1980s, including Bain, were the remarkable years when an ever-resilient America found a way to save itself from becoming what Europe is now—a global has-been."[29]

ENTREPRENEURIAL CREATIVITY IN JUDEO-CHRISTIAN TRADITION

The morality of entrepreneurial creativity is an idea rooted in Judeo-Christian belief. Noted philosopher and theologian Michael Novak has written that Christianity considers "creation left to itself" to be "incomplete." Human beings are meant to be "co-creators with God, bringing forth the potentialities the Creator has hidden."[30]

Judeo-Christian thinking places a high value on the skills of questioning and inquiry that give rise to entrepreneurial innovation. The seventeenth-century philosopher John Locke wrote that the ability to question is fundamental to "reason" and the development of genuine moral convictions: "He that takes away Reason to make way for Revelation, puts out the Light of both."[31] The process of questioning is also fundamental to study of the Talmud.

Democratic capitalism enriches individuals by developing this ability to question and reason. Consider what it takes to start a business, create a new product, or hold down a job. The problem solving required by open markets leads to self-improvement— sharpening our capacity for rational thinking. Michael Novak puts it well:

> Capitalism is very much (as the word suggests) a system of the head. Practical intelligence orders it in every detail. It promotes invention and fresh ideas. It strives constantly for better forms of organization, more efficient production, and greatest satisfaction. It plans for the long run as well as the short. It orders materials, machines, producers, salesmen, and consumers. It organizes means and ends. It constantly studies itself for improvement.[32]

Capitalism's ability to encourage people to go better and farther, and plan "for the long run as well as the short," is illustrated by George Mitchell's fifteen-year quest to develop hydraulic fracturing. In the 1980s, energy experts believed that the supply of natural gas was dwindling. This concern spurred Mitchell, a Houston-based independent energy producer who supplied natural gas to the city of Chicago, to look for a way to replace his critical reserves. A geology report he'd read convinced him there was plenty of gas. The problem, though, was that it was locked in shale, the extremely dense layer of rock under Dallas and Fort Worth.[33]

Nearly everyone, including Mitchell's own engineers, was skeptical that gas could be extracted from the dense rock for a reasonable cost. But he nonetheless persisted, working on a method for fifteen years at his own expense. The result was an enhanced version of a technique called hydraulic fracturing— "fracking"—that extracts natural gas by expanding natural or man-made fractures in rock.

Mitchell's innovation is transforming the energy industry. The United States will eventually become a net energy exporter for the first time in over a half century. Shale gas has rapidly increased from 1 percent to about 25 percent of American natural gas supplies—and future finds are expected to drive this share still higher. Despite the allegations from some (though not all) environmentalists, shale gas is a clean form of energy that has fewer downsides than not only oil but also coal and nuclear. And it will also become a new fuel for heavy vehicles, such as trucks.

The energy entrepreneur—who sold his company in 2002 for more than $3 billion—helped advance a technology that, Big Government permitting, will bring cleaner, cheaper energy to hundreds of millions.

Mitchell's achievement has geopolitical implications. Shale gas discoveries in nations like France and Poland promise to decrease European dependence on oil and gas imports. Russia, a key exporter to Europe, will suffer a major loss of political leverage. With exports no longer propping up its government-dominated economy, it may finally have to enact deeper market reforms.

American society reveres the explorers and pioneers who settled the nation. We admire the astronauts who ventured into space and walked on the moon. No one would question the morality and bravery of these feats of exploration. Entrepreneurial innovation and risk taking of entrepreneurs like George Mitchell and others originate from a similar impulse, in the words of economist and Nobel laureate Edmund Phelps, "to take a plunge, to leap into the unknown." He writes

> This quest to do better, to go farther, to extend our reach is part of what makes us human. . . . I personally hold that the classical spirit of challenge and self-discovery is a fundamental human trait . . . what Augustine called our "restlessness of heart." This is the better part of our human nature. Societies that suppress this restlessness stagnate and die.[34]

* * *

BIG GOVERNMENT: THE ANTI-INNOVATOR

Government suppresses market creativity, as we've noted, because its core competency is maintaining order and security. When it dominates a market, it tends to minimize the risk taking, randomness, and disruption that foster innovation.

You don't have to look far for examples. Take a simple one: the yellow public school bus. School buses are the result of a government-dominated oligopoly. Only a handful of companies manufacture them, and the government—that is, local school districts—is the only customer. Because they reflect the priorities—and budgets—of local education bureaucracies, they have been especially slow to advance.

Manufacturing standards were established in 1939 by a group of educators, manufacturers, and officials brought together by Dr. Frank Cyr, a former school superintendent.[35] Despite their critical responsibility for transporting the nation's children, school bus design has changed less than the design of buses used by public transit. Modern city buses have flat-nosed designs that allow drivers a better view of the street—and pedestrians. But the most common school bus today is still the chunky truck-style vehicle whose design dates back to the 1930s and that affords drivers far less visibility. National safety requirements were last upgraded more than three decades ago.[36] To the dismay of many parents, most school buses still don't contain seat belts.[37] This is especially remarkable when you consider that a national law has required seat belts in passenger cars for nearly fifty years.

Government officials believe that it's hard to get a bus full of kids to use them and that the expense isn't worth the money. The buses, they insist, are safe. However, critics like Dr. Alan Ross of the National Coalition for School Bus Safety have maintained that school bus accidents have injury rates and fatalities that are underreported.[38] They point to National Highway Traffic Safety Administration data showing that lap-shoulder belts in any vehicle reduce injuries and fatalities by 45 percent. Shoulder restraints would also increase safety by making kids stay in their seats. Besides, they say, many parents want them.

The real reason buses don't have seat belts, they're convinced, is the expense: they add as much as $15,000 to the cost of a new bus.[39] Seat belt advocates have won partial victories in six states, which have agreed within the last several years to require them on larger buses.

The seat-belt controversy may have helped to finally bring about other improvements. Modern "flat-nosed" buses are becoming more common. And new buses are featuring "sleeping child alarms" that make drivers check for stragglers at the end of a route. But the slow pace of change illustrates why Big Government impedes innovation. Decisions are based on budgets and politics.

Not everyone may believe that seat belts belong in buses. But *everyone* agrees that air travel in this country is a mess. The TSA is just a small part of it. Any flight just about anywhere can mean endless delays and cancellations. The Department of Transportation's solution in 2010 was to impose its tarmac delay rule, which fines airlines $27,500 per passenger for any aircraft sitting on the runway for more than three hours. There haven't been many violators because airlines terrified of enormous fines have responded by simply canceling flights, producing still more delays.

As this story might suggest, the real cause of the air-travel nightmare is Big Government mismanagement of the nation's aviation infrastructure.

Government-run airports have been reluctant to implement market-based methods like peak pricing of slots that would direct some traffic into off-hours. Today's air traffic control system relies on outdated 1950s radar technology that gives planes limited ability to adapt to changing conditions. Pilots end up wasting time circling runways, using more fuel and slowing air traffic.

We could fix our antiquated infrastructure by upgrading air traffic control, as other countries have done, with GPS-based air traffic control technology similar to the navigation systems used in passenger cars. Known in the United States as NextGen, the new technology would make it easier for pilots to maneuver and would make controlling air traffic more efficient. The United States is expected to fully implement NextGen by 2025 at a cost of $35 billion. But the project has moved forward at a glacial pace, bogged down by congressional battles over funding.[40]

Washington politics haven't been the only obstacle to reforming the system. Airports have avoided peak slot pricing because they fear antagonizing airlines that don't want to pay higher fees.

However, in a free market, it's easier to overcome such resistance to new ideas. Open markets permit an entrepreneurial outsider to come in and transform an industry—as Steve Jobs did with the record business. You may remember in the late 1990s, when people started downloading music for free off the Internet, music companies' initial response was to sue hapless individual offenders. That got them a lot of bad publicity and didn't stop the flood of illegal downloads. Enter Jobs with iTunes, which enabled companies to make money on downloaded music. At first companies resisted because they would have to break up CD compilations and sell individual songs. But Jobs was able to persuade them that selling individual songs was in their self-interest, the only way to sharply reduce theft.[41]

A Big Government bureaucracy does not have the forward-looking vision or problem-solving ability of entrepreneurs like Steve Jobs. Its solutions are about preserving the present—or recapturing the past. President Obama himself reflected this mind-set when he complained that ATMs and airport kiosks meant "a lot fewer workers."[42] Yet the technology revolution that produced those advances was the very reason why unemployment had been at record *lows* in the three decades before he took office.

BIG GOVERNMENT USA:
THE END OF INNOVATION?

There is indeed a lesson about innovation to be learned from the Sputnik moment—but not the one suggested by President Obama. What Sputnik really shows is that, far from energizing competitiveness—Big Government destroys it.

The Russians may have been able to launch their space program and develop a few successful supercomputers. But their efforts were eventually outstripped by innovations of our own Silicon Valley. The reason, author Michael Strong explains, was America's economic freedom:

> Apple, Atari, Microsoft, Lotus, and others changed the world because anyone could create their own software or device and start-up their own company. In economists' jargon, there were no "barriers to entry." And, in fact, many thousands of high school and college dropouts who were engaged in flow experiences, creating gadgets for the fun of it, changed the world.[43]

Soviet Russia's command-and-control dictatorship was able to concentrate its energies on developing Sputnik and getting a man into space. Those innovations, however, were exceptions. Creativity lags in government-dominated social democracies, thanks to countless rules and regulations. Socialized medicine is a major reason why the bureaucratic nations of Western Europe—as well as those in Asia—trail the United States in biotechnology and medical innovation. New drug development has slowed dramatically in Europe, where price controls of socialized health care prevent companies from recouping their costs and generating the profits needed for investment capital.

America's more open markets and collaborative research culture are the reasons why companies like Novartis are relocating facilities and buying companies in this country. U.S. researchers have published more papers about biology and medicine than any other nation.

It's no accident that the personal computer and other inventions originated in the United States. Heavily regulated European social democracies discourage American-style risk taking and entrepreneurship that is the wellspring of growth-producing creativity. In Germany, companies that reach a certain size are required to have union members on their boards.[44] An entrepreneurial CEO can have a difficult time making needed changes in a company's direction because everyone needs to agree. Corporations are members of confederations that negotiate jointly with unions. This also puts a premium on continuing the status quo.

We explained earlier that Europe, with the exception of the U.K., lacks the deep capital markets of the United States. There are far fewer vehicles such as mutual, pension, equity, and venture funds investing in entrepreneurial businesses. Corporations seeking capital have limited access to bond markets. They're forced to rely on big risk-averse banks. To illustrate: U.S. companies have $1.2 trillion in bank loans; their European counterparts have around $6 trillion.[45]

In this sluggish market, initial public offerings (IPOs) are relatively rare. Rising companies have little choice but to merge with larger corporations. Creative enterprises are also held back by statist labor laws. In Spain and Italy, huge severance costs make it extremely difficult to fire people. It's especially hard for entrepreneurs to launch businesses because the cost of failure is enormous. Would-be start-ups also have to jump through regulatory hoops getting countless permissions and licenses.

In the 1990s, the socialist government of France instituted one law that prohibited people from working more than thirty-five hours a week. Police used to check license plates of cars in company parking lots to make sure they hadn't stayed beyond the requisite seven hours.

The French socialist government actually believed that if each person worked fewer hours, companies would hire more workers. Anyone with any real-world experience knows that you don't create employment by making people work *less.* You do so with a successful product that requires hiring more employees to help meet demand.

Not surprisingly, the French ended up with an economy dead in the water, with barely over 1 percent growth and almost 10 percent unemployment. The law was loosened under President Nicolas Sarkozy. But it has nonetheless made labor more expensive. Working past seven hours is now considered overtime.

Entrepreneurs in the United States for most of our history have largely avoided such micromanaging constraints. Tragically that is now changing. Under Obamacare, the federal government will tell insurers what kind of policies they must offer and what prices they can charge. Dodd-Frank legislation, as we've noted, gives government more power to shut down financial companies. And bureaucracies like the National Labor

Relations Board (NLRB) are telling employers like Boeing how and where they can operate their businesses.

Boeing, incidentally, wasn't seeking to outsource jobs overseas or even move. It still manufactured most Dreamliners in its home state of Washington. The NLRB objected to an *additional* factory the company had built in nonunion South Carolina to meet a backlog of orders. The board eventually backed off after the aircraft maker promised to hire more union workers in Seattle. The intrusion set a disturbing precedent: If it could tell a company where to locate its operation in this country, what else would it be able to do?

Libertarian journalist and Fox Business News commentator John Stossel has also complained about the chilling effect on innovation of countless regulations intended to protect safety. Are all of these rules, he asks, really necessary? Stossel points out that natural gas, widely used for heating homes, kills about two hundred Americans a year. One can only imagine the reaction if such a "hazardous" form of energy were introduced today. And what about swimming pools?

> [They] kill over 1,000 Americans every year. I think it's safe to say that the government wouldn't allow them today if they didn't already exist. What about vehicles that weigh a ton and are driven within inches of pedestrians by 16-year-olds, all while spewing noxious exhaust? Cars, I fear, would never make it off the drawing board.[46]

BIG GOVERNMENT CREATES SCARCITY

Big Government rules don't just hamper the creators of big, flashy ideas. They strangle decision making and problem solving throughout an economy. That's why in command-and-control economies there are frequent shortages of even the basic necessities.

Food is so scarce in North Korea that three million people starved to death in the 1990s. In 2011, the country appealed to some forty nations for more aid—much of which was diverted to the military. Widespread malnutrition has shortened life expectancy. The average North Korean is *three inches shorter* than the average South Korean.

When technology entrepreneur and blogger Joseph Pecar visited Moscow immediately after the fall of communism in the early 1990s, things were so bad that "bare necessities" including fruits, vegetables, and toilet paper were "virtually unavailable to the proletariat":

> Even in government office buildings, one was fortunate to find the only substitute for toilet paper to be scraps of paper torn from old newspapers placed in makeshift triangular paper containers hung on restroom doors.[47]

A common reason for shortages is Big Government price controls. They're intended to curtail "greed" and "gouging." But remember, prices and profits are the market's way of telling producers what products and services are in demand. Without this vital feedback producers don't know where to focus their creative energies. They can't respond to the market. The result: not enough products to meet demand, or shortages because prices are kept artificially low.

Another reason why Big Government command-and-control so often produces shortages is that politicians usually respond to problems with *restrictions*. In contrast, a free market solves problems most often by *creating something new or by increasing supply*. Take annoying telemarketing phone calls. Government had a solution: have people place their names on a no-call list. Problem is, it hasn't stopped those nuisance calls. Nonprofit groups are still allowed to make them, and plenty do.

Telephone companies had their own answer: They offered customers features like caller ID and voice mail that enabled people to screen their calls. These technologies gave customers greater flexibility. They also meant jobs at companies making and selling the new phones.

Bureaucrats, however, rarely respond to problems with entrepreneurial solutions. When someone does, they don't react well. When New York City's Metropolitan Transit Authority, under budgetary pressure, recently cut back bus services, attorney Pamela Golinski found herself without a way to get to work. Golinski and a fellow commuter had a solution: help a private operator run a van service along the route. But the city promptly shut it down because the operator didn't have a license.[48]

Big Government advocates insist their regulations serve the common good. But regulations, taxes, and limits on prices are ultimately controls. Controls almost always mean less of something, not more.

HOW BIG GOVERNMENT KILLS INNOVATION:
THE CASE OF THE FDA

The FDA is a prime example of how Big Government kills creativity and innovation. We need safe drugs and that's why the FDA was created. But this byzantine bureaucracy long ago exceeded the bounds of reasonableness and common sense.

Its labyrinthine and immensely expensive approval process is strangling pharmaceutical research. Thanks to the agency's regulatory maze, the number of years needed to bring a new medicine to market has nearly doubled—from eight in the 1960s to as many as fifteen years today. The cost of this process can reach $1 billion for a single drug.

This hypercaution, like everything else in government, boils down to politics. Approve a medication that has an unintended side effect and congressional headline seekers will be giving officials the third degree. Better to let people die by depriving them of new medicines than to risk your career and be excoriated by demagogues in Congress.

Companies are responding by producing fewer new medicines. Science correspondent Ronald Bailey reports in *Reason* magazine that in 1996, the FDA approved fifty-three drugs. That number fell by more than half in 2010.[49]

The need to recover the billions spent on getting these drugs to market is behind industry strategies critics assail as "greedy." Drug developers focus on coming up with blockbuster drugs and shy away from research that would produce medicines for less common, serious diseases.

Another tactic is "tweaking" existing drugs ever so slightly to create a medication the FDA will consider "new." The result: additional years of patent protection that keeps out competition from generics. Reformulating drugs in this way has enabled manufacturers to win patent extensions on drugs like the antacid medication Nexium (really a tweaked form of Prilosec).

The FDA's circuitous and meddlesome regulatory process is increasing drug shortages. In the spring of 2011, nearly 250 drugs were reported to be in short supply—up from just 70 in 2006.[50]

For the first time, doctors are seeing shortages of common antibiotics—drugs like penicillin that have conquered illnesses such as pneumonia and tuberculosis, saving tens of millions of people. Congressman Henry Waxman called the pharmaceutical industry's inability to develop a reliable new class of antibiotics "market failure." The real cause is bureaucratic failure.

The FDA's stranglehold on the industry doesn't end when a drug is approved. John Goodman, president of the National Center for Policy Analysis, a public policy think tank, has written about rigid FDA "output controls" intended to enforce quality in drug production that are slowing down manufacturing, reducing the availability of much-needed medicines:

> [A] drug manufacturer must get approval for how much of a drug it plans to produce, as well as the timeframe. If a shortage develops (because, say, the FDA shuts down a competitor's plant), a drug manufacturer cannot increase its output of that drug without another round of approvals. Nor can it alter its timetable production (producing a shortage drug earlier than planned) without FDA approval.[51]

These bureaucratic rules, Goodman says, are producing shortages of critical drugs used to treat patients with some of the deadliest cancers, as well as heart attack victims and accident survivors:

> Doctors at the Johns Hopkins cancer center are rationing cytarabine, a drug used to treat leukemia and lymphoma. They are literally deciding who will live and who will die. The drug is also in short supply at the Stanford, Wisconsin and Nebraska university medical centers. Large medical centers in Oklahoma and Maryland have completely run out.[52]

The agency can also drive up the cost of drugs by creating artificial monopolies. That was the case with an off-label drug for expectant mothers at risk for premature births known as "17P." Made for years by pharmacists who informally compounded progesterone, 17P was frequently used by low-income patients. It was cheap—around $10 to $15 a dose. Finally a company called Hologic got the FDA to approve this prenatal progesterone formula. That gave the company exclusive rights to the drug, which it then sold to another drug maker, K-V Pharmaceutical. As a result of having exclusive rights, K-V was able to raise the price of the drug, now called Makena, by *10,000 percent*. Instead of $10 to $15 a dose, Makena now cost $1,500 a shot—as high as $30,000 for a pregnancy.[53]

Not surprisingly, this created an uproar. Politicians and industry groups accused the company of gouging. K-V's greed, however, was a consequence of FDA regulations. It's one thing to verify the safety of a drug. But the FDA went beyond this basic mission by giving K-V monopoly rights to an existing drug. U.S. patent laws give manufacturers an eight- to twelve-year monopoly after a new medicine hits the market. Makena, however, was not new but simply an FDA-approved use of synthetic progesterone, a drug that was already in wide use.[54]

Had the FDA permitted the spontaneous innovation that normally takes place in a free market, K-V would not have been able to charge its astronomical price. Free market forces—i.e., competition—would have curtailed "greed." Eventually that happened. Public outcry forced the FDA to change its rules and permit broader market competition.[55] Pharmacists were allowed to keep compounding their version of the drug. The price instantly dropped. Those who pushed for this solution thought they had triumphed over a greedy company. But they had really scored a victory for free market competition—and *against* constraints by Big Government.

MILITARY INNOVATION? YES, BUT—

Yes, the military does innovate. No one denies the exceptional versatility of heat-seeking missiles or stealth aircraft, or the extraordinary aircraft carriers of the U.S. Navy. But these innovations, however, come at a horrendous cost of dollars and resources.

The awarding of contracts, for example, is highly political. Why do defense companies hire every general and admiral they can? To have lines into all the subterranean agencies and parts of agencies involved in weapons development. Defense contracts are awarded based on an unspoken quid pro quo: whether the project is a new aircraft, ship, or weapons system, the winning bidder makes sure work is subcontracted to numerous suppliers in congressional districts around the country. Is it a coincidence that the New Hampshire congressional delegation was in favor of Lockheed's F-22 fighter because a big part of it was going to be manufactured in the state? (President Obama later canceled the project.)

Government is notorious for refusing to adopt weapons that were not created by the military bureaucracies or persisting with failed weapons systems like the early Vietnam-era M-16 rifle. The M-16 was developed to give the infantryman a rapid-fire weapon on the field of battle. During the early years of the Vietnam War, it became notorious for jamming. Even so, the army was extremely reluctant to make the necessary changes or to junk the weapon and try something else.

The Defense Department procurement systems are woefully out of date. Experts note that they are unnecessarily bureaucratic and add years and endless additional expenses to the development of new weapons systems. No company could compete in private industry with such an antiquated system.

And many military technologies would have never changed society without the efforts of entrepreneurs. The Internet was invented by the Defense Advanced Research Projects Agency (DARPA) in the late 1960s as a way to facilitate the transmission of research data between universities, and as a backup communications network in the event of a nuclear attack. But the Internet as we know it today took off only after the government allowed a private company, Network Solutions, to sell domain names in the early 1990s. In just five years, the number of domains registered to people and businesses passed two million.

The Internet era had begun. Government invented the Web, but it took the private sector to turn it into the revolutionary communications medium and robust job creator that it is today.

BIG GOVERNMENT KILLS INNOVATION BY "ENCOURAGING" IT

In a free market, entrepreneurial creativity is a response to the real-world needs of customers. Consider how cup holders came to be in German cars. German automakers hated the idea of cup holders. In their fastidious culture, people don't eat or drink in cars. From their point of view, it was a sloppy thing to do. But they installed cup holders because they were eager to make automobiles that would appeal to the vast American market. Not only that, engineers poured time and energy into coming up with a cup holder that was *better*—one that would accommodate a sixteen-ounce mug of coffee or a giant Big Gulp cup.

Big Government efforts to encourage innovation—through tax credits and subsidies—rarely if ever end up producing this kind of grassroots creativity. The Chevy Volt is the perfect example. The Volt first appeared as a concept car in 2007. After taking over GM in 2009, the administration made the Volt a centerpiece of its campaign to create "green" jobs and technologies.

The Volt was to be the first step in fulfilling the promise of the new Obama administration to "put 1 million Plug-In Hybrid cars . . . that can get up to 150 miles per gallon—on the road by 2015." The federal government poured billions of taxpayer dollars into its development in the form of grants and low-interest loans. The Korean maker of batteries for the Volt got $150 million. More taxpayer dollars were spent to subsidize Volt buyers, who received a $7,500 tax credit.

It certainly *looked* like the administration was funding innovation. But in its rush to please government backers and get the car to market, GM forgot about meeting the everyday needs of the car user. The Volt is a tiny car for an enormous amount of money—the first one sold for $41,000 before tax credit rebates. And it can't go very far on its "green" battery that needs recharging after around twenty-five or thirty miles—less than the average American round-trip commute. Worse still, tests of the battery have resulted in "thermal events"—i.e., it caught on fire.

The Volt's battery requires only about a dollar's worth of electricity to recharge overnight. But as one critic put it, "you could buy a lot of gas for the roughly $20,000 difference between a regular gas compact car and its $41,000 U.S. electric counterpart."[56] No surprise, the Volt flopped. Production was suspended in 2012.

The Volt may have generated admiring press coverage and praise from environmentalists. But in the end, it's fake innovation. Instead of transporting people more efficiently and cheaply, it's less efficient and more expensive. A step backward and not a step forward. Nissan, which has received taxpayer subsidies for development of green technology, has done even worse with its electric Leaf.

Plenty of cars have died in the marketplace after failing to serve the needs of the consumer, the classic case being the Ford Edsel. But the real moral question is: Should Big Government be using taxpayer dollars to fund political projects disguised as "innovation"? Should Americans struggling to make ends meet in a rough economy have to shell out $7,500 to subsidize the purchase of a "green" car whose primary achievement is to make its buyer feel virtuous?

Even when bureaucrats have a sound concept, the political nature of bureaucracy makes it difficult to develop and implement. In the 1960s, the French government sought to push its high-tech industry by creating massive centers with mainframe computers. The idea was to provide smaller users with access to high-power computing. Nice idea, but the execution flopped because of costs and technical difficulties. Free markets did it better years later with networked PCs and, more recently, with cloud computing.

Big Government politicians seldom grasp that people and markets require freedom to successfully innovate. So they'll try to bring it about artificially through directives and controls. This never works. A notorious example was the "forced access" provision of the 1996 Telecommunications Act. Lawmakers wanted more competitors for traditional telephone companies. They required regional Bell operating companies such as Verizon, BellSouth, and SBC Communications to share their networks with start-ups at artificially low, subsidized rates. What happened? The law created a gold rush into telecom by small companies like McLeodUSA, XO, and others. This artificially created industry eventually imploded. The only kind of government initiative that *does* work is deregulation—for example, the breakup of the government-mandated telephone monopoly of AT&T.

Big Government subsidies, meanwhile, hurt more than help. Big Government didn't use taxpayers' money to help Henry Ford. The pioneering automaker got the capital to develop the Model T, the first affordable automobile for the mass market, from a Detroit lumber mogul, William Murphy, and other investors.

That is how the free market spontaneously generates innovation. People and companies risk their capital on new ideas they think will succeed. Then the marketplace picks the winning technologies *based on what works.*

The ability to subject new ideas to such scrutiny is a critical reason why America has led the world in technology. But this process of natural selection does not take place when government gets involved. Real innovations are prevented from emerging.

Noted author and tech industry watcher George Gilder explains that, when Big Government doles out subsidies or other incentives, private sector investors tend to follow suit. Capital is channeled into government-sanctioned "winners"—political favorites—and diverted from technologies that may truly be more innovative.

That's what's starting to happen today in Silicon Valley. Gilder worries that political pressure and government subsidies for the development of green projects are diverting resources into inefficient technologies with limited prospects:

> Solar panels are not digital. They may be made of silicon but they benefit from no magic of miniaturization like the Moore's Law multiplication of transistors on microchips. There is no reasonable way to change the wavelengths of sunlight to fit in drastically smaller photoreceptors. Biofuels are even less promising. Even if all Americans stopped eating (saving about 100 thermal watts per capita on average) and devoted all of our current farmland to biofuels,

the output could not fill much more than 2% of our energy needs.[57]

Venture capital firms that once funded true innovators like Apple, Amazon, and Google are increasingly investing in questionable "green" start-ups. Gilder writes that, alas, "many have ingenious technology and employ thousands of brilliant engineers, but they are mostly wasted on pork catchers."[58]

Silicon Valley and San Francisco became dynamic centers of innovation precisely because there have been no bailouts—companies with bad ideas were allowed to fail. Many observers fear today that Big Government green subsidies artificially propping up certain companies and technologies will lead to a Chevy Volt mentality in technology. Politics will edge out genuine creativity. Big Government will stifle innovation by preventing the technology industry from learning from failure. Silicon Valley, for decades the engine of American's job creation and prosperity, may go the way of Detroit.

4

PAYCHECKS *or* FOOD STAMPS?

Empowerment Versus Dependence

Free markets empower people. From the beginning of our history, America's free society fostered the entrepreneurial spirit that built this nation. Americans facing starvation and disease in the New World had to learn to survive or quickly perish. Necessity, however, was not the only motivator. Freedom enabled people unleash their energies, sharpen their skills, pursue their dreams—and reap the rewards. The combination of latitude and necessity spurs people to develop their abilities and increase their knowledge. It develops what the philosophers call "autonomy," the capacity to be your own person, to think independently and act responsibly in a free society. Nicholas Capaldi of the National Center for Business Ethics at Loyola University calls autonomy "our greatest ultimate and objective good."[1]

In a very similar way, free markets empower companies. To succeed in the marketplace, organizations must continually improve efficiency and performance. Setbacks can be painful. But these experiences teach people and companies to adapt—and do better. Failure has empowered many of our greatest entrepreneurs to go on and achieve their biggest successes.

The promise of empowerment is why America has remained a beacon of opportunity for people from around the world. Millions of individuals of all nationalities have come here seeking self-determination and personal betterment: the freedom to discover their abilities and channel their energies in ways not possible in other nations.

We need government to safeguard the rights of individuals and allow people to empower themselves. But when government artificially props up people and companies, it creates passivity, preserving old ways of doing things. People are kept from solving problems, sharpening their skills, services, and products. Programs and regulations intended to protect against risk insulate people from the consequences of bad decisions, setting the stage for even more destructive risk taking. The explosion of the housing bubble and the financial meltdown in 2008 illustrate the systemic disaster that can occur when Big Government programs create widespread dependency.

Dependence on government creates an entitlement culture. Entrepreneurial impulses are suppressed. Resources are diverted from wealth creating and productive enterprises to funding political projects of Big Government's bureaucracy. This culture of dependence drags down an economy and corrupts civil society. The connection between effort and reward is severed. People lose the skills and desire to do for themselves.

Politicians are good at selling voters on the idea that Big Government is needed to provide security. But cradle-to-grave social welfare "benefits" and other forms of support carry a high price: higher unemployment, fewer opportunities, a lower standard of living, malaise, and dysfunction. In the social welfare states of Europe, crushing taxation needed to fund the social welfare bureaucracies has produced decades of economic stagnation. Nations like Greece and Italy have been torn apart by fiscal crises and unrest.

During his campaign for the Republican nomination, former House Speaker Newt Gingrich said that the choice between less and more government was essentially a choice between paychecks and food stamps. People needed to choose, he implied, between a society that promoted self-empowering enterprise and personal advancement and one mired in a stagnant culture of entitlement and dependence. What kind of nation do Americans want?

BOTTOM LINE: AREN'T PEOPLE BETTER OFF DEVELOPING THEIR TALENTS AND LEARNING HOW TO HELP THEMSELVES RATHER THAN BEING TRAPPED IN DEPENDENCY ON GOVERNMENT?

PAY PEOPLE FOR SOMETHING— AND GET MORE OF IT

Americans are a compassionate people. For .more than a half-century, they have bought into the statist belief that, in a humane society, Big Government must rescue those in need. The result: more people than ever are dependent on government. According to the Heritage Foundation, which publishes an annual index of government dependency, "67.3 million Americans, from college students to retirees to welfare beneficiaries, depend on the federal government for housing, food, income, student aid, or other assistance once considered to be the responsibility of individuals, families, neighborhoods, churches, and other civil society institutions." Spending on dependence programs per recipient in 2010 exceeded Americans' per capita disposable income.[2]

All of this spending, however, *hasn't* eliminated poverty. More likely, many experts believe, it has perpetuated it. After all, what happens when you pay people for something? You usually get more of it.

Fox Business News commentator and columnist John Stossel got a lot of people angry recently when he pointed out that a lack of government assistance certainly wasn't the cause of the problems that have long plagued Native Americans:

> The U.S. government has "helped" no group more than it has "helped" the American Indians. It stuns me when President Obama appears before Indian groups and says things like, "Few have been ignored by Washington for as long as Native Americans."
>
> Ignored? Are you kidding me? They should be so lucky. The government has made most Indian tribes wards of the state. Government manages their land, provides their health care, and pays for housing and child care. Twenty different departments and agencies have special "native American" programs.[3]

The result of all this aid, Stossel points out, has been generations of malaise. Sixty-six percent of Native Americans are born to single mothers. They have the highest poverty rate and the lowest life expectancy of any group in America. Stossel contrasts this grim picture with the little-known story of the Lumbees, a Native American tribe in North Carolina that never received government assistance—and who are an economic success story.

Dan Mitchell of the Cato Institute points out that, before the launch of the War on Poverty programs of the 1960s, the poverty rate was actually *falling*. In the years since the Johnson administration kicked off massive spending, the poverty rate has remained essentially flat—around 12 to 13 percent—until the recession, when it ticked up to a little over 15 percent.[4] Big Government's mammoth spending changed things very little.

That is what *New York Times* reporter Michael Janofsky found in 1998 when he revisited Appalachia, which had been a major recipient of billions of dollars of state and federal aid under the Johnson programs. The decaying rural area, he reported, "looks much as it did 30 years ago." The town of Booneville, Kentucky, was still so poor that it was called "Ho Chi Minh City" because of its "third world appearance." Janofsky reported, "Many of the houses look like shanties, heated with wood or coal. Children walk around with dirty bare feet. Many people lack telephones and cars."[5]

Big Government welfare programs have been especially toxic for African Americans. Andrew Bernstein, free market author and a professor at SUNY Purchase, is not alone in pointing out that massive government welfare programs slowed the economic progress of blacks who had began making steady advances after World War II.

As they fled the bigotry of the Jim Crow–era South, they began a steady rise into middle-class prosperity in the freer North, where there were better schools and more jobs. The proportion of poor black families had dropped to 47 percent by 1960, and then to 30 percent a decade later. This was an enormous and too-little-known achievement on the part of black Americans. Following the launch of Johnson's Great Society social welfare programs, black economic progress slowed drastically. Black families still moved upward out of poverty but *at a significantly reduced rate.* In the fifteen years from 1980 to 1995, the percentage below the poverty line dropped just slightly, from 29 percent to 26 percent in 1995.[6]

Advocates of limited government from the Founding Fathers to Milton Friedman have acknowledged that a humane society should help the very poor. Benjamin Franklin believed that charity should be given to help people get back on their feet. But that's not how Big Government helps the disadvantaged. Support in too many instances takes the form of an automatic, ongoing subsidy. Assistance is provided to people who may not necessarily be in crisis—but who qualify simply on the basis of a "low income."

Not only pro-market advocates but also many liberals have agreed on the failure of these programs. "Welfare as we know it," formerly known as Aid to Families with Dependent Children, for example, was dramatically curtailed in 1996 under President Bill Clinton.

Big Government "corporate welfare" isn't any more effective. Since the Great Depression, farmers have gotten subsidies to soften the impact of low crop prices. The Heritage Foundation points out that this has only driven prices *down further:* "Granting larger subsidies to farmers who plant the most crops merely encourages them to plant yet more crops, driving prices even lower and leading to calls for larger subsidies."[7] Yet the subsidies have continued for decades—despite the fact that the era of small farms has long past. Today's recipients of benefits are commercial farms with an average net worth of $2 million.

ASSISTANCE—OR ENABLING?

Dependence on Big Government perpetuates problems because it prevents people from solving them.

In 2010, at the height of the recession, a fierce battle raged over a proposal to extend the benefits period for unemployment insurance from twenty-six to ninety-nine weeks. Opponents were accused of lacking compassion. Typical was *New York Times* columnist Paul Krugman, who wrote, "We're facing a coalition of the heartless, the clueless and the confused."[8]

Krugman might, however, consider a story in his own newspaper about the experience of Denmark. That social welfare democracy has long been known, in the *Times*'s words, as "the best place on earth to be laid off."[9] Until recently, jobless people there got benefits *for four years*. And yet, during a recession, Denmark in 2010 moved to cut its lavish benefits in half. Why? Not just because the Danish government, whose finances were also affected by the global economic crisis, could no longer afford to pay for them. But more to the point, according to the *Times*, it was because the Danes found that extending unemployment benefits *prolonged joblessness*:

> Danish studies show that the longer a person goes without a job, the harder it is to find work. Many people get a job within the first three months of entering the system, but many more wait until just before benefits expire to take anything available.[10]

Danish researchers found that regardless of whether benefits ran for four years, or—as they once did—for five years, people always managed to find jobs shortly before government support was due to run out. Danish economist Steen Bocian told the *Times* that government benefits enabled people to look for only "the jobs they would like to have" instead of actively seeking "all the jobs they could get." Danish benefits were encouraging joblessness by allowing people to put off the difficult task of finding employment.[11]

A still more powerful example comes from Germany, Europe's largest economy. Several years ago, the longtime welfare state nonetheless made drastic labor law reforms. "An unemployed person in social democratic Germany today can draw benefits for only about half as long as his counterpart in capitalist America," economic commentator Donald Luskin and policy analyst Lorcan Roche Kelly write in the *Wall Street Journal*. Germany's unemployment rate is now far lower than that of the United States.[12]

Corporations propped up by government similarly put off dealing with challenges. Paul Roderick Gregory of Stanford's Hoover Institution believes that the Obama administration did more harm than good in bailing out GM and Chrysler. The government money kept those companies from dealing with a key cause of their problems—union labor costs. He points out:

> A bankruptcy that followed the rule of law would have "saved" Detroit better than Obama's, which left GM under the federal government's diktat, unable to borrow, and with high labor costs. Obama's favoritism towards the UAW "elevated costs in a way that damage prospects for a successful reorganization."[13]

Make no mistake: plenty of jobs were lost in this costly debacle. Gregory writes,

> Obama did not save GM jobs, he saved UAW pay scales and pensions. UAW members left their jobs with a $25,000 new car and $20,000 cash. (Chrysler employees left with much more).[14]

Gregory compares the Big Government enabling of GM and Chrysler to the "normal" bankruptcy restructuring of American Airlines that began in 2011. No question the experience has been brutal. Jobs were lost and American's suppliers and creditors took "hair cuts." Shareholder equity became virtually worthless. American's pilots and engineers received cuts in salaries and benefits and faced tougher work rules. By the time it's finally over, he acknowledges, "pain will be felt all around." But there's a huge difference: "Decisions will be based on business judgments and not payback politics. The American taxpayer will not pay, and a federal judge, experienced in bankruptcy law, not politicians, calls the shots."[15]

Both GM and American, Gregory says, suffered a 15 percent loss in jobs. But GM is emerging from its Big Government captivity still saddled with labor costs producing the failed Volt. American Airlines, meanwhile, is being streamlined and will be better positioned to compete.[16] In fact, US Airways wants to merge with American.

"MORAL HAZARD": HOW DEPENDENCY CORRUPTS YOUR JUDGMENT

Big Government programs and regulations that artificially insulate both individuals and companies from risk create what economists call "moral hazard." People are more likely to make unwise decisions because they don't have to bear the full consequences of their actions. Instead of establishing basic and sensible "rules of the road," Big Government removes the speed limits and traffic lights. Of course people will get into accidents.

The classic example of moral hazard is government flood insurance subsidies that encourage people to rebuild their homes in dangerous coastal areas or in flood zones. But you see the same risk-enabling effect with all government programs.

People in Appalachia interviewed by *New York Times* reporter Michael Janofsky instinctively grasped this. They told him that the reason poverty programs had failed wasn't too little government money. Quite the contrary: Denise Hoffman, a forty-six-year-old farmer, told Janofsky, "The war on poverty was the worst thing that ever happened to Appalachia. It gave people a way to get by without having to do any work."[17] Lavish poverty subsidies meant that unemployment no longer brought material deprivation. There was no longer any need to earn a living. So people could decide to stay home.

Big Government is not the only creator of moral hazard. Buying homeowner's or auto insurance, to a certain degree, can also make people less concerned about being careful. If there's an accident, your insurance company pays. You may be less concerned about banging up a rental car, for example, if you purchase insurance on it.

However, in the private sector, market forces limit the tendency toward poor judgment and excessive risk taking. Insurance companies create an incentive for people to be more cautious by charging more to insure higher risk situations—or raising their rates after an accident. People who flagrantly abuse their policies and file false claims not only run the risk of losing coverage but also being prosecuted. The insurance industry spends hundreds of millions of dollars each year going after insurance fraud.

But government, as we know, lacks the discipline of the market. Unlike private insurance, Big Government support is often provided for free or for an artificially low cost. There are few if any conditions that encourage an individual receiving assistance to act responsibly or be fiscally prudent.

The size of Big Government programs also means that the moral hazard they create is many times more far-reaching and potentially destructive. The subprime mortgage crisis and subsequent economic meltdown illustrates the magnitude of the disaster that can occur when Big Government creates moral hazard throughout the economy.

By pumping trillions of dollars into the market for highly risky mortgages and propping up unqualified borrowers, Fannie and Freddie facilitated dependency and risk taking of breathtaking magnitude. This was exacerbated by the Federal Reserve's existing low interest rate policies. The resulting sea of cheap dollars made loans so easy to get that you needed little more than a pulse to qualify for a mortgage. No longer were homebuyers asked for the traditional "20 percent down" before buying a house. "Stated income loans" became common practice. Borrowers were simply asked to state their income, which lenders didn't bother to verify. You could give virtually any income figure—which is why these were known as "no-doc" or "liar loans." A homeless drug addict in St. Petersburg, Florida, managed to buy five houses. Speculators rushed into the market.[18]

The end result of all these policies was that Big Government became an enabler of a calamitous level of risk taking throughout the economy—from financial institutions lending and investing in risky mortgages to the individuals who bought homes they couldn't afford.

Big Government, in effect, encouraged people to take enormous risks, only to pull the rug out from under them when the

Fed, in the middle of the decade, raised interest rates. Mortgage rates began to go up. Low-income people found they couldn't pay their mortgages and began to default. The collapse of the subprime mortgage market helped bring on the panic of 2008 and the subsequent recession. Yet Big Government supporters—including many in the mainstream media—have continued to blame the disaster on "greedy Wall Street speculators" and "predatory lenders." They have been largely blind to the role of morally hazardous Big Government policies in encouraging this excessive risk taking.

The sane—and moral—response to the subprime crisis would have been to shut down Fannie and Freddie and encourage a return to traditional lending practices that would restore a healthier market. But the Obama administration, typical of Big Government, has continued in the footsteps of the Clinton and Bush administrations as an enabler of the same irresponsible lending policies that caused the meltdown in the first pace.

BIG GOVERNMENT MORAL HAZARD AND THE BUBBLE OF "UNFAIR" COLLEGE TUITION

It's doubtful that all of these so-called predatory lenders believed they were being predatory when they gave loans to those unqualified mortgage applicants. They thought they were giving them a good deal in a market of easy money and low interest rates. Think about it: Why would lenders make loans they didn't think would be repaid—and jeopardize their own survival? That gets to an important point. Big Government creates moral hazard by encouraging good people to make bad decisions. These decisions may, in retrospect, seem irresponsible. But they're decisions that most people would make in a marketplace distorted by government. We see this with the default crisis in college loans—a result of the Fannie-and-Freddie-style bubble that government has created in college tuition. Most people, including President Obama, see the high cost of college education as a given. They give scant consideration to the role government played in this tuition inflation. Since government money started pouring into higher education in the 1970s, the cost of college has risen an astonishing 400 percent—twice the rate of increase in the cost of health care. The average tuition at a four-year private nonprofit college is now around $35,000.[19]

As with the housing market, Big Government's aim in providing aid was to help make higher education more affordable. But this vast infusion of the loan and grant money—billions of dollars—had the same effect on the tuition market that Fannie and Freddie's cheap loan money had on the housing market. It pushed universities to overexpand, driving the cost of higher education beyond most people's ability to pay.

Most students now have to take out loans. About two-thirds of college students graduate in debt. Total student loan debt has reached $1 trillion, more than the entire nation's credit card debt. An estimated two hundred thousand students graduated in 2008 owing more than $40,000 each. Some graduate with debt as high as $100,000.

When government distorts a market to such an extent, goods and services can seem to lose their value. Behavior suffers. Kids attending school on someone else's dime tend to take more time completing their education; many feel less pressure to take courses that would prepare them for higher-earning careers. The final outcome: millions of college graduates poorly prepared for the job market even in a good economy. The percentage of college-educated Americans "underemployed" in lower-skilled jobs has more than tripled since the 1960s, and it is now around 35 percent. They're ill equipped to repay their loans, and the number of defaults is skyrocketing. Between 2003 and 2009, the default rate doubled from 4.5 percent to 8.8 percent.[20]

The "unfairness" of crushing student debt and soaring costs has been a major grievance of President Obama and Occupy Wall Street activists. In his 2012 State of the Union address, the president threatened that, if colleges did not bring down the cost of tuition, they'd lose government money. Actually he'd be doing everyone a favor by helping to restore sanity to a government-inflated market.

HOW BIG GOVERNMENT KILLS CARING

Distorting judgment, enabling destructive behavior, and encouraging stagnation, Big Government programs do anything but foster a humane society. In fact, they allow people to care *less* about the poor.

Many people now believe that before the great Depression, America largely neglected the poor and that "compassion" originated with the development of the welfare state in the 1930s. Not true. Americans took care of the poor prior to the Depression—only they did so largely without the help of government. Care of those in need was provided by a private sector network of nonprofit institutions, ranging from churches and synagogues to private charities.

In his powerful book *The Tragedy of American Compassion,* author and academician Marvin Olasky has explained that charity was once a transaction between the giver and receiver of aid. Like all free market exchanges, it was reciprocal. Those who gave to the poor often did so with a level of personal involvement rarely seen today. Charitable giving in the early days of our history was thought to have seven fundamental characteristics: "affiliation, bonding, categorization, discernment, employment, freedom and God." Volunteers at charitable organizations acted as "new family members," getting deeply involved in the lives of people who received aid, providing emotional support, and convincing them to turn their lives around.[21]

> Charity volunteers a century ago usually were not assigned to massive food-dispensing tasks but were given the narrow but deep responsibility of making a difference in one life over several years. Kindness and firmness were both essential: The magazine *American Hebrew* in 1898 told of how one man was sunk into dependency, but a volunteer "with great patience convinced him that he must earn his living"; soon he did and regained the respect of his family and community. Similarly, a woman had become demoralized, but "for months she was worked with, now through kindness, again through discipline, until finally she began to show a desire to help herself."[22]

Those who accepted assistance, meanwhile, were expected to reciprocate by making a good-faith effort to turn their lives around. "Giving back" was supposed to work two ways. This approach was seen as strengthening social ties. Olasky notes that over a century and a half ago, none other than Henry Raymond, founder of the *New York Times,* feared that dispensing charity via government bureaucracy would actually *undermine* society's compassion. It would, he believed, "breed indifference in the hearts" of citizens by bringing an end to their personal involvement with the poor.[23]

All of this began to change in the early 1930s. The widespread job losses of the Great Depression produced suffering on an unprecedented scale. Millions were out of work and private agencies were overwhelmed. Clearly something had to be done. In Marvin Olasky's words, "many government programs made moral sense . . . as temporary expedients."[24] However, government went far beyond providing temporary aid. It stepped in and essentially nationalized a big piece of the charitable sector. What should have been *short-term* emergency assistance was made *permanent.* Then came the War on Poverty in the 1960s. Government assistance was no longer perceived as a "backup" or a "fall back" but became an entitlement and a "right."

Social services formerly delivered by a free market were now provided by bureaucracies funded by "forced charity" from taxpayers. By inserting itself between donor and recipient, Big Government transformed—and once again, distorted—what had been an open market exchange. No longer was charity voluntary and reciprocal. The welfare state redefined "compassion" as a faceless transaction: people were forced to "give" to Big Government agencies that automatically dole out subsidies and treat people as numbers.

Social welfare bureaucracies became more concerned with their own internal processes and needs than those of the people they were supposed to serve. There have been many accounts by service-minded individuals who go to work for these bureaucracies and come away demoralized and disillusioned. Olasky cites Nathaniel Dunford, a former *New York Times* journalist, who worked in New York City's Child Welfare Administration during the welfare era. He could take the soul-crushing experience for just two months. The job of helping people, he recalled, took a backseat to bureaucracy and paperwork.

> I got more forms and documents on my first day than I had seen in seven years at *The Times*. . . . Cases would usually arrive in the morning. . . . They would be shifted from desk to desk, getting "attachments"—more forms for the caseworker to fill out. They would eventually reach our supervisor, to sit for a few more hours and a few more "attachments." Nothing was allowed to interfere with the lunch break. Meanwhile, in various parts of the city, the children and the sympathetic adults trying to help them were left to fume.[25]

Dunford eventually quit—to work for a private agency. Since he wrote his story, little has changed. A 2009 study of the Milwaukee County child welfare system found dispirited case managers and turnover as high as 50 percent. As one put it: "High caseload and paperwork are the number one barriers. I can't even see my clients."[26] Sociologist John Hagedorn wrote "Forsaking Our Children: Bureaucracy and Reform in the Child Welfare System" after working in Milwaukee's bureaucracy in the 1990s. Although an enthusiastic liberal, he nonetheless says that the idea that such agencies deliver social services is a "myth"— primarily "useful to state legislatures who must provide funds, to a concerned public, and for internal morale."[27]

Instead of creating a more caring society, Big Government

in many ways has done the opposite. Marvin Olasky believes that its social services bureaucracies enable individuals to ignore problems of the poor "without the sting of conscience." After all, government is responsible. Little wonder that since government started providing social services, mutual aid societies disappeared. Church spending on services for the poor fell some 30 percent. The proportion of philanthropic giving devoted to social welfare declined by more than half.[28]

DEPENDENCE ON GOVERNMENT ERODES YOUR FREEDOM

"A government big enough to give you everything you want is a government big enough to take from you everything that you have," observed President Gerald Ford. Coercion is the flip side of dependency. Those who push for more dependency-creating programs in the name of compassion forget the Golden Rule of Big Government: *He who has the gold makes the rules.*

Thus, when people get "free" Big Government health care, government determines what medical care you get—or if you get it at all. "Free" food courtesy of the Food Stamp program means that certain foods you may like—that bureaucrats do not—may be declared off-limits. And if you are an artist getting government grants from a politically sensitive entity like the National Endowment for the Arts, it can mean that work that offends politicians can lose or not get funding. Advocates of Big Government arts funding will cry "censorship." But genuine censorship is when government tries to suppress what people write or create on their own time. When you're getting someone else's money, there are going to be conditions.

The situation has been no different for corporations bailed out during the financial crisis. The federal government under George W. Bush, you remember, forced all large banks to "accept" an "investment" from Uncle Sam. The largest institutions suddenly received $25 billion each for a special class of preferred stock. Hundreds of other banks received lesser amounts. One institution, BB&T, a fair-sized outfit with over $165 billion in assets, publicly said it didn't need the money. The government responded that this was an offer that BB&T could not refuse as a government-regulated institution. The bank had no choice but to accept.

The bank bailout provided "justification" for the administration to bash banks with a vehemence not seen in decades. The president assailed "obscene" bank bonuses. Regulators became more aggressive in telling institutions how they could compensate their executives. The pressure has led banks like Morgan Stanley to reduce bonuses to a fraction of what they were. Banks also had to get Uncle Sam's permission over the payment of dividends to shareholders. Lenders of home loans were also forced to provide relief to strapped borrowers by forgiving part of their loans.

This coerced "fairness" has damaged both the financial sector and the broader economy. The hostile and uncertain environment inhibited lending to small and medium-size businesses. Bank stocks have seriously lagged the market. The reduced activity and sinking stocks have meant that banks have had to lay off hundreds of thousands of employees. The administration's putative approach has been a major factor behind the slowness of the economy's recovery from the contraction of 2008 and early 2009.

Government slammed the industry again in 2012, forcing

banks to pay $25 billion to some one million borrowers who claimed to be "abused" by bank collection practices. Where did the banks get that $25 billion? Out of the hides of shareholders and higher fees from customers.

John Tamny, editor of RealClearMarkets and Forbes Opinions, aptly summed up this sad situation: "Bailouts are never free, not for the taxpayers who pay for them, nor for the businesses that falsely benefit from them. Politicians always return for their pound of flesh."[29]

BIG GOVERNMENT'S ENTITLEMENT CULTURE

At the conclusion of his 1961 inaugural address, President John F. Kennedy famously asked the nation, "And so, my fellow Americans: ask not what your country can do for you—ask what you can do for your country." Far too often, this rallying cry has now become, "Ask your country how much it can do for you."

The Founding Fathers wrote in the Declaration of Independence that government's role was to protect our "unalienable Rights" to "Life, Liberty and the Pursuit of Happiness." The role of government, the framers stated, was simply "to secure these rights." What would the framers think about today's Big Government, which subsidizes, in one way or another, one in five Americans? Nearly half of U.S. citizens pay no federal income taxes. According to the Heritage Foundation, *70 percent* of Federal spending goes to individual assistance programs. The national debt now stands at over $15 trillion.

In the near future, as the population ages, there will be fewer working taxpayers to support Big Government's ever-growing burden of "mandatory" entitlements such as Medicare and Social Security. Yet in the arrogant mind-set of Washington, Americans have lost the right to question the scope or financing of these programs—or for that matter, their impact on our economy and our culture.

Taxpayers are having to foot the bill for ever-expanding aid programs based on a constantly loosening definition of "need." Take the Food Stamp program, which was supposed to help the very poor and is today used by a growing number of college students. The program actually advertises and invites people to enroll and become clients. The number of participants has exploded—going from twenty-six million in 2007 to forty-six million as of 2012.

Salon.com, a liberal publication, has reported on the growing number of twenty- and thirtysomething college graduates, "hipsters on food stamps," who use them between jobs. One of the recipients interviewed was "Mak," a thirty-one-year-old who "grew up in New York's Westchester County, graduated from the University of Chicago, and toiled in publishing in New York during his 20s before moving to Baltimore with a meager part-time blogging job."[30]

> About half of his friends in Baltimore have been getting food stamps since the economy toppled, so he decided to give it a try; to his delight, he qualified for $200 a month. "I'm sort of a foodie, and I'm not going to do the 'living off ramen' thing," he said, fondly remembering a recent meal he'd prepared of roasted rabbit with butter, tarragon, and sweet potatoes. "I used to think that you could only

get processed food and government cheese on food stamps, but it's great that you can get anything."[31]

In the 1970s, the Nixon administration established the Section Eight voucher program to provide housing subsidies to the needy. The Department of Housing and Urban Development subsidizes more than two million households—payments can reach as much as $2,800 per household or more. The program's budget was $19 billion in 2011, up from $7 billion in 1994.

Section Eight was intended to help the homeless. But this mission has expanded along with the program's budget. Howard Husock of the Manhattan Institute reports that in New York City, where many Section Eight participants live, "homeless" has become a "slippery term."

[I]ts meaning [is] based on the quality of a family's living arrangements rather than whether or not it has a roof over it. The [city] will classify a household arriving at a shelter "homeless" simply because it finds their living arrangements "not appropriate" . . . the department frequently declares inappropriate a relatively commonplace situation in which a new teen mother, still living at home with her mother or grandmother until her baby's presence sparks a family fight, runs off to seek shelter as "homeless"—in order to get herself moved into a government-subsidized first home.[32]

These programs not only create widespread dependency. They are changing the way we see ourselves and our capabilities as a nation and as individuals. Supporters of more government in various ways suggest that ideals like enterprise, ingenuity, and self-reliance are outdated. Are they? Those who still believe in them were startled by "The Life of Julia," a slide show by the Obama campaign. It looked at how the administration's welfare state programs and policies "help one woman over her lifetime"—from pre-kindergarten in Head Start to college grants to small business loans as an adult, and finally, to Medicare and Social Security. "Julia" is depicted, in the words of the *National Review*'s Rich Lowry, as a "featureless version of Dora the Explorer." This image of a bland and faceless non-person, he says, "inadvertently captured something important about the progressive vision."

> Julia's central relationship is to the state. It is her educator, banker, health-care provider, venture capitalist, and retirement fund. . . . Every benefit she gets is cut-rate or free. She apparently doesn't worry about paying taxes. It doesn't enter her mind that the programs supporting her might add to the debt or might have unintended consequences. She has no moral qualms about forcing others to pay for her contraception, and her sense of patriotic duty is limited to getting as much government help as she can.[33]

Lowry calls this statist vision "condescending" and "creepy" because it suggests that "giving people things will distract them from larger considerations."

Nationally syndicated radio commentator and ethics columnist Dennis Prager observes that today's entitlement state, instead of instilling altruism, is creating a culture of selfishness. "The welfare state," he writes, "enables—and thereby produces—people whose preoccupations become more and more self-centered as time goes on." People care mainly about what they can get for themselves, such as, he says:

How many benefits will I receive from the state?

How much will the state pay for my education?

How much will the state pay for my health care and when I retire?

What is the youngest age at which I can retire?

How much vacation time can I get each year?

How many days can I call in sick and get paid?

How many months can I claim paternity or maternity care money?[34]

Wall Street Journal columnist Evan Newmark writes that the entitlement mind-set causes people in all different ways to game the system—from police who fix traffic tickets for family and friends to the explosion of frivolous lawsuits.[35]

People who feel entitled often have a sense of grievance and are quick to sue when they believe that their "rights" have been violated. According to one study, lawsuit abuse costs the economy about $261 billion a year—about $880 a person.[36] One Southern California restaurant owner was sued because the handicapped mirror in his men's restroom—which customers had defaced—had been replaced with a mirror that was two inches higher than required by law. *Two inches.* The lawsuit is costing more than the restaurant made in a single year.[37] In New York, a 290-pound man sued the White Castle hamburger chain. His complaint: the restaurant chain's uncomfortable booths violate the civil rights of fat people.[38] And then there's the Florida man who sued Winn-Dixie Stores and a flower importer for $15,000 in damages for . . . pricking his finger on a rose bouquet.[39]

Entitlement mania distorts society's priorities. Values become centered around the redistribution of existing wealth—instead of on spurring enterprise and innovation needed for new growth and prosperity. Growth takes place in the entitlement-dispensing bureaucracy instead of the private sector. *Wall Street Journal* columnist Steve Moore wrote about this in a much-talked-about op-ed entitled "We've Become a Nation of Takers, Not Makers." The entitlement culture, he says, has become an industry in itself:

> Today in America there are nearly twice as many people working for the government (22.5 million) than in all of manufacturing (11.5 million). This is an almost exact reversal of the situation in 1960, when there were 15 million workers in manufacturing and 8.7 million collecting a paycheck from the government.[40]

He observes, "More Americans work for the government than work in construction, farming, fishing, forestry, manufacturing, mining and utilities combined."

You can't generate the wealth that pays for entitlements in an economy based on government bureaucracy. The only way to "win the future" and generate the kind of prosperity that truly helps the poor is, in Moore's words, "to grow the economy that makes things, not the sector that takes things."[41]

✳ ✳ ✳

FREE MARKETS AND AMERICA'S
ENTREPRENEURIAL SPIRIT

Today's belief in the morality of an entitlement-based society is a dramatic departure from the values that built this country. Before the growth of government in the twentieth century, free markets were seen as empowering. What is today called "assistance" or "bailouts" was then called "handouts" and considered a last resort. American society was based on a culture of work and self-reliance.

These ideals reflected America's experience as a frontier nation, and also its British political heritage. South America was colonized by Spain and Portugal. There, too, settlers had to fend for themselves. But they did not develop the same entrepreneurial spirit. The Spanish and Portuguese brought with them a rigid, hierarchical tradition, as did the French who settled parts of North America. All were accustomed to depending on guidance from a powerful government. By contrast, Great Britain never had the all-powerful central governments that dominated Western Europe.

The English legal tradition was different from that of the Continent. Philosophers like John Locke emphasized the idea that governments were formed by individuals, rather than being handed down from God. The English were influenced by Reformation theologians like John Calvin, who also emphasized the spiritual value of work. America therefore had a very different environment from French North America (Quebec) or the Spanish and Portuguese colonies. British immigrants to the New World greatly expanded the self-governing traditions of their homeland. English governance of the colonies was far less controlling than France, which kept a tight rein on its North American settlements. Thus by the mid-eighteenth century French North America had a population of only sixty thousand while British North America had a population of over two million.[42]

This heritage engendered in the Americans of the New World a new culture of liberty, self-governance, and mobility. The nineteenth-century philosopher and historian Alexis de Tocqueville wrote that Americans' "taste for material en-joyments" created in them a restlessness that translated into "an irresistible need for action." In this culture of enterprise, Tocqueville wrote, "To change is to improve." Some people could become fixated on these goals. But overall, he suggested, this determination to better one's circumstances had an empow-ering effect on America's free society.

> It is not a question of building vast palaces, of vanquish-ing or of deceiving nature, of exhausting the universe, in order to satisfy better the passions of a man; it is a matter of adding a few feet to his fields, of planting an orchard, of enlarging a house, of making life easier and more comfort-able each moment, of avoiding discomfort and satisfying the slightest needs effortlessly and almost without cost.[43]

The Frenchman observed that this "passion" to improve cut across class lines, unlike in Europe, "where aristocracy domi-nates society and keeps it immobile." In America's open society, where "ranks are mingled and privileges destroyed," the poor could become rich and the rich could lose their fortunes. Every-one therefore understood the meaning and value of work.

Tocqueville saw America, in the words of the Manhattan In-stitute's Steve Malanga, as "a remarkable society in which . . . all 'honest callings are honorable' and in which 'the notion of labor is therefore presented to the mind on every side as the necessary, natural, and honest condition of human existence.'" Malanga writes,

> Unlike in Europe, where aristocrats and gentry often scorned labor, in the United States, "a wealthy man thinks

that he owes it to public opinion to devote his leisure to some kind of industrial or commercial pursuit, or to public business. He would think himself in bad repute if he employed his life solely in living."[44]

Benjamin Franklin was among the first to articulate the principles of the American ethic of work and self-reliance. We think of Franklin most often as the multifaceted Founding Father and inventor whose visage graces the hundred-dollar bill. But he was also a highly successful entrepreneur. Franklin published what may have been the first self-improvement guide, *The Way to Wealth*. Franklin's advice included, "There are no gains, without pains"; "One today is worth two tomorrows"; "Time is money"; "Have you somewhat to do tomorrow, do it today"; "The eye of a master will do more work than both his hands"; and "Early to bed, and early to rise, makes a man healthy, wealthy and wise."[45]

Franklin's maxims may be nothing new for readers of today's self-help books. But this wisdom helped him rise from modest beginnings as the son of a candle maker to become one of the most influential figures in American history, while amassing a fortune that allowed him to retire from business at age forty-two.[46]

NECESSITY IS THE MOTHER OF ENTERPRISE

Free markets foster the opposite of moral hazard. The necessity of having to compete compels individuals and companies to make better decisions. They learn how to manage risk and adapt to adversity. In the end most improve. The challenge of overcoming obstacles pushes people to discover new capabilities and come up with innovations.

We're taught in grade school that Thomas Edison invented the incandescent bulb because he wanted to create better lighting. But that's not the whole story. *Forbes* magazine founder B. C. Forbes once asked Edison if the legend about his real motivation for developing the incandescent lightbulb was true. Edison responded that he was, in fact, angry at the local gas company:

> I was paying a sheriff 5 dollars a day to postpone a judgment on my small factory. But then came the gas man and he cut off my gas. That made me so mad that I looked up to see if electricity couldn't be made to replace gas and give them a run for their money. I stuck to it for four years but I was so poor an economist that I didn't hurt them at all, except lately. [Signed, "Edison."][47]

Edison may not have done away with the gas man, but his invention brought electric light to millions and, yes, changed the world.

McDonald's had dominated the fast-food sector since the 1950s. But by the late 1990s the restaurant giant was showing worrisome signs of decay. The quality of its franchises was visibly declining. The menu was regarded as stale and the changes it made were quick market flops. The company was being challenged by a new generation of nimble competitors, like Starbucks, which was offering more food along with coffee. In 2002 the *New York Times* even ran a story with suggestions for saving the chain from high-profile customers.

What a humiliation. But McDonald's resurrected itself. It came up with new salads that were edible and healthy. It changed its coffee so that it didn't taste like leftovers from commercial airlines. To compete with Starbucks, McDonald's opened up "McCafés" in the United States and Europe that served very tasty pastries as well as espressos. The company also shut down a number of lagging units. McDonald's came roaring back with its stock reaching new highs.

Free markets in a similar fashion strengthen individuals. People learn how to delay gratification, and how to work successfully with others. They acquire the skills to bootstrap their way up.

They develop ingenuity and self-reliance. A few years ago, a twenty-six-year-old named Adam Shepard decided he wanted to find out for himself if it was true that—as so many insisted— the American Dream of upward mobility was a thing of the past. With a knapsack on his back and $25 in his pocket, he had himself dropped off in Charleston, South Carolina, a city he picked out of a hat. He started working in menial jobs. In several months he had saved up enough money to buy a used truck and get an apartment. After a year he had a car and $5,500. He told *ABC News,* "I was able to do it because I made sacrifices."[48]

This idea of having to sink or swim in a free market without government assistance may sound harsh to some people. But is it really? Consider John Stossel's story of the Lumbees, a little-known North Carolina Indian tribe. Because they were not recognized as a "tribe" by the federal government, they did not receive the assistance the government provided other Native Americans. What happened? Stossel was amazed to discover,

> Lumbees own their homes and succeed in business. They include real estate developer Jim Thomas, who used to own the Sacramento Kings, and Jack Lowery, who helped

start the Cracker Barrel Restaurants. Lumbees started the first Indian-owned bank, which now has 12 branches.

The Lumbees' wealth is not from casino money. "We don't have any casinos. We have 12 banks," says Ben Chavis, another successful Lumbee businessman. He also points out that Robeson County looks different from most Indian reservations.

"There [are] mansions. They look like English manors. I can take you to one neighborhood where my people are from and show you nicer homes than the whole Sioux reservation."[49]

Stossel acknowledges that the U.S. government stole the Indians' land and "caused great misery." But the treaties meant to redress this "brought the Indians socialism. It's what keeps them dependent and poor." The Lumbees, who were not given special treatment, were left free and were able to prosper.

Dr. Ben Carson, an African American and son of a single mother, rose from the Detroit ghetto to become one of the nation's leading brain surgeons. An active educational philanthropist who gives away millions in educational scholarships, the physician regularly speaks to young people around the country about personal empowerment. He credits his success to his mother's personal example of self-reliance and discipline. A third-grade dropout, she worked three jobs to stay off welfare, because, she would tell him, "I never saw anyone go on welfare and come off of it."[50]

Carson told Fox News: "If somebody can show me where depending on government handouts and welfare programs and entitlements lead to a great society, I'm all ears. I haven't seen it."[51]

THE VALUE OF FAILURE

Statists typically say we need Big Government to promote "safety and security," and to protect people and companies from failure. What they seldom grasp is that life's ups and downs, while painful, teach valuable lessons that empower people to succeed later.

The first venture that Bill Gates and former partners Paul Allen and Paul Gilbert started during high school was a company called Traf-O-Data. It read information from roadway traffic counters that track cars for local governments and traffic engineers. That company failed, but it got them into the software writing business, laying the groundwork for the launch of Microsoft. Gates later declared, "Success is a lousy teacher. It seduces smart people into thinking they can't lose."[52]

There may be no better example of free market empowerment than the story of iconic retailing entrepreneur James Cash Penney. Born in 1875 to a struggling farm family with twelve children (only half of whom survived), his early years were framed by hardship. Penney was eight years old when his father told him he would have to clothe himself. In order to do so, he worked on neighboring farms, growing watermelons and raising pigs. He later endured a bout with tuberculosis, the failure of an early business, and the devastating deaths of two wives.

Penney began working as a salesman for the Golden Rule chain of stores in 1898. He so impressed the owners that they made him a partner in one location. The partnership expanded and eventually he bought out his partners and incorporated as J.C. Penney. By the end of the 1920s he had 1,400 stores and had expanded into real estate and a dairy business. All of this came to a halt with the 1929 stock market crash. Penney personally lost the astronomical sum of $40 million. Facing a $7 million debt—big numbers even today—he had to sell almost all his assets to pay creditors. In his midfifties, he found himself nearly broke and sick enough to enter a sanitarium. Convinced that he was about to die, he wrote farewell letters to his friends and family.

Then one day a hymn emanating from the hospital chapel, with the words "God will take care of you," struck an inner chord, which caused him to rally. Eventually Penney borrowed money that enabled him to start over. He regained control of his empire and rebuilt his fortune. He lived until the age of ninety-five and built a business that continues to this day. Penney once said of perseverance, "It is a natural thing to want to succeed, but all are not willing to pay the price of success. Some folks have a wishbone instead of a backbone."[53]

Adaptability—the ability to learn from failure in a free market—is essential to innovation, as we discussed in chapter 3. But even more important, it's critical to avoiding the worst disasters.

Free market failure "saved" IBM by propelling the company to adapt. The company was the largest mainframe manufacturer in the world and was a formidable presence in software and microchips. It was so immensely powerful that it was once the subject of a federal antitrust suit. But in the 1980s the world drastically changed. Mini-computers and PCs undermined the market for mainframes. Despite unprecedented cost cutting and layoffs, IBM was in dire straits by the early 1990s. Had the company been headquartered in France, where the government plays a dominant role in directing the economy, the response would have been massive infusions of aid to protect a "flagship" company. Taxpayers would have faced years of multibillion-dollar bailouts. Instead, IBM's board of directors brought in Lou Gerstner, who had turned around American Express credit card operations and RJR Nabisco. Between 1990 and 1995, the company shed 150,000 jobs. Gerstner invested heavily in software and dramatically reshaped the company. Today, IBM offers new products and services, like technology integration. The company employs more people than when Gerstner took over.

Many believe the fact that as many as 10 percent of U.S. firms go bankrupt every year is actually *good* for our nation's economy. *Financial Times* columnist and author Tim Harford makes the intriguing observation that, much like people, the most successful markets and economies are those that are allowed to experience more failures: "To get an instinctive grasp of this, just compare the astonishing failure rate of Silicon Valley firms with the situation of the Big 3 in Detroit, who seem to be in a perpetual state of slow-motion failure without ever quite leaving the economic stage."[54]

BEFORE BIG GOVERNMENT:
LESS DYSFUNCTION

Many people are concerned with the growing dependency on Big Government. But the feeling often is "What's the alternative?" Without many government programs, they insist, people would starve, and care of the poor would revert to the Dickensian conditions of the nineteenth century. That is a myth. For one thing, we forget that those classic images partially reflect the fact that life was many times harder for *everyone* in the nineteenth century. We seldom appreciate that a social safety net existed long before Big Government programs were first established in the 1930s. As we noted earlier, people took care of the poor through an effective network of private charities.

Clifford Thies of the Independent Institute, a noted free market think tank, writes in "Work and Housing for 19th Century Poor and Paupers" that in urban areas, the larger private charities were sophisticated self-help agencies that provided a compendium of services. These included "thrift institutions, consumer cooperatives, and employment agencies, along with *workhouses* that assured that no person would be without food and a place to stay for lack of work."[55]

The conditions in many of these facilities, Thies acknowledges, were "minimal." But the institutions fulfilled their role as a safety net: no one starved. But at the same time, few able-bodied individuals were tempted to become dependent. "[R]elatives, friends, neighbors, and co-workers recognized the Spartan housing conditions offered by the poorhouses, and therefore often were willing to open their own homes to the elderly, disabled, and orphaned."

Today we often think of the Industrial Revolution of the nineteenth century as an era of rampant "greed" and rise of the so-called robber barons. That's a misconception. Most were actually innovative entrepreneurs. Even less well known is that the rise of the great private fortunes also ushered in today's era of modern philanthropy. Hundreds of organizations sprang up to help the needy.[56] *The growth of commerce gave rise to a broad-based culture of giving.*

The 1800s saw the founding of major philanthropic, community service, and educational institutions that continue to this day. They include the Cleveland Foundation, Jane Addams

Hull House, and the Henry Street Settlement to the Rockefeller Foundation and Cooper Union (a free university for science and art education), among others.

By the 1820s, larger cities had almost an overabundance of charitable organizations. Consortiums and coalitions began to develop among charities. Thanks to better communication, local societies became regional and, later, national in scope.

How well did these organizations do? Historian Gertrude Himmelfarb has written about how the rise of such charitable institutions in both pre-welfare state England as well as the United States was followed by less crime and social dysfunction:

> In England between 1856 and 1901, the rate of serious crimes declined by almost 50 percent. . . . National crime statistics for the United States start only in 1960, but local statistics suggest that, as in England, crime generally decreased from the latter half of the nineteenth century into the early twentieth century.[57]

Since Big Government took over social services functions previously performed by these private charities, billions of dollars—money taken forcibly from taxpayers—have been channeled into the fight to end poverty. This "investment" has been a disaster. Not only did it fail to end poverty, it produced declining rather than improving moral statistics—more and not less social malaise, and a spike in crime that only began to come down in the past twenty years.

FROM "WELFARE AS WE KNOW IT"
TO EMPOWERMENT

The ending of the welfare program in the late 1990s illustrates how people in a free economy become self-reliant when not tethered to government. In 1996, President Bill Clinton signed the Personal Responsibility and Work Opportunity Reconciliation Act that ended "welfare as we know it." Aid to Families with Dependent Children ceased being an automatic entitlement. It required recipients to work after two years of receiving benefits. Among other measures it placed a lifetime limit on welfare benefits a person could receive from the federal government.

Opponents warned that ending welfare would bring calamity. Then New York Democratic senator Daniel Patrick Moynihan predicted "scenes of social trauma such as we haven't known since the cholera epidemics."[58] They never materialized. On the tenth anniversary of reform, former president Bill Clinton wrote in the *New York Times,* in the article "How We Ended Welfare, Together,"

> In the past decade, welfare rolls have dropped substantially, from 12.2 million in 1996 to 4.5 million today. At the same time, caseloads declined by 54 percent. Sixty percent of mothers who left welfare found work, far surpassing predictions of experts. Through the Welfare to Work Partnership, which my administration started to speed the transition to employment, more than 20,000 businesses hired 1.1 million former welfare recipients.[59]

What became of the individuals who supposedly would have died or ended up on grates without welfare? Many of them got jobs. Michelle Gordon was a thirty-year-old single mother with four kids when Clinton signed the law. Since then she's held a succession of low-paying jobs, including working at a call center, as a nurse's aide, at a grocery store, and doing janitorial work at a drug rehabilitation center. Another single mom, Mary Bradford, took a job filling orders at a Victorian Trading center where her earnings have since more than doubled.[60]

A number of people also went back to school. The bottom line is, they have become productive. *USA Today* reported in 2006: "Earnings for the poorest 40% of families headed by women doubled from 1994 to 2000, before recession wiped out nearly half the gains." And instead of kids sleeping on grates, the paper reported, "poverty rates for children fell 25% before rising 10% since 2000."[61]

COMPASSION WITHOUT DEPENDENCY

A moral society helps those in need. But there are better ways to do this than through dependency-creating subsidies. Advocates of Big Government often have a difficult time imagining alternatives. Welfare reform, however, shows the success of a reciprocal work-for-aid arrangement, closer to what private sector charity once provided.

Immigrant entrepreneurs who rise from poverty without government assistance show that it's possible to help others without creating dependency. Koreans, for example, help each other generate capital for new businesses by taking part in a lending circle known as a "kye." Members pool their money, which is then loaned to participants who pay it back so that everyone gets access.[62]

Few people would consider the Amish an uncaring society. In the 1960s, the Anabaptist Christian sect, whose adherents live in rural Pennsylvania and Ohio, obtained a historic exemption from paying Social Security taxes. The Amish also do not pay or receive Social Security, or, for that matter, Medicare or Medicaid, or Worker's Compensation. With some exceptions, they also have not accepted agricultural subsidies, even though they are farmers. Donald Kraybill, author of several books on the sect, writes that they refused to sell their cows in a federal buyout program in the 1990s or to accept payment for letting farmland sit idle. The community places an exceptionally high value on mutual aid, responsibility, and self-reliance. Kraybill writes that the result is "a society virtually free of crime and violence." It's also "a social system without poverty"—indeed, the community's wealth is increasing.[63] It is true that the Amish are an insular, highly religious society that rejects modern ways, but they are a powerful reminder of what happens when individuals take responsibility in empowering themselves and caring for others—instead of relying on dependency-creating government bureaucracy.

5

APPLE *or* SOLYNDRA?

Meritocracy Versus Cronyism

An open market economy is a meritocracy. If you're offering something people want, they'll buy it, whether that may be a new technology, a better smoothie, or your own workplace skills. Your ability to meet the needs of the market matters more than personal background and social status. Productive individuals and companies are rewarded for the value they provide others.

Alexander Hamilton had a unique appreciation of the meritocracy of markets. Born in the West Indies to a single mother, he made his way to Colonial America in 1772 while in his midteens, rising to become America's first treasury secretary under George Washington. In the words of biographer Forrest McDonald, he keenly understood that "money is oblivious to class, status, color and inherited social position; money is the ultimate, neutral, impersonal arbiter." Hamilton created a financial system based on money and markets because he wanted America to be "a society fluid and open to merit."[1]

In a free market economy, not everyone has the drive or the desire to become a Forbes 400 billionaire like Warren Buffett or Bill Gates. But the openness of democratic capitalism provides the fairest chance for those who want to try. Free markets are equal-opportunity environments for individuals and companies alike. And those that make it won't stay on top if they stop meeting the needs of others. Consider the list of the one hundred largest U.S. corporations, published when Forbes *magazine first appeared in 1917. Only twelve survive today.*

What about the often-heard complaint that the meritocracy of democratic capitalism promotes inequality by enabling a few to become rich? It's true, in a free market economy there is "income inequality." There is political and economic inequality in all societies. But the meritocracy of a free market offers the greatest *opportunity for people to rise through the creation and accumulation of wealth. Studies show that more than half of families in the bottom quintile of income in the United States move up within ten years, while at least half of those in the top quintile move down.*

Critics miss the fact that "income inequality" in American society is often a by-product of economic growth and wealth creation that is simultaneously lifting living standards for everyone. Respected economists like Brian Wesbury have pointed out that during times of technological innovation, incomes increase more rapidly for those at the top. Bill Gates and Mark Zuckerberg get fantastically rich from their innovations in technology. But the rest of us are also benefiting—through higher living standards and greater access to consumer goods. Products considered "luxuries" available to an elite few very quickly become necessities available to the majority of people. In 1900, John D. Rockefeller was the richest man on the planet. But despite spending an astounding sum of a half-million dollars—the equivalent of more than $11 million today—he was unable to prevent his grandson from dying of scarlet fever. Today, scarlet fever is almost unheard of—even among the poor—because of modern antibiotics.[2]

The openness and access of free markets contrast dramatically with Big Government–run economies or industries, where politics trumps merit. There's far less and often no connection between effort and reward. People and companies too often rise, and get rich, based on how well they meet the needs of those in power. Government policies benefit political cronies or those with high-powered lobbyists and the resources to curry favor.

Big Government cronyism can mean that powerful industries like sugar producers get government subsidies for decades. Or that the influential steel industry gets tariffs imposed on imports from foreign competitors. With Obamacare, for example, Big Government favoritism has meant that companies with connections got waivers exempting them from having to comply with the law.

This favoritism is immoral not only because it's unfair, but also because society pays. Protectionist tariffs and regulations put in place to please powerful industries or unions result in higher prices for products like steel, tires, and automobiles. Big Government sweetheart deals propping up "green" technologies or other politically favored projects can mean more wealth-destroying taxes. Capital is diverted from companies that lack political connections but have better technologies.

The choice between free market meritocracy and Big Government cronyism is illustrated by the contrast between Apple and the solar panel maker Solyndra. Apple succeeded because of innovations that met market needs in new and historic ways. Solyndra had an innovative product. But the main reason that it rose, as we explain later, was the political connections of a key financial backer—which helped the company get a $535 million government loan. The company's solar technology, however, was too expensive. The company went belly-up, at the expense of the taxpayers.

Do Americans want an open meritocracy that produces job-creating innovators like Apple—or government-dominated markets that give cronies like Solyndra unfair advantages and often taxpayer dollars? The end result of this kind of favoritism: a slower-growing economy with less job creation. Just ask people who have lived in the developing world or in communist nations—from the former Soviet Union to Argentina—where a politically connected aristocracy thrives and everyone else suffers.

BOTTOM LINE: IS IT FAIR FOR PEOPLE TO GET AHEAD BASED ON POLITICAL CONNECTIONS INSTEAD OF THE REAL VALUE THEY PROVIDE TO OTHERS?

FREE MARKETS BREAK DOWN BARRIERS

Few people today appreciate the role that money and markets have played in creating America's open society. The colonists may have come to the New World seeking freedom from the restraints of Europe. But in Alexander Hamilton's time the gateways to upward mobility were closing. In the words of Hamilton biographer Forrest McDonald, "Status and power [were] monopolized, in most American communities, by a handful of intermarried families which, for the most part, were closed to newcomers."[3]

Hamilton sought to change this by making it easier for outsiders to create wealth. Believing that—as he wrote in Federalist Paper No. 36—*"The door ought to be equally open to all,"* he instituted a sound currency and capital markets to provide the liquidity to stimulate entrepreneurial commerce.

Hamilton has not been the only one to recognize how money and markets break down social barriers. In his thought-provoking book *The History of Money,* Jack Weather-ford explains how the invention of gold coins in the city-state of Lydia during ancient times created markets that transcended social boundaries. The Lydians traditionally conducted trade mainly within small kinship-based communities where people bartered with each other. But with the advent of a uniform currency, this dramatically changed.

> Money became the social nexus connecting humans in many more social relationships, no matter how distant or transitory, than had previously been possible . . . it weak-ened the traditional ties based on kinship and political power.[4]

Their new mercantile system took hold in the region and became a source of power that helped the neighboring Greeks prevail over their adversaries, the Persians, despite the latter's military superiority. Coins gave Lydian women the ability to make their own dowries and choose their own husbands.

Money and markets became a force for upward mobility. Weatherford quotes seventeenth-century Japanese writer Ihara Saikaku, who observed that, in the markets that money created, "birth and lineage mean nothing."

How markets break down barriers between people is vividly illustrated by the classic free market allegory "I, Pencil," written in the 1950s by noted free market economist Leonard Read. Recounting its story in the form of a children's tale, the pen-cil explains how "millions of human beings have had a hand in my creation, no one of whom even knows more than a very few of the others."[5] From the cutting of lumber in California to extracting rapeseed oil in Indonesia to make erasers, the process of making the pencil brought together strangers from different cultures. People who would not normally associate with each other cooperate and form alliances.

The medical device maker EndoStim is a modern-day "I, Pencil" story. Tom Friedman writes in the *New York Times* that the company, which makes a medical device to treat acid reflux, "was inspired by Cuban and Indian immigrants to America and funded by St. Louis venture capitalists." Friedman marvels, "Its prototype is being manufactured in Uruguay, with the help of Israeli engineers and constant feedback from doctors in India and Chile. Oh, and the CEO is a South African, who was educated at the Sorbonne but lives in Missouri and California, and his head office is basically a BlackBerry."[6]

With all the heated rhetoric coming out of the Middle East, few would expect Israelis and Palestinians to be working together in the technology sector that is now blossoming in the region. Companies in Israel employ Palestinian workers, including high-paid engineers. Israeli venture capitalist Yadin Kaufman began a partnership with Palestinian software engineer Saed Nashef after discovering that there was technological potential in the Palestinian territories, but no one to fund it. "It is an untapped opportunity," Kaufman told the *Christian Science Monitor.* Ramallah-based Asal Technologies specializes in IT business outsourced to Palestinian territories and does 40 percent of its business with Israeli companies. Company founder Murad Tahboub says such ventures are not only bringing prosperity to the region, but they're also "an investment in peace."[7]

BUT IS MERITOCRACY MORAL?

Free market meritocracies may break down barriers. However, critics like the Occupy Wall Street protesters suggest that markets are nonetheless unfair becase they create inequality. After all, doesn't the Declaration of Independence say that "all men are created equal"? In fact, if you read the entire sentence, you'll find that the Founders wrote something different: "We hold these truths to be self-evident, that all men are created equal, *that they are endowed by their Creator with certain unalienable Rights, that among these are Life, Liberty and the pursuit of Happiness*" (our italics). People are equal because they have equal *rights*—in other words, *equality of opportunity*.

Luigi Zingales of the University of Chicago Booth School of Business explains that the notion of equal rights was then a radical concept:

> In the eighteenth century, the social order throughout the world was based on birthrights: nobles ruled Europe and Japan, the caste system prevailed in India, and even in England, where merchants were gaining economic and political strength, the aristocracy wielded most of the political power. The American Revolution was a revolt against aristocracy and the immobility of European society, but unlike the French Revolution, which emphasized the principle of equality, it championed the freedom to pursue happiness.[8]

Statists, however, believe in something else: *equality of outcome*. This is a very different idea. It's one thing to believe that everyone should have equal rights under the law—quite another to believe that people and companies should be rewarded regardless of their level of productivity. "Equality of outcome" is also unfair because it penalizes merit in the name of equality. We see this, as we discuss later, with antitrust laws that punish companies for being too successful.

Americans have long believed in equality of opportunity, not of outcome. The prosperity of America's open markets, Zingales says, "cemented in the collective perception the benefits of assigning rewards and responsibilities according to merit."

A survey of twenty-seven developed countries by Pew Charitable Trusts found that Americans more than any other people believe in the connection between merit and reward. Only a third of Americans believe it's the government's role to reduce income inequality, compared with 44 percent in Canada and 89 percent in Portugal. An overwhelming majority of Americans saw our economic system as being "fair." Only 19 percent thought, for example, that coming from a wealthy family was important for getting ahead, a far smaller percentage than in other countries, where the median response was 28 percent.[9]

This belief in rewarding effort is ingrained even in equality-minded Berkeley students. In a recent experiment, a group of undergraduates played a game in which they were asked to divide a sum of money between themselves and an anonymous individual. In one version, they were told the anonymous recipient worked hard; in another, they were told the person had done nothing. The students were more willing to reward those who worked than those who hadn't.[10]

Even equality-minded Occupy Wall Street protesters share this impulse. In the New York protest, volunteers preparing food around the clock for the protesters objected to having to feed "squatters," vagrants and ex-cons who had infiltrated the Zuccotti Park encampment—and who were seen as *undeserving*. They went on strike and stopped serving food for two hours.[11]

The real dispute today is not about the morality of rewarding "merit," but rather what constitutes "merit" and how it should be rewarded. One reason why intellectuals and members of the political class have problems with open market meritocracy is, as Zingales puts it, "Lady Gaga makes a lot more money than Nobel laureates do." Or, for that matter, a hedge fund manager who doesn't appear to "make things" can make tens of millions of dollars more than a physician or a teacher. In a free market, people who work hard are rewarded—but sometimes the reward may not meet expectations. Or it can seem excessive to others. That's because markets first and foremost reward value—i.e., innovation. Economist Bryan Caplan points out that value and merit are correlated in the market, but not perfectly.[12]

Luigi Zingales believes this is a key reason that meritocracy is a "politically fragile" principle, "difficult to sustain in a democracy. Any system that allocates rewards on the basis of merit inevitably gives higher compensation to the few, leaving the majority potentially envious."

In order to maintain a merit-based, free society, he says, it's especially important that people understand why free market meritocracy benefits everyone.

HOW BILL GATES MAKES YOU RICHER

Bill Gates is fantastically rich because Microsoft, the corporation he co-founded, has helped make computing more affordable. Hundreds of millions of people worldwide have bought his company's products. But the jobs, innovations, and opportunities created by Gates and the rest of the 1 percent are the reason why Americans enjoy a higher standard of living, including those on the lower rungs. For example, more than 72 percent of "poor" households in the United States own a car. More than 76 percent have air-conditioning. The percentage who have a microwave is 73.3. Some 55 percent have two or more TV sets—and 26 percent have a widescreen TV.[13] Studies have shown that being "poor" in the United States would not be considered poverty in other countries—including democratic socialist countries like Sweden. A study by the Swedish free market think tank Timbro put it this way,

> Poverty is a highly relative concept . . . for example, 40 per cent of all Swedish households would rank among low-income households in the USA, and an even greater number in the poorer European countries would be classed as low-income earnings by the American definition.[14]

In addition, Timbro points out, "The average American household has a home that is 80 per cent larger than its average European counterpart." The study concludes, "Good economic development, in other words, results in even poor people being relatively well off."[15] In a free market meritocracy, more wealth is created—for everybody.

The greater openness and wealth created by free markets mean that more people can get ahead. It's no accident that the most dramatic stories of entrepreneurial start-ups coming out of nowhere and challenging the establishment are found in markets with the least government interference—such as in computer and information technology. Many of those start-ups have been college students or dropouts like Facebook founder Mark Zuckerberg, and, decades earlier, Michael Dell, who founded his eponymous company in his dorm room. Microsoft was launched by Bill Gates and Paul Allen when they were barely into their twenties. These visionaries did not cultivate powerful bureaucrats to become successful. They simply had an idea that took off and attracted investors.

Until the financial crisis and the recent growth of government, the United States was far more hospitable to entrepreneurs than other nations, which is why we attracted ambitious people not only from Asia but also from France and Germany. Liberals may like to talk about the "end of the American Dream." However, the U.S. Treasury study found that in the decade from the mid-1990s to the mid-2000s most people who had been in the fourth or fifth quintile of income moved up at least one quintile or more.[16]

It's true that in recent years real incomes have indeed stagnated. This too is a consequence of bad policy, namely the Federal Reserve–created weak dollar. The weakening of the dollar means that wages don't go as far. If history repeats itself, the decline should be temporary. A similar phenomenon occurred in the 1970s, which led to pressure to stabilize the dollar.

Immigrants to this country have never cared about "income inequality." They came seeking opportunity—the chance to get ahead no matter where you come from.

ANOTHER REASON "INEQUALITY" IS FAIR

If tougher jobs didn't pay more money, people wouldn't bother taking them. Why put up with all the headaches and risks of being a CEO if you only got the pay of an executive vice president? You might as well stay where you are. But we need CEOs and people in other higher paying positions. Stingy reimbursements from Medicare and Medicaid that don't pay physicians enough for their services is one reason many are choosing to leave the profession.

As we have noted elsewhere, Friedrich von Hayek has explained that prices and profits are really the way the market conveys information about what's better and what's in demand. *You* benefit from knowing more about the value of products and services. For example, if all computers cost $1,500, how would you know which one was better?

Higher pay and prices for better work mobilize people. As we noted in chapter 3, higher profits signal to producers to increase production. They also encourage people to improve the quality of their services and become more efficient. One of the problems in our educational system, for example, is that there is no such financial incentive to improve. We're not necessarily talking about "merit pay" for teachers but the bigger picture: No matter what they do, schools stay in business and teachers keep their jobs. This would change if there were a real consumer market in education. Better schools would be rewarded for merit by attracting more students and staying in business. Lagging schools would not survive as they do today.

THE REAL REASON BIG GOVERNMENT DISTRUSTS "THE RICH"

Free markets don't create "aristocracies." They destroy them. Politically as well as economically, free markets undermine permanence.

In medieval Europe, the marketplace became a source of power that allowed people to challenge the ruling monarchs. Historian Jack Weatherford cites the twelfth-century example of the Templars—the Military Order of the Knights of the Temple of Solomon. The fighting knights were also a religious charity that employed seven thousand people, owning a network of castles and houses extending from Europe to Jerusalem. They helped finance the Crusades, evolving into what may have been the world's first international banking corporation. The Spartan lives of individual Templars belied their immense power. The order itself, in Weatherford's words, "grew rich and fat but seemingly beyond the control of any nation or king."[17]

In 1295, King Philip IV "The Fair" of France, like heads of state before and since, had an insatiable need for more money. He trumped up charges of immorality against the Templars as an excuse to seize and plunder their wealth. He eventually had the order abolished. Fifty-four of their leaders were burned at the stake.

The Templars may have met defeat. But the spirit of enterprise in Europe was far from extinguished. In the fifteenth century, the Medici family of bankers and merchants rose in Templar-like fashion, amassing vast wealth and influence. They, too, incurred the wrath of a king. Charles VIII of France expelled the family and confiscated their property after he invaded Florence in 1494.[18]

Monarchs and other authoritarian rulers have never liked concentrations of wealth outside their control. Open markets have repeatedly led to the overthrow of dictators. The classic example of their democratizing power is Chile. Strongman Augusto Pinochet removed price controls, privatized government companies and the social security system, and increased trade. Eventually calls for democracy led to a plebiscite on his future. He lost.

Wealth generated by markets creates powerful new political constituencies. People who get used to voting with their money for goods and services sooner or later want to choose their officials.

China was once among the world's most brutal dictatorships. But since the Chinese government liberalized its economy, people have been increasingly challenging the nation's ruling elite. In 2007, then ninety-year-old Li Rui, Mao Zedong's former secretary and biographer and a former senior official under Deng Xiaoping, issued an astonishing warning: the Communist Party must end its "privileged status." China must democratize or see its economic progress reversed:

> Our Party must lead the way in exemplary enforcement of the Constitution and guaranteeing that the people enjoy their civic rights of freedom of expression, freedom of news, freedom of publication and freedom of association.[19]

Thanks to the democratizing power of markets, a onetime associate of Chairman Mao is singing the praises of freedom and democracy in words that could have been written by America's Founding Fathers.

* * *

BIG GOVERNMENT "FEW-DALISM": PRIVILEGES FOR THE FEW

Big Government is supposed to promote "equal opportunity," "fairness," and "equality." But it actually encourages *few-dalism*. Political cronyism and crony capitalism channel privileges to the favored few—the bureaucratic elite and their special interest constituents. The most egregious examples of political aristocracy are found within the biggest governments, especially socialist or communist regimes ostensibly dedicated to "equality."

In communist Cuba for many years only elite government officials, those with political connections, were allowed to legally buy cell phones or stay in the best hotels. The old Soviet Union was notorious for its special stores that were off-limits to ordinary citizens, catering only to government apparatchiks and foreigners.

In the Big Government health care systems of Canada and Europe, well-connected people often jump to the front of the "queue"—those interminable waits when care is rationed—and get faster treatment. As one frustrated Canadian complained to the *New York Times,* "If you are not bleeding all over the place, you are put on the back burner, unless of course you have money or know somebody."[20]

Big Government few-dalism determined the controversial and widely covered granting of Obamacare waivers. The law's myriad regulations and restrictions made it impossible for some employers to provide insurance to large numbers of transient employees. Thus, after the law was passed, you may recall that McDonald's and hundreds of others sought exemptions. As of spring 2011, the administration had granted more than thirteen hundred waivers to employers covering an estimated three million people or families.

No one was surprised when McDonald's, which had been first in line, got an exception. What *was* galling, however, were the hundreds of waivers granted to Big Labor unions that are among the administration's biggest financial supporters. They included, to name just a few, UFCW Allied Trade Health & Welfare Trust, IBEW No. 915, Asbestos Workers Local 53 Welfare Fund, Plumbers & Pipefitters Local 123 Welfare Fund, and on and on.[21]

Then there was the wave of waivers issued in 2011 to companies that just happened to be in the congressional district of former House Speaker Nancy Pelosi. The Daily Caller news website reported that these new recipients were not just big corporations and unions but "fancy eateries, hip nightclubs and decadent hotels," which were the "first major examples of luxurious, gourmet restaurants and hotels getting a year-long pass from Obamacare." This included establishments like Boboquivari's, a restaurant that, according to the news site, "advertises $59 porterhouse steaks, $39 filet mignons and $35 crab dinners."[22]

Why should these businesses, which are no different from countless other small employers across the nation, be exempt from a law that the Obama administration insists is good for all Americans?

Big Government cronyism does anything but promote fairness. It undermines the impartial rule of law critical to a moral society. If we are ever to maintain a functioning democracy, it's essential, in the words of Michael Barone of the American Enterprise Institute, that "laws apply to everybody."[23]

Republicans as well as Democrats have been guilty of Big Government few-dalism. The administration of George W. Bush was widely criticized for favoritism in awarding construction contracts in the wake of Hurricane Katrina. Few-dalism can also take the form of granting companies monopoly rights, as Congress officially did in 1984 to local cable operators. Companies that won rights to become the cable operator in a local municipality had to shell out huge sums to fund various pet projects of local politicians, in addition to paying franchise fees. What happened? Cable bills rose twice as fast as the rate of inflation. As is typical of Big Government few-dalism, the favored few benefit while the public pays.

FROM RAGS TO RENT-SEEKING

Occupy Wall Street protesters and their supporters think there would be greater "fairness"—less of a gulf between haves and have-nots—if government were given more power.

This is woefully misguided. It may be harder to get rich in state-dominated societies. But some people manage to do it. However, rather than offering products and services providing genuine value, they often profit from what economists call "rent-seeking"—that is, capitalizing on the political environment.

Paul R. Gregory of the Hoover Institution explains the distinction between free market wealth creation and the rent-seeking that takes place in a government-run society. In a free economy, he explains, wealth is created

> as a result of innovation, hard work, brilliant insights, or even luck. Entrepreneurs create enormous wealth when they have a better idea (Henry Ford's assembly line), discover and develop new products (Microsoft Windows or Google's search engine), see a new business model (Sam Walton), or are simply at the right place at the right time . . .
>
> A second and negative route to personal wealth is through political connections, lobbying to obtain benefits from the state, violence to remove competitors, or outright theft of public resources. Those who earn their fortunes the first way create jobs, raise productivity, and contribute to economic welfare. Those who use the second route are "rent seekers" who subtract from growth and welfare for their own benefit.[24]

In a Big Government economy, moving from rags to riches is not accomplished by working your way up, Horatio Alger–style, through a free market meritocracy. It's *rags to rent-seeking*. The bigger and more capricious government gets, the more wealth creation becomes dependent on how good you are at currying political favor.

There is still a "1 percent" in government-dominated nations. The difference is that the rich in those societies reap their gains from political favors—and they're even wealthier relative to the general population.

Hoover's Paul Gregory makes a fascinating observation: Oligarchs in state-run societies are far more powerful than the

1 percent in market economies like the United States. Entrepreneurial wealth creators such as Bill Gates, Warren Buffett, and Larry Ellison account for a smaller share of GDP than Russian billionaires whose wealth was state created.

> In those countries (U.S., EU, South Korea) where the top wealth holders play primarily entrepreneurial roles, their share is between *one and two* percent. Viewed in the light of their contribution to the economy, their wealth reward seems rather modest. In Ukraine and Russia, the share of GDP of the top ten is between *four and six* percent—a rather substantial return to those making negative or questionable contributions to output and welfare. [Our italics.][25]

Most of Russia's "1 percent" were given control of formerly state-owned assets based on government connections. The United States may not have Russian-style oligarchs. But Big Government cronyism in this country is indeed creating millionaires. Among members of Congress, rent-seeking has long been a bipartisan tradition. In his widely acclaimed and disturbing book, *Throw Them All Out,* Peter Schweizer of Stanford's Hoover Institution reveals that profiting from political influence and inside information is commonplace. Congress is not known for paying high salaries. Nonetheless, the job of U.S. senator or representative, he writes, can be highly lucrative.

One study, Schweizer writes, found that members of Congress "were 'accumulating wealth about 50% faster than expected' compared with other Americans." Lawmakers, he says, "saw their net worth soar, on average, an astonishing 84%

between 2004 and 2006." *It even increased, though far less dramatically, during the recession,* when the rest of the country grew poorer.[26]

National legislators who make laws affecting the nation's corporations were, until recently, permitted to trade stocks without private sector constraints on insider trading. A study of four thousand stock trades that senators made found that, on average, they beat the market by 12 percent a year—a higher percentage than investors who are corporate insiders. (Members of the House of Representatives also have a pretty good record.)

Thanks to the uproar caused by the publication of Schweizer's book, Congress finally passed laws banning insider trading in 2012. However, Schweizer is not impressed. Given the way Washington works, he doesn't believe these prohibitions will be effectively enforced. After all, the SEC and the FBI get their appropriations from . . . Congress.

Legislators also make money in other ways. Dennis Hastert, who served in Congress for twenty years and was Speaker of the House from 1999 to 2007, purchased more than a hundred acres of farmland. He put an earmark in a transportation bill to build a $220 million highway nearby. That doubled the value of the land and he made a couple million dollars upon selling the property.[27]

"A lot of [Washington lawmakers] come in of modest means and leave as millionaires and that is just simply wrong," says Schweizer.

Cronyism also influences who gets government loans and subsidies. To cite just one example: Department of Energy grants and government-guaranteed loans doled out under the 2009 economic "stimulus" often went to—you guessed it—Obama campaign donors. The most prominent case of "green graft" was Solyndra—the ill-fated solar panel company backed by Obama fund-raiser George Kaiser that went bankrupt after receiving $535 million in taxpayer dollars.

Another beneficiary: former vice president Al Gore. Some have predicted that Gore could become the world's first carbon billionaire, thanks to lucrative government contracts awarded to Kleiner Perkins, the venture capital firm where he is a partner.[28]

This kind of deal making—in green technologies and elsewhere—means that political connections and influence are replacing fairness and genuine competition, Schweizer writes:

> Hard work and innovation should be driving the American economy, but in Washington, crony connections have thrown these stable economic helmsmen overboard.[29]

Big Government crony capitalism, by the way, is a major source of those Wall Street profits and bonuses that Occupy Wall Street protesters and others have decried as "unfair." Fred Siegel of the Manhattan Institute makes the point, overlooked by virtually everybody, that government distortion of the financial sector is often what's driving these outsized gains. Bush and Obama bailouts, along with economic stimulus money and near-zero interest rates, he says, artificially propped up big banks. The growth of government since the Great Society of the 1960s also helped create the giant government unions whose pension funds are major sources of Wall Street money. As Siegel observed in the *Wall Street Journal*: "Wall Street makes money off the bonds that have to be floated to pay the public sector workers in New York." The Occupy Wall Street protesters, he suggests, don't have it all wrong. But they should be protesting the ways of Washington—and not those of Wall Street.[30]

HOW BIG GOVERNMENT CORRUPTS

Crony capitalism is generally blamed on "greedy" corporations. But Big Government, and not business, drives this corruption. Government, after all, is the dispenser of favors. Shortly after taking office, President Obama announced that his administration would dramatically cut back on hiring lobbyists for political posts. He demanded that his White House post all meetings with representatives of lobbying firms.

Condemned by both left and right, the proliferation of lobbyists is seen as symptomatic of excessive corporate influence. Critics, however, forget why lobbyists exist. The more powerful government becomes, the greater its ability to destroy or help your business. Broadcasters have traditionally had a powerful lobbying effort, for example, because Big Government determines who has access to the airwaves. Big box retailers like Walmart want the government to force banks to charge lower swipe fees on debit cards. Big Government wealth also attracts businesses looking for lucrative contracts.

Author and *National Review* columnist Jonah Goldberg has observed, "As the size and scope of government have grown, so have the numbers of businesses petitioning the government. In 1956, the *Encyclopedia of Associations* listed 4,900 groups. Today it lists over 23,000."[31]

Companies that do business the old-fashioned way, focusing exclusively on their customers and their competition, do so at their peril. For twenty years, Microsoft paid no attention to Washington. The result? A mammoth antitrust action that dragged on for years, costing the company billions of dollars in fines and legal fees. Today the company has a major presence in Washington, D.C., and employs numerous powerful lobbying firms and individual lobbyists to protect its interests.

Facebook, which became a multibillion-dollar giant in the few years since it was founded in 2004, was not about to make the same mistake. In 2011, the company, concerned by potential government privacy restrictions, opened up a spanking new eight-thousand-square-foot office in Washington with a staff that includes a former privacy expert from the American Civil Liberties Union. Google, another start-up-turned-giant, is spending each year many millions of dollars on lobbying.

The reason these and countless other companies are writing big checks for lobbying is simple: they've come to the conclusion that if you don't do what it takes to get political protection, regulators and ambitious Department of Justice lawyers will eat you alive. Virtually every major industry and company has a presence in Washington—from broadcasters and telecom companies to the National Restaurant Association.

Government power—and the fear of it—is what draws so much favor-seeking. How many lobbyists would there be if we didn't have so many bureaucracies, rules, and regulations? Far fewer than there are today.

This corruption breeds additional corruption as firms seeking to protect their interests look for ways to shape government decisions and policies. Typical of Big Government cronies, the regulated often end up influencing the regulators.

One of the worst recent examples was the incestuous relationship that evolved between the federal government and those now-infamous mortgage giants Fannie Mae and Freddie Mac. Both began as government agencies and later became "government-sponsored enterprises" (GSEs)—public corporations created by the federal government.

Fannie and Freddie were for years regarded as de facto arms of Uncle Sam because they had lines of credit with the Treasury Department. But they were public corporations subject to oversight. Unfortunately for us, they received little or none. Their relationship with the federal government was worse than corrupt and was a major factor in the widespread collapse of the housing market.

Gretchen Morgenson and Josh Rosner chronicle the unhealthy symbiosis that developed between the two mortgage leviathans and a succession of administrations in their excellent book *Reckless Endangerment: How Outsized Ambition, Greed, and Corruption Led to Economic Armageddon.* They recall that, in the 1990s, Fannie Mae and the Clinton administration formed an "unprecedented partnership." Both sides had a shared mission and each served the needs of the other. Bill Clinton was pushing the goal of 70 percent home ownership. This strategy, however, was not in response to bad economic times. Morgenson and Rosner point out that it was crassly political: "An owner in every home. It was the prosperous, 1990s version of the Depression-era 'A Chicken in Every Pot.' "[32]

Fannie and Freddie's high-risk business model fit the political needs of politicians. And Fannie Mae became hyperaggressive in promoting it. The authors write that Fannie Mae "perfected the art of manipulating lawmakers, eviscerating its regulators and enriching its executives."[33]

Money was spread everywhere. According to *Investors Business Daily,* some 384 politicians got donations from Fannie and Freddie, which spent $200 million on lobbying and political activities between 1989 and 2008.[34] Money went to political campaigns and to mute criticism from pressure groups like the Association of Community Organizations for Reform Now (ACORN). Congressman Barney Frank, the then powerful chairman of the House Financial Services Committee and Fannie Mae's fervent advocate, was among those receiving campaign donations from Fannie and Freddie. Fannie even made "sizable contributions" to the Committee to End Elder Homelessness, cofounded by Frank's mother, and hired his partner as an executive.[35] Presidential contender Newt Gingrich attracted considerable criticism for accepting lucrative consulting fees from Freddie Mac. Others getting campaign dollars included then senator Christopher Dodd, chairman of the Senate Banking Committee at that time, as well as then senator Barack Obama.

Thanks to these efforts, Fannie was able to successfully push practices like relaxing underwriting to permit loans based on just a 5 percent down payment. These standards were adopted by the rest of the industry, and contributed to the lending mania that set the stage for the explosion of the housing bubble and financial crisis. Washington's massive corruption and Big Government cronyism very nearly brought down the entire U.S. economy.

Things can get particularly tawdry at the local level. Cronyism is rampant throughout the immense political bureaucracies of New York State, and especially New York City. In 2011, the Indian Community and Cultural Center managed to buy four and a half acres from the old Creedmoor Hospital, a state-owned property, for $1.8 million—an appallingly low sum in a region renowned for high real estate prices. The market value of the land was said to be closer to $7.3 million.

Normally state land in New York is auctioned off to the highest bidder. Heather Haddon reported in the *New York Post* that an exception was made in the case of the Creedmoor property. Special legislation passed in 2006 authorized the sale to the group at below market value. Permission was also granted for a community center and apartment buildings to be built on the property. What makes these special privileges even more remarkable was that the buyers were broke. The Indian community group ran a $22,000 deficit in 2009.

Clearly, state officials went to great lengths to engineer this sale of state land to a money-losing community group at a below market price, at the expense of the taxpayers. Why? Haddon answers, "The group is rich in political capital, including ties to the growing concentration of Indian-Americans living in eastern Queens."[36]

No surprise that investment decisions made by large state employee pension funds can be equally rife with corruption and cronyism. Private equity firms jockey to win the business of these funds, which are controlled by state officials and can mean investments in the tens or hundreds of millions. In 2011, former New York State comptroller Alan Hevesi, a former candidate for New York City mayor, was sentenced to up to four years in prison after pleading guilty to receiving "pay-to-play" kickbacks of more than $1 million for approving $250 million in pension fund investments in Markstone Capital Partners, a private equity fund.[37]

Also getting jail time was Hevesi's longtime political adviser, Hank Morris. Working as a middleman or "placement agent,"

Morris steered pension fund business to investment firms, raking in $19 million in fees. Along the way, he solicited contributions to Hevesi's reelection campaign. Pay-to-play accusations have also been made against pension fund officials and investment fund managers in other states, including California, where a pension fund invested in Wetherly Capital Group, another firm represented by Morris.[38]

Big Government's control over vast resources, its power over industries—not to mention the need for officials and bureaucrats to please their political backers—amount to a recipe for political corruption. Making matters worse is the fact that, unlike in the private sector, officials can exercise their immense power without having to answer to customers or shareholders. There's no fear that their actions will cause their employer (the government) to go out of business. There's little in the way of transparency and accountability. It's possible for dishonest individuals to get away with almost anything—and some do.

BIG GOVERNMENT CRONYISM CRUSHES THE LITTLE GUY

Politicians will tell you that Big Government rules and regulations are necessary to fight "injustice" and help the "little guy." The real injustice is the amount of damage done to the economy—and to the American people—by politicians selling regulations based on this myth. It is true, as we have emphasized, that government with a small "g" is needed to protect individuals and businesses from fraud and other wrongdoing. But intrusive, overbearing Big Government rules that micromanage the economy rarely help small players or level the playing field. They crush smaller, less established players, while cementing the position of incumbents.

The twenty-three-hundred-page Dodd-Frank financial "reform" legislation passed by Congress in 2010 was supposed to protect the little guy by preventing future financial traumas like the panic of 2008. But this monster legislation—the financial industry version of Obamacare—does nothing of the sort. It ignores the causes of the financial crisis, including, as we've said, the role of Fannie Mae, Freddie Mac, and the Federal Reserve.

The bill helps big players by unintentionally codifying the "too big to fail" doctrine. The law places more power in the hands of regulators who, typical of bureaucrats, are highly unlikely to admit mistakes in oversight. Thus they will rescue an institution rather than letting it fail. Bigger institutions end up benefiting: they're able to obtain capital at lower costs because the market believes they'd be rescued by government.

This has already happened. A smaller institution, CIT Financial, was recently allowed to go bankrupt. When the firm emerged from bankruptcy, its borrowing costs were higher than those of General Electric, a larger competitor. A big part of the difference in their borrowing costs was not their respective sizes but rather the belief that Uncle Sam wouldn't let GE go belly up.

CIT's experience reflects how Dodd-Frank is devastating smaller institutions. Former FDIC chairman William Isaac writes that the Dodd-Frank financial reform effectively throws seven thousand small banks "under the bus." The legal monstrosity, in Isaac's words, "will heap at least 10,000 pages of new regulations on community banks." The cost of complying will be enormous. When the dust clears, only the biggest players—the Citibanks and the Bank of Americas—will be able to compete. Isaac writes,

> At a recent meeting in Washington of 1,000 bankers from all size of banks, members of the audience were asked to raise their hand if they believed banks with assets of less than $100 million in size had a future. Virtually no hands were raised. The same question was asked about $500 million-asset banks and there was a 50 percent show of hands. This does not bode well for America's smaller communities and businesses.[39]

Big Government cronyism is also at the heart of eminent domain rights abuses. Local governments forcibly take private property of individuals and businesses for commercial development. "Eminent domain" refers to the "Takings clause" inserted by James Madison in the Fifth Amendment to the U.S. Constitution. It states that *private property shall not be taken for public use, without just compensation.* Writing in the *Public Corporation Law Quarterly,* Daniel P. Dalton explains that Madison "hoped that the clause would 'impress on the people the sanctity of property.'"[40]

Before the 1940s, government evoked "eminent domain" and confiscated private land when it was needed for public works projects like freeways, waterways, defense installations, and government and public buildings. The definition of "public use" began to change with the growth of activist government during the Great Depression and the subsequent urban renewal movement of the 1940s and 1950s. "For the first time," Dalton writes, "government proposed large-scale condemnation of residential property with the intention of reconveying it to private developers." Today the law has become, as he puts it, "a favored method for urban development, creating shopping malls, and building big-box retail stores."

In the notorious case of *Kelo vs. New London* in 2005, the Supreme Court ruled that the Connecticut town could take private property for the "public purpose" of economic development—that is, projects that result in job creation. Homeowner Susette Kelo was forced to move her pink cottage to another location. Her neighbors, the Cristofaros, were forced to buy another home.

Did the public benefit? New London had intended the confiscated land for a tony retail shopping center that would entice nearby Pfizer Inc. to expand its operations. But Pfizer and its fourteen hundred jobs ended up leaving anyway. Even if the development had come to pass, the *Kelo* decision, and the hijacking of eminent domain to please political cronies, remain morally wrong and an abuse of government power.

If anyone doubts the cronyism implicit in eminent domain, consider the case of the Deepdale Golf Club located on Long Island's affluent North Shore. In 2006, the club successfully spurned an attempt by the town of North Hills to confiscate its land. Although *Kelo* had already passed, Deepdale supporters managed to get special legislation passed by the state legislature prohibiting North Hills from taking the property.[41] How did the golf club avoid the fate of Susie Kelo and the Cristofaros family? The reason may have had something to do with the political connections of the historic club, whose members have included financial and media heavy hitters like Tom Brokaw, Sean Connery, and Pete Peterson.[42] The moral of the story is that in

Big Government crony capitalism, the players with the deepest pockets get favors. And the little guy gets screwed—a scenario that is neither moral nor fair.

THE MORAL SHAM OF ANTITRUST

What about antitrust laws? Aren't they supposed to protect smaller players? Think again. Antitrust laws put in place in the name of "equality" show how Big Government can unfairly penalize "too much success."

The idea that government is needed to subdue big companies with too much "market power" is virtually a religion. Yet companies targeted by antitrust actions have rarely behaved as monopolies—or, for that matter, harmed consumers. Economist Dominick Armentano studied fifty-five historic antitrust actions and found that, in every single case, companies were innovating, lowering their prices, and expanding production, providing more benefit to their customers.[43] So why were these companies targeted for violating antitrust laws? Because politically connected, rent-seeking *big* competitors convinced regulators that these companies had "unfair advantages."

The famed Microsoft antitrust case, for example, was propelled by large corporations like Sun Microsystems and Oracle. Was Microsoft really becoming too powerful? Hardly. Ten years ago, most people used PCs. But even then there were alternatives to Microsoft's browsers that could be installed on your computer.

Antitrust, like most Big Government intervention, cements the position of incumbents and penalizes entrepreneurial upstarts. Microsoft survived the global antitrust assault. More than a decade later, the company faces its own challenges in a fiercely competitive market from a new generation of upstarts like Google. What does it do? In 2011, Microsoft filed its own antitrust suit in Europe against Google, accusing the online giant of engaging in anticompetitive behavior.

In the United States, a stunned Eric Schmidt, executive chairman of Google, was summoned by the Senate Judiciary Antitrust Subcommittee to answer similar allegations that the company is a monopolist. In an interview with the *Washington Post,* he made little secret of his incredulity:

> So we get hauled in front of the Congress for developing a product that's free, that serves a billion people. OK? I mean, I don't know how to say it any clearer. . . . It's not like we raised prices. We could lower prices from free to . . . lower than free? You see what I'm saying?[44]

HOW CRONY CAPITALISM DESTROYS WEALTH CREATION

Big Government few-dalism is immoral not just because it's unfair. It also drags down the economy. That's because—as we've explained—big companies are usually the ones to get the breaks. The smaller companies that create the most growth and innovation in the economy are kept from rising up. Entrepreneurship, innovation, and job creation suffer. Wealth is not created but destroyed. Bruce Chapman of the Discovery Institute has cited the example of Illinois. Overwhelmed by debt, the state recently gave special tax breaks to Motorola, Continental Tire, and other big companies whose jobs and tax dollars it could not afford to lose. Meanwhile, he writes, "not getting tax breaks are the little guys, the small and medium-size businesses that would like to become big someday—if government didn't keep piling costs on them."[45]

Politicians are always talking about the need for Americans to increase manufacturing and export more products. Big Government crony capitalism can lead to trade wars that make this goal even more difficult. A recent example: the 2009 ban on Mexican commercial trucks entering the United States, imposed by the administration under pressure by the Teamsters Union. Instead of simply crossing the border into the United States, the Mexican trucks were required to unload their cargo, which was placed on American trucks driven by members of the Teamsters. Mexico responded by slapping $2.4 billion in tariffs on U.S. goods. The result? Thanks to the administration's political favors to Teamsters, produce exported to Mexico from farmers in states such as California, Washington, and elsewhere cost 20 percent more. The United States and Mexico finally agreed to end both the ban and the retaliatory tariffs in the spring of 2011.

Not only do prices rise with Big Government cronyism, many products and services never get developed because the economy's capital has been diverted toward political purposes—like those green jobs. Not only do we end up with a slumping economy, but also something potentially more dangerous: a decline of faith in the system.

Researchers at Harvard University and MIT studied the influence of the perception of "fairness" on national policies and voting patterns in the United States and Europe. They discovered a vicious cycle:

If a society believes that individual effort determines income, and that all have a right to enjoy the fruits of their effort, it will choose low redistribution and low taxes. . . . If instead a society believes that luck, birth, connections and/or corruption determine wealth, it will tax a lot, thus distorting allocations and making these beliefs self-sustained as well.[46]

Big Government cronyism is especially insidious because it is self-perpetuating. The worse it becomes, the more likely people turn to government as the solution. Far too frequently, they end up voting in new regulations and restrictions—less fairness and less liberty.

THE UNITED STATES OF ARGENTINA?

More than one observer has expressed fear that the United States today is becoming a North American version of Argentina. That beleaguered South American nation has lurched from one economic crisis to another as a consequence of policies shaped by Big Government cronyism. In a widely lauded article in the *Financial Times,* journalist Alan Beattie reminds us that Argentina at one time, believe it or not, was seen as a land of opportunity.

A short century ago the US and Argentina were rivals. Both were riding the first wave of globalisation at the turn of the 20th century. Both were young, dynamic nations with fertile farmlands and confident exporters. Both brought the beef of the New World to the tables of their European colonial forebears. Before the Great Depression of the 1930s, Argentina was among the 10 richest economies in the world. The millions of emigrant Italians and Irish fleeing poverty at the end of the 19th century were torn between the two: Buenos Aires or New York? The pampas or the prairie?[47]

Both the United States and Argentina began as agrarian states, with frontier movements. But the key difference, Beattie says, is that the United States opted to create a decentralized, open society while Argentina placed control of the nation's land and other resources in the hands of a wealthy aristocracy and a centralized government. He continues:

Both countries opened up the west, the US to the Pacific and the Argentines to the Andes, but not in the same way. America favoured squatters: Argentina backed landlords. Thus was privilege reinforced. European emigrants to Argentina had escaped a landowning aristocracy, only to recreate it in the New World. The similarities were more than superficial. In the 1860s and 1870s, the landowners regarded rural life and the actual practice of agriculture with disdain. Many lived refined, deracinated lives in the cities, spending their time immersed in European literature and music. The closest they came to celebrating country life was elevating polo, an aristocratised version of a rural pursuit, to a symbol of Argentine athletic elegance. Even then it took an elite form: the famous Jockey Club of Buenos Aires. By the end of the 19th century some were sending their sons to Eton.[48]

Argentina's economic policies ever since have focused on preserving the interests of ruling elites. The country's famed strongman, Juan Perón, in the mid-1940s encouraged, in Beattie's words, "a cult of personality and urged Nazi-style economic self-sufficiency and 'corporatism'—a strong government, organised labour and industrial conglomerates jointly directing and managing growth."[49]

Argentina's elitist, protectionist policies caused it to turn inward. The country taxed exports and discouraged foreign trade. The nation instituted a welfare state. To pay for this profligate spending, Argentina borrowed heavily and stimulated its economy by printing more pesos and suffered the economic equivalent of an amphetamine overdose. In recent decades, the nation has endured a succession of currency crises with breathtaking bouts of hyperinflation of as high as 5,000 percent. Beattie recounts that in 1989 hyperinflation wiped Argentinians' life savings in a matter of months. He quotes one journalist who complained that during the time it took to write a piece about the disaster, "the price of the cigarette that he was smoking went from 11 to 14 australes [a new currency that lasted a matter of weeks]."[50]

The sad saga continues. Argentine prices in 2011 were rising at a rate of around 25 percent per year, second only to socialist Venezuela. The situation is so severe that one grocery chain owner is forced to "change prices in his stores daily as suppliers send him new lists, with increases on some products ranging from 5 percent a month to as much as 5 or 10 percent in a single week." He told the reporter, "If I didn't change the prices, maybe I'd end up selling goods at a price below the new costs."[51]

The Cato Institute's Dan Mitchell, like Beattie, believes Argentina's story is "a warning to America":

Argentina's economy, for all intents and purposes, is one giant Fannie Mae/Freddie Mac/Obamacare/General Motors/Goldman Sachs Obamaesque dystopia. Government has enormous influence over every major economic decision. It's like being in the middle of *Atlas Shrugged,* as political connections are the way to get rich.[52]

The question is what the future will bring with the growth of Big Government regulation, spending, and taxes reaching new levels under Barack Obama. *Forbes* publisher and columnist Rich Karlgaard has pointed out that U.S. prosperity since World War II has been based on annual GDP growth averaging 3.3 percent. This growth is not propelled by larger companies but the meritocracy of our markets—the ability of small upstarts to get big. Research from the Kaufman Foundation, the entrepreneurial think tank, shows that "the X factor of America's historical success," the single most important contributor to a nation's economic growth, is the number of start-ups that grow to a billion dollars in revenue within twenty years. Karlgaard says,

Yes, we want our large multinational companies—the Apples and IBMs, Walmarts and Exxon Mobils—to be successful. But their success, while necessary for a healthy economy, won't grow the economy much more than a Western Europe–like 2% per year (a rate of growth, as we've learned, that feels moribund to an American).[53]

What happens when crony capitalism of bigger government makes it harder for newcomers to rise up and become the

Netflix and Google of tomorrow? You get precisely what the United States has experienced since the financial crisis: a stagnant European-style economy with high unemployment, less opportunity, and growing despair about "unfairness" and the death of the American Dream.

6

THE SPIRIT OF REAGAN
or OBAMA?

Optimism and Cooperation Versus Pessimism and Distrust

Free markets are rooted in moral optimism. Buying, selling, and investing require trust—the optimistic belief that it is in the other person's self-interest to live up to agreements and make good on one's promises. Investing in new ventures requires faith. People stake their capital, time, and reputations on the ideas and creativity of others. America's history abounds with stories of entrepreneurs—from Thomas Edison to Steve Jobs—who reached the zenith of wealth and achievement because they had the courage to take such risks.

The openness of markets to these entrepreneurial upstarts and newcomers also fosters the optimistic perception that anyone who works hard enough can get ahead. The American Dream of success and upward mobility is the reason why this country has throughout its history been a magnet for millions of individuals seeking to realize their own visions of success.

We call the optimism of the market moral optimism *because it promotes the betterment of society by fostering cooperation, entrepreneurial creativity, and innovation—what some call "human flourishing." Without such faith in people and the future, individuals would be unable to work together in a voluntary economy. Markets and businesses couldn't function. Entrepreneurial individuals would not invest and innovate. Society and people would not move forward.*

The moral optimism of the market lies in stark contast to the pessimism that drives Big Government and its supporters. To a certain degree, this is as it should be. Government's core competency is protecting people from the bad behavior of others and maintaining order. Therefore its focus is on what can go wrong and on the baser side of human nature. The problem with Big Government, however, is that its policies, political culture—indeed, its entire worldview—are based on this negative perspective.

In the mind-set of Big Government supporters and bureaucrats, unregulated markets are chaotic places, where law abiding individuals are endangered by the forces of "greed" and "injustice." Thus the only "solution" must be controls that safeguard people and minimize risk. Without protection from government, the future can only hold disaster—whether that may be totally unaffordable health insurance, economic depression, or "the end of the American Dream." Pessimism also colors statists' views of rich and poor, who are seen as mutually antagonistic groups with opposing interests.

The contrast between the moral optimism of enterprise and the negative assumptions of Big Government is reflected in the differing visions of Ronald Reagan and Barack Obama. As we point out later on in this chapter, both came to office in troubled times. But Reagan, a champion of limited government and open markets, believed that the historic ingenuity of the American people would prevail. His moral optimism led him to reduce the high taxation and regulation that were constraining enterprise—producing twenty-five years of historic growth, prosperity, and innovation.

Barack Obama takes a bleaker view, believing Big Government is necessary to rescue people from "greed"—from themselves.

His Big Government pessimism has led to punitive regulations and policies meant to control "greed" that have slowed the economy and polarized people. Instead of bringing more hope, they have produced more despair. In 2011, at a time when government has never been bigger, a USA Today/Gallup poll found the nation's optimism about the future at an all-time low. More than half the nation, 55 percent, believed that today's youth would not have a better life than their parents. Their pessimism was even greater than at the beginning of the recession in 2008.[1]

BOTTOM LINE: DO WE WANT A GOVERNMENT WITH FAITH IN PEOPLE THAT PROMOTES PROSPERITY—OR ONE THAT DIVIDES SOCIETY, PUNISHES ENTERPRISE, AND RESTRICTS OUR FREEDOM?

THE "APOCA-LIBERAL" VISION OF BIG GOVERNMENT BELIEVERS

In a 2011 *New York Times* op-ed, "The Kids Are Not All Right," Joel Bakan, a law professor at the University of British Columbia, bemoaned the dangers faced by today's teenagers "absorbed by the titillating roil of online social life, the addictive pull of video games and virtual worlds."

As he watches his kids "stare endlessly at video clips and digital pictures of themselves and their friends," Bakan "feels like something is wrong. . . . There is reason to believe that childhood itself is now in crisis." Video games and Internet addiction, he says, are just the tip of the iceberg. He enumerates a long list of what he describes as growing dangers to kids from greedy corporations. These include not only video games, but everything from junk food advertising that helps bring on obesity to "toxic chemicals" and "potentially harmful psycho-tropic drugs."[2]

Not surprisingly, Bakan is the author of a book called *Childhood Under Siege: How Big Business Targets Children*. The problem, he says, isn't just business. Bakan gets to what he sees as the real issue: not enough government control. "Deregulation, privatization, weak enforcement of existing regulations and legal and political resistance to new regulations have eroded our ability, as a society, to protect children."

Bakan's worldview is typical of what we call the *apoca-liberal* vision of Big Government statists, who all too frequently perceive even mildly objectionable circumstances as harbingers of impending disaster—not just for kids but for "society" and "the planet." These "crises" can almost never be solved through reasonable solutions undertaken voluntarily by individuals. Rather, they are systemic catastrophes requiring some massive intervention by government.

Bakan laments that many kids "spend more hours engaging with various electronic media . . . than they spend in school."[3] No question many parents today are frustrated by kids who pay more attention to text messages than to their homework or family conversation. But does that mean, as Bakan suggests, that childhood is in "crisis"? As he describes his children staring at online pictures of themselves and their friends, one hardly gets the feeling that they're under assault. They're simply enjoying themselves—being kids.

Are the dangers that Bakan describes really threats to childhood? Certainly they pale in comparison to what kids endured centuries ago, when people worried about diseases like cholera, typhoid, and diphtheria, major causes of infant death in the

1800s. Many kids never made it past their fifth birthday. They were lucky to have a childhood. And if they did have one, it was often brutal. Toys were simple and there were far fewer of them compared with today. And children from poor families also faced something far worse than obesity—starvation.

Even in the first half of the twentieth century, conditions were much harsher than they are now. Until recently, corporal punishment—beating children in schools to enforce discipline—was common. Polio, afflicting hundreds of thousands of American children, was a constant threat.

A lot of what Bakan complains about, such as advances like the Internet, are *good things*. Yes, kids *and adults* waste time with social media. And parents and teachers need to warn against the dangers of predators, online and offline. But the educational benefits of the Web far outweigh the negatives. And most would agree that interacting with video games and Internet media, which requires reading, writing, and decision making, is an improvement over spending hours passively staring at the TV. Instead of the Big Government rules and regs that Bakan wants, what about more parental ground rules like: "no Facebook until you've done your homework"? Schools that do a better job of teaching kids would also help.

Bakan's complaints are typical of Big Government statists, who all too often exaggerate the downsides of products and technologies that are mainly beneficial. You see this with health scares that swirl around products certain people think should be more heavily regulated. In 2011, people became alarmed about reports of arsenic in apple juice. Arsenic is a lethal poison present throughout the environment. In apple juice it exists in trace amounts. None of the stories reporting this supposed danger mentioned a single case of a toddler falling ill with arsenic poisoning. Even the Food and Drug Administration itself eventually acknowledged that the levels of arsenic in apple juice were of little concern.

Unfortunately, such common sense has often not prevailed when it comes to other "hazards." Gilbert Ross, M.D., the medical director at the American Council on Science and Health, points out that health "risks" decried by Big Government activists are frequently overstated. Phthalates, a plastic softener found in some toys, as well as in critical medical products, is one of those chemicals often said to be "dangerous." Tests show it's poisonous to rats at high exposures. Detectable levels have been found in people's blood. But does that mean it's seriously hazardous? Ross's organization points out on its website, "The presence of a chemical does not necessarily mean that it is harmful . . . it is the dose that makes the poison."[4]

The apocalyptic thinking of Big Government activists all too often results in overreaction—demands for outright bans or restrictions on products and technologies that do far more good than harm. In the worst instances, the hysteria of Big Government apoca-liberals can end up depriving people of desperately needed products, services, and technologies.

This is the case with the breakthrough technology of hydraulic fracturing. As we discussed in chapter 3, "fracking" promises to dramatically boost domestic supplies and turn the United States into a leading gas exporter. The technology could be a godsend in economically lagging parts of New York State. But, as always, activists pressed the state to ban the process, insisting it would poison groundwater and cause other environmental disasters.

In fact, the percentage of chemicals in this water is minuscule: 99.5 percent of the fluid injected into the rock is water and sand.[5] Not surprisingly, the moratorium in New York was later partially lifted.

It's worth noting that in Pennsylvania, which did not have crippling restrictions on the technology, natural gas exploration has flourished. Over seventy-two thousand high-paying jobs have been created.[6] Pennsylvania's state government collected in a single fiscal year an unanticipated $700 million in revenue from this additional economic activity.

MIRED IN MYOPIA

Even when things are going well, statists see potential disaster. In 1995, when U.S. unemployment was at a low of 5.6 percent, Jeremy Rifkin, a longtime advocate of Big Government and a notorious gloomsayer, published *The End of Work: The Decline of the Global Labor Force and the Dawn of the Post-Market Era*, a book predicting that the rise of information technology would eliminate tens of millions of jobs and produce a worldwide epidemic of joblessness.

However, a decade later, before government policies thrust the economy into the Great Recession, work didn't end. Instead, U.S. unemployment dropped still further—to 4.6 percent by 2007.

Andrew Stern, then president of the Service Employees International Union, lamented to the *New York Times* during that same year that parents "cannot see where the jobs of the future are that will allow their kids to have a better life than they had."[7]

Responding to Stern's complaint in the *Times,* George Mason University economist Donald Boudreaux asks, "when could Americans of any generation foresee future jobs?" Did the telegram-deliverer in 1950 foresee his child designing software for cell phones? Did the local pharmacist in 1960 foresee his daughter's job as a biomedical engineer?[8]

Donald Boudreaux's questions highlight another flaw of apoca-liberal pessimism: it's fixated on the present. Unlike entrepreneurs who think in terms of the future, bureaucrats and their supporters are stuck in the here and now. They see market conditions like high prices as permanent and can't imagine how things could possibly change—even though they always do.

In the case of health care, statists believe government is the only answer "because health care is so astronomically expensive." It's impossible for them to grasp the idea that, if you removed today's innumerable government constraints that are inflating the cost of both care and insurance, the entire universe would instantly change. Prices would fall if you cut back cost-inflating federal and state regulations, allowed competition, and enabled people—and not companies—to make the buying decisions. You'd see a flowering of creativity throughout the industry—new ways to provide insurance and medical care— that do not exist today. Remember the Staples principle we discussed in chapter 3. In a healthy, consumer-driven market, companies competing for business always seek to improve offerings and make prices cheaper.

To a certain degree statists' myopia is understandable. Some problems can seem so immense that it's hard for people to imagine *any* solutions, much less those arising spontaneously from entrepreneurial, free markets. Reminding people that free markets have always solved problems in the past also doesn't help. In many instances "progress is so gradual that a few pockets of decay hide it from the public view," observes George Mason University economist Bryan Caplan in his book *The Myth of the Rational Voter.*[9]

There's no question that, for many people, a downbeat narrative can seem more compelling than sunny, "Pollyanna" optimism. The public has traditionally had what Caplan calls a "pessimistic bias"—"a tendency to overestimate the severity of economic problems and underestimate the (recent) past, present, and future performance of the economy."[10]

American Enterprise Institute scholar Arthur Herman reminds us that, to a certain degree, pessimism is part of human nature. "Virtually every culture past or present has believed that men and women are not up to the standards of their parents and forebears."[11]

PROBLEM-MONGERING: "THE SUREST PATH TO POWER"

Remember the now famous quip from President Obama's former chief of staff Rahm Emanuel: "You never want a serious crisis to go to waste." Politicians on both sides have throughout history seized on crises as opportunities to advance an agenda. But Big Government politicians and activists have a particular tendency to see through the glass darkly. Their gloom-and-doom rhetoric implies that solutions to big, systemic problems are beyond the power of individuals and demand Big Government intervention. Donald Boudreaux reminds us, "Problem-mongering is the surest path to power."[12]

We're so accustomed to these forecasts by promoters of Big Government that we seldom notice that they rarely, if ever, come true. When President Clinton enacted the North American Free Trade Agreement (NAFTA), doomsayers predicted a "giant sucking sound" of jobs leaving this country for Mexico. Yet U.S. unemployment continued to *fall* for the next fifteen years, until the 2008–2009 recession. As we noted in chapter 3, many people in the 1970s subscribed to the Malthusian belief that overpopulation would create scarcity and starvation among the world's poor countries. Instead, as Julian Simon predicted, we entered three decades of increasing abundance as nations worldwide liberalized their economies. *We're now concerned about how to compete with the countries we once feared would starve.*

THE MORAL FALLACY OF "CLASS WARFARE"

With their myopic, downbeat worldview, it's easy to understand how statists see rich and poor as fixed groups with opposing interests. In the 2004 presidential election campaign, Democratic vice presidential candidate John Edwards best summed up this belief when he spoke of "two Americas . . . one privileged, the other burdened . . . one America that does the work, another that reaps the reward. One America that pays the taxes, another America that gets the tax breaks."[13]

The fundamental notion of antagonistic "class warfare" is part of a populist tradition that has long driven the policies and strategies of promoters of more government.

In September 2011, President Obama, announcing his plan to create jobs, declared that Americans had a choice: "Should we keep tax breaks for millionaires and billionaires? Or should we put teachers back to work so our kids can graduate ready for college and good jobs? Right now, we can't afford to do both. This isn't political grandstanding. This isn't class warfare. This is simple math."[14]

Not only does the president's "math" pit Americans against each other, it does not add up. After spending over a trillion federal dollars on a "stimulus" that went largely to state and local governments, the unemployment rate still remained historically high. If the president really wanted to generate more revenue to pay for teachers, he would have implemented pro-market policies to increase the nation's tax base by spurring economic growth.

Such moves by both Republican and Democratic administrations have benefited not only "billionaires" but also the entire economy. Big Government opponents, nonetheless, keep insisting that tax reductions are for "the rich." More than simply a divisive tactic to stir up political support, the rhetoric of class warfare reflects a profound and misguided cynicism.

The idea of "rich" and "poor" being at cross-purposes is rooted in the Marxist vision of class struggle. Marx portrayed "the poor"—or as he liked to put it, "the proletarians"—as a permanent underclass forever victimized by "the rich." This critique is based on a profound misperception of history.

Marx lived in nineteenth-century Europe during the Industrial Revolution, a time of economic and social change. A growing middle class—what he and others preferred to call "the bourgeoisie"—was beginning to undermine an aristocratic hierarchy that originated with the feudal society of medieval Europe. Kings, queens, and nobles still held sway, but a new meritocracy was emerging based on commerce.

In other words, Marx's perceptions of markets were colored by his personal experience in a hierarchical, postfeudal society. He confused the riches won by aristocracies in "a status or caste society" with wealth generated by a free market economy. Noted Austrian economist and social philosopher Ludwig von Mises powerfully delineates the distinction in his book *Theory and History*. The "feudal property" of aristocrats, like kings and queens,

> came into existence either by conquest or by donation on the part of a conqueror.
>
> The owners of feudal property did not depend on the market, they did not serve the consumers; within the range of their property rights they were real lords. But it is quite different with the capitalists and entrepreneurs of a market economy. They acquire and enlarge their property through the services they have rendered to the consumers, and they can retain it only by serving daily again in the best possible way.[15]

To paraphrase Mises, people may refer to a successful pasta manufacturer as "the spaghetti king." But this king did not build his empire through wars and conquest, but by selling pasta people like. What Marxists totally miss, Mises writes, is that "the rich" in free markets do not get their power by impoverishing wage earners—but by producing goods that improve their standard of living.

Marx always labored under the deceptive conception that the workers are toiling for the sole benefit of an upper class of idle parasites. He did not see that the workers themselves consume by far the greater part of all the consumers' goods turned out.[16]

Marx's hostility to markets was undoubtedly colored by his era's widespread anxiety over changes taking place in society as a result of the Industrial Revolution. He reacted like many statists do today—rejecting the new and instead looking backward and refusing to give up old ideas.

WHOSE "GREED"?

"Greed" is the bedrock of Big Government pessimism. It is the cause of all evils—from Wall Street bonuses and CEO salaries to high energy and drug prices, the financial collapse, and the subsequent recession. Companies that have become large and successful, or whose labor practices incur the wrath of powerful unions, are almost always accused of being "greedy." These charges can be effective in intimidating political opponents. They are too often taken at face value by the media, as well as by voters.

The real question we should be asking is: *Whose greed are we really talking about?*

In the 1930s, Huey Long, a salesman-turned-lawyer, famously used the greed mantra to advance his political ambitions. He became governor of the state of Louisiana and later a U.S. senator, one of the most powerful and controversial figures of his time. In the 1920s, Long fueled his rise in state politics by attacking corporate interests—namely, Standard Oil—and "the rich." His 1934 "Share the Wealth" radio speech, made while he served in the U.S. Senate in advance of a potential run for president, sounded themes that, in today's era of Occupy Wall Street, are all too familiar:

> It is not the difficulty of the problem which we have; it is the fact that the rich people of this country—and by rich people I mean the super-rich—will not allow us to solve the problems, or rather the one little problem that is afflicting this country, because in order to cure all of our woes it is necessary to scale down the big fortunes, that we may scatter the wealth to be shared by all of the people.[17]

In his autobiography, Long expressed the classic statist view of wealth as being "zero sum"—produced by malevolent taking from others:

> But when one man must have more houses to live in than ninety-nine other people; when one man decides he must own more foodstuff than any other ninety-nine people own; when one man decides he must have more goods to wear for himself and family than any other ninety-nine people . . . that one man, through his gluttonous greed, takes over ninety-nine parts for himself and leaves one part for the ninety-nine. . . .
>
> [H]e can say: "This food and these clothes and these houses are mine, and while I cannot use them, my greed can only be satisfied by keeping anybody else from having them."[18]

The real story, of course, was Long's own greed for power. As Louisiana governor, he became a virtual dictator. He replaced thousands of state employees with supporters who were

expected to contribute a portion of their salaries to his political machine. He also embarked on aggressive public works
and infrastructure building that created more patronage jobs.
Giveaways of textbooks and cheap energy further shored up his
power.

Long's tightfisted control of Louisiana, his ruthless tactics,
and his over-the-top rhetoric frightened even his fellow
Democrats—including FDR—who saw him as a demagogue
and a dictator.

There are plenty of greedy individuals. However, suggesting
that the market—or its problems—are driven by greed is not
simply divisive. It's just plain wrong. Eminent economist and
political philosopher Thomas Sowell of Stanford University's
Hoover Institution points out that no amount of "greed" will
make someone get rich unless they provide a product or service
that somehow benefits others:

> Think about it: I could become so greedy that I wanted a
> fortune twice the size of Bill Gates'—but this greed would
> not increase my income by one cent.
>
> If you want to explain why some people have astronomical
> incomes, it cannot be simply because of their own desires—
> whether "greedy" or not—but because of what other peo-
> ple are willing to pay them.[19]

The idea that CEO salaries or the prices of pharmaceuticals
should instantly appear reasonable to everyone is characteristic
of what Sowell calls "the Greed Fallacy."

Sounding a little like Hayek, the economist explains that it's
impossible even for educated, highly intelligent people to know
all the conditions of a market:

As Will Rogers said, everybody is ignorant, but just about different things. Should computer experts tell brain surgeons how to do their job? Or horse trainers tell either of them what to do?

One of the reasons why central planning sounds so good, but has failed so badly that even socialist and communist governments finally abandoned the idea by the end of the 20th century, is that nobody knows enough to second guess everybody else.[20]

Sowell makes a final point: allegations of greed wax and wane with the political climate. When oil prices went up several years ago, accusations of oil company greed and calls for more energy taxes and regulation dominated the news. When prices dropped, so did the name-calling. "Does that mean," he asks, "that oil companies have lost their 'greed'?"

As for Wall Street "greed," Sowell raises this question: Were people really less interested in making money in the 1990s? But you didn't hear about "greed" then. And the Obama administration didn't cry "greed" when executives of Fannie Mae and Freddie Mac gave its top ten executives nearly $13 million in bonuses.

Yet Fannie and Freddie have done anything but deliver value to the economy. Like the big private sector banks, these two government-created mortgage entities also had to be bailed out. They were a major cause of the excessive risk taking, overexpansion, and collapse of the housing market. Shareholders who invested in them (they were ostensibly spun off by the federal government as public companies) took a bath. Not long after the award of those bonuses, the Securities and Exchange Commission sued the former CEOs of these entities for misleading investors about the risks of Fannie and Freddie's sub-prime mortgage loans. But politicians who had decried private sector bank bonuses were silent on the subject of bonuses for the two former government agencies that, as public companies, have long functioned as Washington ATMs.

Milton Friedman acknowledged years ago that, to a very great extent, "greed" is something that happens to other people. Or as he put it: "Of course none of us are greedy; it's only the other fellow who's greedy."[21]

"KUMBAYA?"—NOT!

Richard Wilkinson, a British academic, expresses a widely held belief when he writes that "inequality is divisive and socially corrosive."[22] Big Government advocates will claim that ending "inequality"—whether that may be in health care, housing, or elsewhere in the economy—will bring fairness and more social harmony. There would be more cooperation. People would get along better.

Really? Pessimistic Big Government, in various ways, *destroys* cooperation in markets, companies, and among people. Today's polarized political environment of finger-pointing, ramped-up greed rhetoric, and economic paralysis is symptomatic of what happens when an overbearing government destroys trust.

Overly meddlesome government creates a society focused on grievance politics. Groups vie for Big Government subsidies and political favors. People are divided into competing interests: Medicare patients versus the privately insured, the "1 percent" versus the "99 percent," younger workers versus older employees.

Big Government destroys trust in another way, too. Friedrich von Hayek has written that free markets have natural mechanisms of "truth telling and promise keeping," such as credit ratings, contracts, and financial statements. Such tools, he explained, are fundamental to "market morality" and trust in a free economy. When they are corrupted, the market's self-regulating moral behavior goes awry.

The corruption of such mechanisms of trust by Big Government helped bring about the financial crisis. Bruce Yandle, former executive director of the Federal Trade Commission, explains that decades of affordable housing policies (see chapter 2), along with the flood of market-distorting mortgage money from Fannie and Freddie, destroyed vital "trust technology"—such as credit ratings. By flooding the mortgage market with money, Fannie and Freddie encouraged banks to be *too trusting* and lend to many untrustworthy borrowers.[23] So did Federal Reserve Bank low-interest-rate "easy money" policies.

Further destroying market trust was the return of a little-known accounting rule known as mark-to-market. When the financial crisis began in the summer of 2007, the rule perversely forced institutions to understate the value of their loans, making them look weaker than they were. Short sellers swooped in like vultures, shorting bank stocks and bonds. Banks had to write down value of capital even more, which put them in a death spiral. This led to the crash of the stock market and a destruction of trust throughout the entire U.S. financial system. A credit squeeze virtually froze lending in the country in late 2008.

This implosion of market trust rippled not only throughout the United States but the global economy and shook people to their very core. It was a financial and emotional trauma from which we haven't recovered. The kind of social unrest we've seen in Europe and the Occupy Wall Street protests in the United States are symptomatic of this massive destruction of trust.

When trust is destroyed, the link in the public mind between effort and reward is undermined. Seemingly undeserving players such as oil companies and Wall Street banks get outsized profits. Meanwhile, smaller businesses are damaged. Through no fault of their own they suddenly have their bank credit denied or restricted. People lose their faith in financial institutions, in government—and in each other.

Michael Lewis in *Vanity Fair* explains (in "Beware of Greeks Bearing Bonds") that this fraying of the social fabric is precisely what happened in Greece. "The Greek state," he writes, "was not just corrupt but also corrupting."

Greek people have [difficulty] saying a kind word about one another. Individual Greeks are delightful: funny, warm, smart, and good company. I left two dozen interviews saying to myself, "What great people!" They do not share the sentiment about one another: the hardest thing to do in Greece is to get one Greek to compliment another behind his back. No success of any kind is regarded without suspicion. Everyone is pretty sure everyone is cheating on his taxes, or bribing politicians, or taking bribes, or lying about the value of his real estate. And this total absence of faith in one another is self-reinforcing. The epidemic of lying and cheating and stealing makes any sort of civic life impossible; the collapse of civic life only encourages more lying, cheating, and stealing. Lacking faith in one another, they fall back on themselves and their families.[24]

Greece's government intended to further the common good. But the society it has produced, in Lewis's words, "is the opposite of a collective. Its real structure is every man for himself. Into this system investors had poured hundreds of billions of dollars. And the credit boom had pushed the country over the edge, into total moral collapse."

This is not surprising. Political economist Francis Fukuyama, whose work we explore later in this chapter, observes that people in societies with a history of government domination—China, France, and southern Italy—show lower degrees of trust. A dominant state, he believes, can "undermine civil society." Citizens are consequently "much less able to promote strong bonds of special solidarity or the moral fabric that underlies community."[25]

This is why you often see more corruption and criminality in low-trust states with a history of government domination, such as Russia and China. While both are moving toward market economies, government still continues to dominate. Trust-promoting business practices and standards have been slow to develop.

✳ ✳ ✳

DEMOCRATIC CAPITALISM'S
MORAL OPTIMISM

Contrast Big Government's narrow, bureaucratic pessimism with the entrepreneurial spirit of free markets, which focuses on the positive. In his seminal book *Wealth and Poverty*, George Gilder writes powerfully of how activities in a free market are propelled by "faith in man, faith in the future, faith in the rising returns of giving, faith in the mutual benefits of trade, faith in the providence of God."

All are necessary to sustain the spirit of work and enterprise against the setbacks and frustrations it inevitably meets in a fallen world; to inspire trust and cooperation in an economy where they will often be betrayed; to encourage the forgoing of present pleasures in the name of a future that may well go up in smoke; to promote risk and initiative in a world where the rewards all vanish unless others join the game.[26]

To launch a business, invest in a new venture—to work toward any goal under hostile conditions and against the odds—requires confidence in people and the future. *New York Times* columnist David Brooks describes the market's entrepreneurial faith as a "manic energy."

Pioneers and immigrants endured hardship in the present because of their confidence in future plenty. Entrepreneurs start up companies with an exaggerated sense of their chances of success. The faith is the molten core of the country's dynamism.[27]

Faith in the future enabled hundreds of thousands of entrepreneurs to launch start-ups in the Great Recession, the worst time for business since the Depression. And it is the reason why many of today's biggest and best-known companies were launched in past downturns, including CNN and Amgen (both

1980), MTV (1981), General Electric (1890), and IBM (1896). Microsoft, Apple, FedEx, Oracle, and others were launched during the economically stagnant 1970s.

Entrepreneurial faith rooted in Judeo-Christian belief is the reason why Europeans progressed faster and further than other civilizations. Noted thinkers like Rodney Stark, Michael Novak, Matthew Ridley, and others have pointed out that Judeo-Christian belief in reason and progress is the reason why Europe surged ahead of India and China, even though those peoples had access to advanced technologies. Rodney Stark has observed that "Although many civilizations had pursued alchemy, the study led to chemistry only in Europe." He asks, "Why was it that, for centuries, Europeans were the only ones possessed of eyeglasses, chimneys, reliable clocks, heavy cavalry, or a system of music notation? How had the nations that had arisen from the rubble of Rome so greatly surpassed the rest of the world?" Not only that, "Why did Europeans excel at metallurgy, shipbuilding, or farming?"[28] His answer:

> Christian faith in reason and in progress was the foundation on which Western success was achieved . . . science arose only in Europe because only there did people think that science could be done and should be done, a faith "derivative from medieval theology." Moreover the medieval Christian faith in reason and progress was constantly reinforced by actual progress, by technical and organizational innovations.[29]

The faith that drives markets is not "magical thinking" or "irrational exuberance." It's based on real-world knowledge that the determination of individuals, and the collective ingenuity of the market, has solved problems throughout history.

Democratic capitalism's moral optimism does not make you a starry-eyed idealist. Financier Bernard Baruch lived through the Great Depression and two world wars. In a 1953 essay, "Thought for Tomorrow," he admitted that his faith in a better future was shaken by "thunder of war, the stench of concentration camps, the mushroom cloud of the atomic bomb." But it was not destroyed.

> I still believe in it. If I sometimes doubt that man will achieve his mortal potentialities, I never doubt that he can. I believe that these potentialities promise all men a measure beyond reckoning of the joys and comforts, material and spiritual, that life offers. Not utopia, to be sure. I do not believe in utopias. Man may achieve all but perfection. . . .
>
> Tragedy will be with us in some degree as long as there is life, but misery we can banish. Injustice will raise its head in the best of all possible worlds, but tyranny we can conquer. Evil will invade some men's hearts, intolerance will twist some men's minds, but decency is a far more common human attribute, and it can be made to prevail in our daily lives.
>
> I believe all this because I believe, above all else, in reason—in the power of the human mind to cope with the problems of life. . . .
>
> Because I place my trust in reason, I place it in the individual. . . . I have known, as who has not, personal disappointments and despair. But always the thought of tomorrow has buoyed me up.[30]

HOW MORAL OPTIMISM PROMOTES
TRUST AND COOPERATION

Barack Obama in his 2012 State of the Union address openly admired the cooperation within the military. Americans, he said, would solve their problems if they could only put aside their differences and work as a "team."[31] We have already been doing this for generations in free markets—collaborating and solving problems in those greedy corporations.

What are corporations, after all, but communities of people cooperating and working toward a common goal? The difference is that in a corporation you solve problems voluntarily. In the military, you're often forced to do so—especially when a draft makes you sign up.

Critics of capitalism usually focus on violations of trust by individuals like Bernard Madoff. But such episodes are exceptions. The daily reality of a free market is millions of people—total strangers of widely differing backgrounds—working together, cooperating in what Francis Fukuyama calls "networks of trust."[32] Leonard Read's story "I, Pencil" predates Fukuyama by several decades. But it illustrates what he's talking about. The simple act of manufacturing a pencil brings together countless individuals from around the globe—from "the miner of graphite in Ceylon and the logger in Oregon"[33] to factory workers in Mississippi who help process the graphite to even American utility workers who help supply the factories with power.

Networks of trust are taken for granted by Americans in our market economy. Indeed, even the president seemed not to recognize them. They are in many ways miraculous. Fukuyama points out that they are not the norm in other societies. "High trust" market nations like the United States contrast with "low trust" societies, where trust extends primarily to the people in your family or ethnic group.

Fukuyama's observations are confirmed by researchers who have found that societies where there are open markets tend to be more trusting. University of British Columbia social scientist Joseph Henrich and his colleagues studied two thousand people from a range of different cultures. Some were hunters and gatherers, while others lived in market-based societies. Henrich's subjects were asked to play a game in which they won a prize. They were then given a choice: they could share a prize with anonymous strangers—or they could choose to keep it.

Who were the most generous and cooperative? People who lived in market cultures. Henrich's winners were Walmart shoppers who lived in the small town of Hamilton, Missouri.

Henrich echoes Fukuyama when he speculates that shoppers in market societies may be more inclined to show fairness to strangers because they have more experience in "successful exchange and interaction" beyond their immediate kinship circles. In other words, they are more capable of trust.[34]

We may not find it especially startling that small-town Americans are trusting. However, researchers from Cornell University and Tohoku University report something truly surprising: studies have found that Americans are more trusting than the Japanese. Given Japan's polite, homogenous culture—and America's diversity and frequent discord—you'd expect the opposite. But the researchers say that doing business with strangers in open markets has made Americans better at assessing others—and thus better able to trust. Japanese collectivism and conformity, in contrast, nurtures "parochial tendencies toward protection and in-group favoritism."[35] They explain, "[People] rarely encounter strangers and thus remain highly parochial, trusting only their neighbors and avoiding open-market transactions with outsiders."

Naysayers who once feared Japanese competition have long underestimated America's entrepreneurial culture of trust and moral optimism. Yet it is why, despite their gloomy forecasts, we continue to lead Japan's economy.

A TALE OF TWO PRESIDENTS

The contrast between the pessimistic assumptions of Big Government and the moral optimism of democratic capitalism is illustrated by a tale of two presidents. Barack Obama and Ronald Reagan both took office at a time of economic turmoil. Reagan delivered his inaugural address in 1981, as the economy, wracked by double-digit inflation, was descending deeper into recession. Nearly three decades later, Barack Obama came to power with the nation reeling from a historic financial crisis. Both men delivered widely praised inaugural addresses describing the problems facing Americans—but from thoroughly divergent perspectives.

Obama presented a bleak vision of an America whose economy was "badly weakened, a consequence of greed and irresponsibility on the part of some, but also our collective failure to make hard choices. . . . Our health care is too costly, our schools fail too many—and each day brings further evidence that the ways we use energy strengthen our adversaries and threaten our planet."[36] The nation, he maintained, was afflicted by the "sapping of confidence across our land; a nagging fear that America's decline is inevitable, that the next generation must lower its sights."

While not going so far as to declare America in actual decline, the new president painted a picture of a country troubled by "conflict and discord" that was clearly on the brink.

On this day, we come to proclaim an end to the petty grievances and false promises, the recriminations and worn-out dogmas that for far too long have strangled our politics. We remain a young nation. But in the words of Scripture, the time has come to set aside childish things.[37]

Was America still a great country, the world's beacon of freedom and democracy? Obama's answer is a qualified "yes, but—."

In reaffirming the greatness of our nation we understand that greatness is never a given.[38]

Ronald Reagan also acknowledged that the United States of 1980 was "confronted with an economic affliction of great proportions. We suffer from the longest and one of the worst sustained inflations in our national history."[39] Reagan did not minimize the challenges we faced. He acknowledged that "the economic ills we suffer have come upon us over several decades" and threatened to "shatter" people's lives.[40]

But, unlike Barack Obama, he did not see these problems as reflections of a declining America or the moral weaknesses of its citizens. Rather they were the effects of an economic storm that he was confident would ultimately pass. The nation's troubles, he said, "will not go away in days, weeks, or months, but they will go away" because of the ingenuity of the American people.

> They will go away because we, as Americans, have the capacity now, as we have had in the past, to do whatever needs to be done to preserve this last and greatest bastion of freedom.[41]

Instead of warning that America was in danger of slipping into decline, Reagan assured an anxious citizenry that our country's greatness—the fundamental strength of our democracy and free economy—was indeed a given. It was the reason why the clouds would pass and our strengths as Americans would get us through.

There is an implied subtext in the speeches of both men: Barack Obama believes in government solutions because he is ultimately unsure about the American system and thinks less of individuals who, he implies, are mired in "greed" and "conflict." Profoundly optimistic about the capabilities and character of the American people, Ronald Reagan believed the solution lay with the efforts of individuals allowing the American free enterprise system to work. Barack Obama admonishes citizens to put aside "childish things"; Reagan focused on the strengths in the American character: "I believe we, the Americans of today, are ready to act worthy of ourselves, ready to do what must be done to ensure happiness and liberty for ourselves, our children and our children's children." That is the reason, he concluded, that things will get better.

> If we look to the answer as to why, for so many years, we achieved so much, prospered as no other people on Earth,

it was because here, in this land, we unleashed the energy and individual genius of man to a greater extent than has ever been done before. Freedom and the dignity of the individual have been more available and assured here than in any other place on Earth.[42]

Two stark and contrasting visions, one based on a profound belief in the capacity of a free people to do great things. The other—a belief in the need for Big Government to guide us because we are unable to guide ourselves. Optimism versus pessimism, choice versus coercion, redistribution versus wealth creation, mobility versus stagnation. We must now decide: Which vision will guide America and the world?

Notes

Introduction: A Battle for the Soul of America

1. Richard Rahn, "Will the Market Rise or Fall?" *Washington Times,* December 29, 2009, http://www.washingtontimes.com/news/2009/dec/29/will-the-market-rise-or-fall/; Chris Edwards, Testimony before the Senate Finance Committee, July 26, 2011. http://finance.senate.gov/imo/media/doc/edwards%20senate%20finance%20testimony.pdf.
2. Peter Ferrara, "Obama's Budget: The Decline and Fall of the American Economy," *Forbes,* February 16, 2012. http://www.forbes.com/sites/peterferrara/2012/02/16/obamas-budget-the-decline-and-fall-of-the-american-economy/.
3. Lydia Saad, "Americans Express Historic Negativity Toward U.S. Government," Gallup, September 26, 2011. http://www.gallup.com/poll/149678/americans-express-historic-negativity-toward-government.aspx.
4. Michael Grunwald, "Obama's Agenda: Get America Back on Track," *Time,* November 5, 2008. http://www.time.com/time/specials/packages/article/0,28804,1856381_1856380_1856375,00.html.
5. Mark Drajem and Catherine Dodge, "Obama Wrote 5% Fewer Rules Than Bush While Costing Business," Bloomberg.com, October 25, 2011. http://www.bloomberg.com/news/2011-10-25/obama-wrote-5-fewer-rules-than-bush-while-costing-business.html.
6. United States Misery Index. http://www.miseryindex.us/default.aspx.
7. "Employer Heath Benefits: 2011 Annual Survey," Kaiser Family Foundation and the Health Research and Educational Trust, September 2011. http://ehbs.kff.org/pdf/2011/8225.pdf.
8. "Historical Debt Outstanding—2000–2010," TreasuryDirect.gov, U.S. Department of the Treasury, Bureau of the Public Debt. http://www

245

.treasurydirect.gov/govt/reports/pd/histdebt/histdebt_histo5
.htm.

9. Stephen Moore, "A Fairness Quiz for the President," *Wall Street Journal,* February 7, 2012. http://online.wsj.com/article/SB10001424052 970204369404577206980068367936.html?mod=googlenews_wsj.

10. Sami Moubayed, "iSad in Damascus: Syria Reclaims Jobs," *Asia Times,* October 8, 2011. http://www.atimes.com/atimes/Middle _East/MJ08Ak01.html.

11. Library of Congress, "Places in the News: Syria/Israel," January 2000. http://www.loc.gov/today/placesinthenews/archive/2000arch/ 20000112_syriaisrael.html.

12. Rob Stein, "Should Doctors Be 'Parsimonious' About Health Care?" *Shots* (NPR's Health Blog), January 3, 2012. http://www.npr .org/blogs/health/2011/12/30/144485098/should-doctors -be-parsimonious-about-health-care.

13. Jeff Stier, "No Kugel for You! Mike's Homeless-Gift Ban," *New York Post,* March 18, 2012. http://www.nypost.com/p/news/opinion/oped columnists/no_kugel_for_you_N4VuTrqavfOiApSHngxuMJ.

14. William McGurn, "Bill Maher's 'Fatwa,'" *Wall Street Journal,* March 13, 2012. http://online.wsj.com/article/SB100014240527023045379 04577277703463103794.html?mod=WSJ_Opinion_LEADTop.

15. Greg Smith, "Why I Am Leaving Goldman Sachs," *New York Times,* March 14, 2012. http://www.nytimes.com/2012/03/14/opinion/ why-i-am-leaving-goldman-sachs.html?pagewanted=all.

16. Peter Cohan, "Greg Smith Quits, Should Clients Fire Goldman Sachs?" *Forbes,* March 14, 2012. http://www.forbes.com/sites/peter cohan/2012/03/14/greg-smith-quits-should-clients-fire-goldman -sachs/2/.

17. Bryan Caplan, "Myth of the Rational Voter," *Cato Unbound,* Cato Institute, November 6, 2006. http://www.cato-unbound.org/2006/ 11/06/bryan-caplan/the-myth-of-the-rational-voter/.

18. Patrice Hill, "In Throes of Recession, D.C. Stands Apart," *Washington Times,* October 17, 2010. http://www.washingtontimes.com/ news/2010/oct/17/in-throes-of-recession-capital-stands-apart/ ?page=all.

19. Bacchus Barua, Mark Rovere, and Brett J. Skinner, "Waiting Your Turn: Wait Times for Health Care in Canada," Fraser Institute, December 2011. http://www.fraserinstitute.org/uploadedFiles/fraser-ca/

Content/research-news/research/publications/waiting-your
-turn-2011.pdf.

20. Clifford Kraus, "Canada's Private Clinics Surge as Public System
Falters," *New York Times,* February 28, 2006. http://www.nytimes
.com/2006/02/28/international/americas/28canada.html?pa.

CHAPTER 1: FEDEX *or* THE POST OFFICE?

1. Adam Smith, *Wealth of Nations* (London: J.M. Dent & Sons Ltd.,
1957), originally published in 1776.

2. John Maynard Keynes, *The General Theory of Employment, Interest
and Money* (New Delhi: Atlantic Publishers & Distributors, 2006),
p. 144.

3. Walter Isaacson, *Steve Jobs* (New York: Simon & Schuster, 2011),
p. 567.

4. "2011 FedEx Rate Changes," FedEx.com, FedEx, January 3, 2011.
http://www.fedex.com/us/2011rates/ratechanges.html and "Postal
Service Adjusts Mailing Services Prices for 2012," United States
Postal Service press release, October 18, 2011, on USPS website.
http://about.usps.com/news/national-releases/2011/prll_116.htm.

5. State of New Jersey, The Governor's FY 2013 Budget Summary, Section 1, February 12, 2012. www.state.nj.us/treasury/omb/publications/
13bib/BIB.pdf.

6. House Committee on the Budget, Chairman Paul Ryan of Wisconsin, "The Path to Prosperity: Restoring America's Promise," Fiscal Year 2012 Budget Resolution. budget.house.gov/UploadedFiles/
PathToProsperityFY2012.pdf.

7. C. Northcote Parkinson, *Parkinson's Law* (Boston: Houghton Mifflin
Co., 1957, reprinted by Buccaneer Books, 1996), p. 2.

8. Ibid.

9. Ed O'Keefe, "Government Overlap Costs Taxpayers Billions, GAO Reports," *Washington Post,* March 1, 2011. http://www.washingtonpost
.com/blogs/federal-eye/post/government-overlap-costs-taxpayers
-billions-gao-reports/2010/12/20/ABRVMYN_blog.html.

10. Government Accountability Office, *Opportunities to Reduce Potential
Duplication in Government Programs, Save Tax Dollars, and En-
hance* Revenue, March 2011. http://www.gao.gov/new.items/d11318
sp.pdf.

11. Thomas J. DiLorenzo, "The Futility of Bureaucracy," *The Free Market* 20, no. 7 (August 2002). http://mises.org/freemarket_detail.aspx ?control=409.

12. ("41 percent") Chris Edwards, "The Damaging Rise of Federal Spending and Debt," Testimony before the Joint Economic Committee, United States Congress, September 20, 2011. http://www.cato .org/publications/congressional-testimony/damaging-rise-federal -spending-debt; ("not even 7 percent"). Brandon R. Julio, "The Growth of Government in 20th Century," Special Report 93, March 1, 2000. http://www.taxfoundation.org/news/show/754.html.

13. Dennis Cauchon, "For Feds, More Get 6-Figure Salaries," *USA Today*, December 11, 2009. http://www.usatoday.com/news/washington/ 2009-12-10-federal-pay-salaries_N.htm.

14. William Voegeli, *Never Enough: America's Limitless Welfare State* (New York: Encounter Books, 2010), p. 4.

15. Quoted in Milton Friedman, *Free to Choose: A Personal Statement* (Orlando, FL: Houghton Mifflin Harcourt, 1990), p. 155.

16. Jessica Holzer and Jamila Trindle, "Schapiro Defends Bed for SEC Funding Boost," *Wall Street Journal*, March 10, 2011. http://online.wsj .com/article/SB10001424052748704823004576192381898229572 .html.

17. Associated Press, "General Motors Corp. Will Give the United Auto Workers Union up to 20 Percent of Its Common Stock," *New York Daily News*, May 26, 2009. http://www.nydailynews.com/news/ money/general-motors-corp-give-united-auto-workers-union-20 -percent-common-stock-article-1.374945#ixzz1rHOwE8kv.

18. Bill Vlasic and Nick Bunkley, "Obama Is Upbeat for G.M.'s Future," *New York Times,* June 2, 2009. http://www.nytimes.com/2009/06/02/ business/02auto.html?_r=2

19. Joseph Tepper and Michael J. Feeney, "Protected Bike Lanes in E. Harlem Stir Controversy," *New York Daily News,* December 9, 2011.

20. J. David Goodman, "Expansion of Bike Lanes in City Brings Backlash," *New York Times*, November 22, 2010. http://www.nytimes .com/2010/11/23/nyregion/23bicycle.html.

21. Michael Tanner, "'Death Panels' Were an Overblown Claim—Until Now," *The Daily Caller,* May 27, 2010. http://dailycaller.com/2010/ 05/27/death-panels-were-an-overblown-claim-until-now/.

22. Barack Obama, interview by David Leonhardt, *New York Times*,

April 28, 2010. http://www.nytimes.com/2009/05/03/magazine/03Obama-t.html?pagewanted=all.

23. "The Pro-Diabetes Board," *Wall Street Journal,* Review and Outlook, March 18, 2011. http://online.wsj.com/articleSB100014240527487046626045762028839134684422.html.

24. Sally Pipes, "Even ObamaCare's Supporters Don't Support the Rationing Board," Forbes.com, June 13, 2011. http://www.forbes.com/sites/sallypipes/2011/06/13/even-obamacares-supporters-dont-support-the-rationing-board/.

25. Daniel Henninger, "Obama's Two Economies," *Wall Street Journal,* September 15, 2011. http://online.wsj.com/article/SB10001424053111904060604576570821884273638.html.

26. Ryan Ellis, "Obama's 'Tax Trigger' Takes Aim at Jobs and Growth," Americans for Tax Reform website, April 18, 2011. http://www.atr.org/?content=taxtrigger#ixzz1rHTBfQbR.

27. Brendan Scott and Fredric U. Dicker, "Cuomo Exposes Dirty Budget Trick," *New York Post,* February 1, 2011. http://www.nypost.com/p/news/local/cuomo_exposes_dirty_trick_DRgwu2QVC7WnpgORXaWZzM#ixzz1jZlUKwCo.

28. Daniel DiSalvo and Fred Siegel, "The New Tammany Hall," *The Weekly Standard,* October 12, 2009. http://www.weeklystandard.com/Content/Public/Articles/000/000/017/031citja.asp.

29. Dennis Cauchon, "Federal Workers Earning Double Their Private Counterparts," *USA Today,* August 13, 2010. http://www.usatoday.com/money/economy/income/2010-08-10-1Afedpay10_ST_N.htm.

30. Daniel Henninger, "The Fall of the House of Kennedy," *Wall Street Journal,* January 21, 2010. http://online.wsj.com/article/SB10001424052748704320104575015010515688120,00.html.

31. William K. Rashbaum, "11 Charged in L.I.R.R. Disability Fraud Plot," *New York Times,* October 27, 2011. http://www.nytimes.com/2011/10/28/nyregion/charges-in-lirr-disability-scheme.html?_r=1&pagewanted=all.

32. Daniel Hannan, "A European's Warning to America," *Wall Street Journal,* March 11, 2011. http://online.wsj.com/article/SB10001424052748703559604576176620582972608.html.

33. Daniel Hannan, *Why America Must Not Follow Europe* (New York: Encounter Books, 2011), p. 11.

34. Brian Domitrovic, *ECONOCLASTS: The Rebels Who Sparked the Supply-Side Revolution and Restored American Prosperity,* chapter 1, "That 70s Funk" (Wilmington, DE: Intercollegiate Studies Institute, 2009).

35. Michael Lewis, "Beware of Greeks Bearing Bonds," *Vanity Fair,* October 1, 2010. http://www.vanityfair.com/business/features/2010/10/greeks-bearing-bonds-201010.

36. Ibid.

37. Ibid.

38. George Gilder, *Wealth and Poverty* (San Francisco: ICS Press, 1993).

39. Charity Navigator, "Giving Statistics," http://www.charitynavigator.org/index.cfm?bay=content.view&cpid=42.

40. Milton Friedman, *Free to Choose: A Personal Statement.*

41. Collectors Weekly, "Antique and Vintage Waterman Pens," http://www.collectorsweekly.com/pens/waterman.

42. Victoria Barret, "Best Small Companies: Dropbox," *Forbes,* October 19, 2011. http://www.forbes.com/forbes/2011/1107/best-companies-11-drew-houston-steve-jobs-ferdowsi-dropbox-barret.html.

43. Ibid.

44. Walter Isaacson, *Steve Jobs,* p. 61.

45. Steve Forbes, "Private Equity, Public Benefits," *Wall Street Journal,* July 25, 2007. http://online.wsj.com/article/SB118532670875877067.html.

46. Kimberly Palmer, "The Store of YOU," *U.S. News & World Report,* October 27, 2008. http://money.usnews.com/money/personal-finance/articles/2008/10/27/the-store-of-you.

47. Joseph Pine II, "Beyond Mass Customization," Harvard Business Review Blog Network, May 2, 2011. http://blogs.hbr.org/cs/2011/05/beyond_mass_customization.html.

48. Jed Horne, "New Schools in New Orleans," *EducationNext* (Spring 2011). http://educationnext.org/new-schools-in-new-orleans/.

49. Dan Lips, "School Choice in Sweden: An Interview with Thomas Idergard of Timbro," The Heritage Foundation, Web memo 2828, March 8, 2010. http://www.heritage.org/research/reports/2010/03/school-choice-in-sweden-an-interview-with-thomas-idergard-of-timbro.

50. Fred L. Smith Jr. and Braden Cox, "Airline Deregulation," *The Concise Encyclopedia of Economics,* Library of Economics and Liberty. http://www.econlib.org/library/Enc/AirlineDeregulation.html.

51. Robert W. Crandall, Ph.D., and Jerry Ellig, Ph.D., "Texas Telecommunications: Everything's Dynamic Except the Pricing," Research Report for the Texas Public Policy Foundation, January 2005 (information based on authors' analysis of data from Bureau of Labor Statistics, page 8).

52. Moria Herbst, "East Germany 20 Years After Reunification," Bloomberg BusinessWeek.com, November 5, 2009. http://www.businessweek.com/globalbiz/content/nov2009/gb2009115_550451.htm.

CHAPTER 2: FREEDOM *or* BIG BROTHER?

1. Milton Friedman, *Free to Choose: A Personal* Statement (Orlando, FL: Houghton Mifflin Harcourt, 1990).

2. Friedrich August Hayek, *The Road to Serfdom: Text and Documents, The Definitive Edition—The Collected Works of F. A. Hayek, Volume II,* edited by Bruce Caldwell (Chicago: University of Chicago Press, 2007), p. 113.

3. Ibid.

4. *Respectfully Quoted: A Dictionary of Quotations from the Library of Congress,* Congressional Quarterly Press, edited by Suzy Platt, 1989 (online edition). http://www.bartleby.com/73/754.html.

5. James Madison, "The Structure of the Government Must Furnish the Proper Checks and Balances Between the Different Departments," *The Federalist Papers* No. 51, Wednesday, February 6, 1788.

6. Milton Friedman, *Free to Choose.*

7. Timothy Williams, "Jailed for Switching Her Daughters' School District," *New York Times,* September 26, 2011. http://www.nytimes.com/2011/09/27/us/jailed-for-switching-her-daughters-school-district.html.

8. Bill Mears, "Supreme Court Divided Over Health Care Mandate," CNN.com, March 27, 2012. http://www.cnn.com/2012/03/27/justice/scotus-health-care/index.html.

9. *State of Florida* v. *US Department of Health and Human Services,* Case No.: 3:10-cv-91-RV/EM (Northern District of Florida, January 31, 2011).

10. Betsy McCaughey, "How Obamacare Destroys Your Privacy," *New York Post,* June 15, 2011. http://www.nypost.com/p/news/opinion/opedcolumnists/how_obamacare_destroys_your_privacy_zItwZSGo I661FeB1iC5POI.

11. Betsy McCaughey, "Impact on Your Doctor," Defend Your Health-care. http://craftcampaigns.com/dyh/obama-health-law-101/impact-on-your-doctor/#.

12. Compiled with some modification from George Amberg, "The Tax Path Away from Liberty," LewRockwell.com, January 15, 2005. http://www.lewrockwell.com/orig6/amberg1.html; Tom Nugent, "Taxes: What the Hell Happened?" National Review Online, September 26, 2003. http://old.nationalreview.com/nrof_nugent/nugent092603.asp.

13. Rev. Robert A. Sirico, "The Sin Tax Crazy: Who's Next?," *Acton Commentary*, April 27, 2004. http://www.acton.org/pub/commentary/2004/04/28/sin-tax-craze-whos-next.

14. Kathleen Purvis, "No You Can't Order a Rare Burger—Yet," Charlotte Observer.com, April 13, 2011. http://www.charlotteobserver.com/2011/04/13/2218811/no-you-cant-order-a-rare-burger.html#story link=cpy.

15. Julie Gunlock, "Lunch Nazis on the Attack," *New York Post,* February 15, 2012. http://www.nypost.com/p/news/opinion/opedcolumnists/lunch_nazis_on_the_attack_tGyUoxc3mKetWmBpZz41rN.

16. Rich Lowry, "The War on Lemonade," *National Review*, August 5, 2011. http://www.nationalreview.com/articles/273739/war-lemonade-rich-lowry.

17. "Employer Health Benefits: 2009 Summary of Findings," Kaiser Family Foundation. http://ehbs.kff.org/pdf/2009/7937.pdf.

18. Suzanne Sataline and Shirley S. Wang, "Medical Schools Can't Keep Up," *Wall Street Journal,* April 12, 2010. http://online.wsj.com/article/SB10001424052702304506904575180331528424238.html.

19. Joe Romm, "Why Did Environmentalists Pursue Cap-and-Trade and Was It a Doomed Strategy?" Think Progress.com, April 21, 2011. http://thinkprogress.org/climate/2011/04/21/207932/cap-and-trade-doomed/.

20. John Tierney, "Findings: When Energy Efficiency Sullies the Environment," *New York Times,* March 8, 2011. http://query.nytimes.com/gst/fullpage.html?res=9C03E6DD1E3FF93BA35750C0A9679D8B63&pagewanted=all.

21. "Washing Machine Buying Guide," *Consumer Reports*, January 2011. http://www.consumerreports.org/cro/washing-machines/buying-guide.htm?pn=0.

22. Phillip Matier and Andrew Ross, "Low-Flow Toilets Cause a Stink in

SF," *San Francisco Chronicle,* February 28, 2011, p. C-1. http://www
.sfgate.com/cgi-bin/article.cgi?f=/c/a/2011/02/27/BAVP1HUSUD
.DTL#ixzz1vABOKpfS.

23. Deroy Murdock, "The All-American Light Bulb Dims as Freedom
Flickers," *National Review,* July 2, 2010. http://www.nationalreview
.com/articles/243383/all-american-light-bulb-dims-freedom-flickers
-deroy-murdock?pg=1.

24. Quoted in John Tierney, "Findings: When Energy Efficiency Sullies
the Environment."

25. Robert Poole, "Don't Federalize Airport Security," Reason Foundation, October 24, 2001. http://reason.org/news/show/dont-federalize
-airport-securi.

26. Philip K. Howard, "Too Much Law Suffocating America," CNN,
February 22, 2010. http://articles.cnn.com/2010-02-22/opinion/
howard.too.much.law_1_health-care-entitlements-partisanship?_s
=PM:OPINION.

27. Laurie Goodstein, "Church Battle Over Mandate Was at Ready,"
New York Times, February 10, 2012, p. A1.

28. *Brief Summary of the Dodd-Frank Wall Street Reform and Consumer
Protection Act.* http://banking.senate.gov/public/_files/070110_Dodd
_Frank_Wall_Street_Reform_comprehensive_summary_Final.pdf.

29. James Gattuso, "New Consumer Bureau Will Run Free of Any Leash,"
Heritage Foundation Commentary, April 12, 2011. http://www
.heritage.org/research/commentary/2011/04/new-consumer-bureau
-will-run-free-of-any-leash.

30. Grover G. Norquist, "Trickle-Down Taxation," *Wall Street Journal,*
April 17, 2012, p. A15. http://online.wsj.com/article/SB10001424052
702304299304577347610737753148.html.

31. Louise Radnofsky, Gary Fields, and John R. Emshwiller, "Federal
Police Ranks Swell to Enforce a Widening Array of Criminal Laws,"
Wall Street Journal, December 17, 2011.

32. Ibid.

33. Paul Craig Roberts and Lawrence M. Stratton, preface to *Tyranny of
Good Intentions: How Prosecutors and Law Enforcement Are Trampling
the Constitution in the Name of Justice* (New York: Three Rivers Press,
2008), p. xxi.

34. Paul Rosenzweig and Brian W. Walsh, eds., *One Nation Under Arrest:
How Crazy Laws, Rogue Prosecutors, and Activist Judges Threaten Your
Liberty* (Washington, DC: The Heritage Foundation, 2010).

35. John R. Emshwiller and Gary Fields, "Federal Asset Seizures Rise, Netting Innocent with Guilty," WSJ.com, August 22, 2011. http://online.wsj.com/article/SB1000142405311190348090457651225326507380.html.
36. Ibid.
37. Philip K. Howard, "Too Much Law Suffocating America."
38. Ibid.
39. Jerry B., "Unions Will Never Understand . . ." Activistsandairplanes.com; also email correspondence. http://activistsandairplanes.com/2011/04/15/unions-will-never-understand/.
40. Frédéric Bastiat, *The Law* (Auburn, AL: Ludwig von Mises Institute, 2007), p. 7.
41. Brian Heater, "Texas PC Repair Now Requires PI License," *PC Magazine,* June 30, 2008. http://www.pcmag.com/article2/0,2817,2324217,00.asp.
42. Robert McNamara, "D.C.'s Problem with 'Describing Without a License,'" *Washington Post,* September 17, 2010. http://voices.washingtonpost.com/local-opinions/2010/09/dcs_problem_with_describing_wi.html.
43. Agnes Wierzbicki, "The Cuban Black Market," unpublished, Fall 2005. www.photosbymartin.com/south_america/cuban_black_market.pdf.
44. F. A. Hayek, *The Road to Serfdom: Text and Documents,* ed. Bruce Caldwell (Chicago: University of Chicago Press, 2007), p. 77.
45. Frederick Jackson Turner, *The Frontier in American History* (Ann Arbor, MI: Scholarly Publishing Office, University of Michigan Library, 2005).
46. Ibid.
47. Ibid.
48. George C. Leef, "What's So Bad About Big Government Anyway?," *The Freeman* 47, no. 12 (December 1997). http://www.thefreemanonline.org/featured/whats-so-bad-about-big-government-anyway/.
49. John Locke, *Second Treatise on Civil Government,* Ch. V, Sect. 27, retrieved from http://constitution.org/jl/2ndtr05.txt.
50. Rodney Stark, *The Victory of Reason: How Christianity Led to Freedom, Capitalism, and Western Success* (New York: Random House, 2005), pp. 23–24.
51. William L. Anderson, "A Primer on Regulation," *The Free Market* 24, no. 5 (May 2004). http://mises.org/freemarket_detail.aspx?control=485.

52. Benn Steil and Manuel Hinds, *Money, Markets & Sovereignty* (New Haven, CT: Yale University Press, 2009), p. 23.

53. Bruce Benson, "It Takes Two Invisible Hands to Make a Market: *Lex Mercatoria* (Law Merchant) Always Emerges to Facilitate Emerging Market Activity," *Studies in Emergent Order* 3 (2010), p. 100. http://docs.sieo.org/SIEO_3_2010_Benson.pdf.

54. Ibid.

55. Charles Gasparino, "Faith in Government Doomed Corzine," *New York Post*, November 4, 2011. http://www.nypost.com/p/news/opinion/opedcolumnists/faith_in_government_doomed_corzine_y9pk8VLfhQRyrH0fQkguVP.

56. "Does the Free Market Corrode Moral Character?" John Templeton Foundation (Autumn 2008), p. 8. http://www.templeton.org/market/PDF/BQ%20Market%20Essays.pdf.

57. Michael Novak, "Does the Free Market Corrode Moral Character? No! And, Well, Yes." John Templeton Foundation website. http://www.templeton.org/market/.

58. Ibid.

59. Ben Franklin, April 17, 1987, Washington, Jefferson & Madison Institute. http://www.wjmi.org/FF/FoFaFrank.html.

60. Amanda Carpenter, "Clinton: 'Something Has to Be Taken Away from Some People,'" TownHall, June 4, 2007. http://townhall.com/columnists/amandacarpenter/2007/06/04/clinton_something_has_to_be_taken_away_from_some_people.

61. Deirdre McCloskey, "Bourgeois Dignity: A Revolution in Rhetoric," *Cato Unbound*, Cato Institute, October 4, 2010. http://www.cato-unbound.org/2010/10/04/deirdre-mccloskey/bourgeois-dignity-a-revolution-in-rhetoric/.

62. Jeff May, "The Best Country to Start a Business . . ." *Wall Street Journal*, November 15, 2010. http://online.wsj.com/article/SB10001424052748703859204575525883366862428.html.

63. Edward Younkins, "Private Property Rights: The Moral and Economic Foundation of a Free Society," *Liberty Free Press*, April 15, 2000. http://www.quebecoislibre.org/younkins5.html.

64. Ibid.

65. Frederick Jackson Turner, *The Significance of the Frontier in American History* (New York: Henry Holt and Company, 1921), p. 31.

66. Daniel Griswold, "Trading Tyranny for Freedom: How Open Markets Till the Soil for Democracy," Cato Institute, January 6, 2004.

http://www.cato.org/publications/trade-policy-analysis/trading
-tyranny-freedom-how-open-markets-till-soil-democracy.

67. Sebastiano Bavetta and Pietro Navarra, "Economic Freedom and the Pursuit of Happiness," *2011 Index of Economic Freedom* (Washington, DC: The Heritage Foundation and Dow Jones & Company, Inc., 2011), p. 68. http://www.heritage.org/index/PDF/2011/Index2011 _Chapter5.pdf.

68. Justin Connaher, "Part 2: A Cuban Refugee's Odyssey to America," *Fond du Lac Reporter*, May 25, 2010. http://www.fdlreporter .com/article/20100526/FON0101/100525143/PHOTOS-STORY -VIDEO-Part-2-Cuban-Refugee-s-Odyssey-America.

69. Justin Connaher, "Part 1: A Cuban Refugee's Odyssey to America," *Fond du Lac Reporter*, May 24, 2010. http://www.fdlreporter.com/ article/20100525/FON0101/100524059/PHOTOS-STORY -VIDEO-PART-1-Cuban-refugee-s-odyssey-America.

70. Ami Dodson, "A Conversation with Professor Lan Cao," William & Mary Law School's Faculty Spotlight. http://law.wm.edu/faculty -spotlight/cao-profile-spotlight.php.

Chapter 3: Silicon Valley *or* Detroit?

1. Edmund Phelps, "Economic Justice and the Spirit of Innovation," *First Things*, October 2009. http://www.firstthings.com/article/2009/ 10/economic-justice-and-the-spirit-of-innovation.

2. Tim Harford, *Adapt: Why Success Always Starts with Failure* (New York: Farrar, Straus and Giroux, 2011), p. 12.

3. Remarks by the President in State of Union Address, January 25, 2011. http://www.whitehouse.gov/the-press-office/2011/01/25/remarks -president-state-union-address.

4. Friedrich Hayek, "The Use of Knowledge in Society," *American Economic Review* XXXV, no. 4, pp. 519–30. American Economic Association, September 1945. http://www.econlib.org/library/Essays/ hykKnw1.html.

5. John T. Edge, "How the Microplane Grater Escaped the Garage," *New York Times,* January 11, 2011.

6. Karen Eley and Stephen Watt-Smith, "A New Surgical Tool—the IKEA Pencil," *British Medical Journal* 341:c6595 (December 9, 2010), retrieved April 8, 2012, from http://www.sciencedaily.com/ releases/2010/12/101209201946.htm.

7. Henry Adams, *The Education of Henry Adams* (Lexington, KY: Feather Trail Press, 2009), p. 165.
8. "Moore's Law," Wikipedia.org. http://en.wikipedia.org/wiki/Moore %27s_law.
9. "The Future of National Security, by the Numbers," Brookings Institution, May 2011. http://www.brookings.edu/articles/2011/05 _national_security_singer.aspx.
10. Michael Novak, *The Spirit of Democratic Capitalism* (New York: Simon & Schuster, 1982), p. 16.
11. Ibid.
12. Matt Ridley, *The Rational Optimist* (New York: Harper, 2010), p. 12.
13. Ibid., p. 20.
14. Michael Strong, *Be the Solution: How Entrepreneurs and Conscious Capitalists Can Solve All the World's Problems* (Hoboken, NJ: John Wiley & Sons, 2009), p. 57.
15. Council on Environmental Quality, *The Global 2000 Report to the President*, Volume I (Washington, DC: U.S. Government Printing Office, 1980), p. 11.
16. Julian L. Simon and Herman Kahn, *The Resourceful Earth: A Response to Global 2000* (New York: Blackwell, 1984).
17. Brian Palmer, "Has the Earth Run Out of Any Natural Resources?," Slate.com, October 20, 2010. http://www.slate.com/articles/news _and_politics/explainer/2010/10/has_the_earth_run_out_of_any _natural_resources.html.
18. Justin Gerdes, "Daniel Yergin: On Energy, Security, and the Remaking of the Modern World," Climate One, The Commonwealth Club HQ, October 13, 2011. http://climate-one.org/blog/daniel-yergin -energy-security-and-remaking-modern-world.
19. "Environmental Kuznets Curves," Wikipedia.org. http://en.wikipedia .org/wiki/Kuznets_curve#Environmental_Kuznets_Curves.
20. Paul B. Farrell, "Population Bomb: 9 Billion March to WWIII," *MarketWatch*, June 28, 2011. http://www.marketwatch.com/story/ population-bomb-9-billion-march-to-wwiii-2011-06-28 ?pagenumber=1.
21. UNCTAD Sees New Opportunities in the ICT Sector for the Poor, United Nations Conference on Trade and Development, Press Release, October 14, 2010. htttp://www.unctad.org/templates/webflyer.asp ?docid=13953&intItemID=1528&lang=1.
22. Leonard Waverman, Meloria Meschi, and Melvyn Fuss, "The Impact

of Telecoms on Economic Growth in Developing Countries," London Business School, 2005. http://web.si.umich.edu/tprc/papers/2005/450/L%20Waverman-%20Telecoms%20Growth%20in%20Dev.%20Countries.pdf.

23. Bill Gates, "Creative Capitalism," Speech at Davos 2008, January 28, 2008. http://www.egovmonitor.com/node/16877.

24. "Slumdog Thousandaire: What the Celebrated Film Can Teach America about Economic Stimulus," Interview with Shikha Dalmia, Reason TV. http://reason.tv/video/show/slumdog-thousandaire.

25. Interview with Michael Moore, *Piers Morgan Tonight,* CNN.com, September 26, 2011. http://transcripts.cnn.com/TRANSCRIPTS/1109/26/pmt.01.html.

26. Michael Levenson, "Newt Gingrich Attacks Mitt Romney's Bain Record," Boston.com, January 9, 2012. http://www.boston.com/Boston/politicalintelligence/2012/01/newt-gingrich-attacks-mitt-romney-bain-record/jYogmlKKuDbUXhejARvvQO/index.html.

27. Thomas Sowell, "Is Anti-Semitism Generic?" *Hoover Digest,* no. 3, (July 30, 2005). www.hoover.org/publications/hoover-digest/article/7727.

28. Hatim Tyabji and Vijay Sathe, "Venture Capital Firms in Europe Vs. America: The Under Performers," *Ivey Business Journal,* March/April 2011.

29. Daniel Henninger, "Bain Capital Saved America," *Wall Street Journal,* January 19, 2012, p. A13.

30. Michael Novak, *The Spirit of Democratic Capitalism*, p. 39.

31. John Locke, *An Essay Concerning Human Understanding* (A. Churchill, 1721), vol. 2, p. 318. http://books.google.com/books?id=TDMVAAAAQAAJ.

32. Michael Novak, *The Spirit of Democratic Capitalism,* p. 43.

33. Daniel Yergin, "Stepping on the Gas," *Wall Street Journal,* April 2, 2011. http://online.wsj.com/article/SB100014240527487037125045762325829900089002.html.

34. Edmund Phelps, "Economic Justice."

35. "School Bus," Wikipedia.org. http://en.wikipedia.org/wiki/School_bus#Industry_contraction_.281980-2005.29.

36. Ibid.

37. Ibid.

38. Nancy Bauder, "Seatbelts on School Buses," testimony presented to

the National Transportation Safety Board, 1994. http://www.ncsbs
.org/testimonies/testimony_nbauder.htm.

39. Alex Johnson, "Why Your Child's School Bus Has No Seat Belts,"
    MSNBC.com, December 29, 2010. http://www.msnbc.msn.com/
    id/40820669/ns/us_news-life/t/why-your-childs-school-bus-has-no
    -seat-belts/#.T4Ggob9GijE.

40. Robert Poole, "Air Traffic Control Reform Newsletter #86," Reason
    Foundation, August 30, 2011.

41. Walter Isaacson, *Steve Jobs* (New York: Simon & Schuster, 2011),
    pp. 398–402.

42. Alex Fitzsimmons, "Obama Blames High Unemployment on ATMs,
    Media Shrug Off Gaffe," MSNBC, June 15, 2011. Read more: http://news
    busters.org/blogs/alex-fitzsimmons/2011/06/15/obama-blames-high
    -unemployment-atms-media-shrug-gaffe#ixzz1kUUNGHvX.

43. Michael Strong and John Mackey, *Be the Solution* (New York: John
    Wiley and Sons, 2009), p. 60.

44. Wikipedia.org, "Codetermination in Germany." http://en.wikipedia
    .org/wiki/Codetermination_in_Germany.

45. Steve Forbes, "Are You There Banks? It's Me, Mike Mayo" (interview
    with Mike Mayo, managing director at Credit Agricole Securities),
    Forbes.com, February 15, 2012.

46. John Stossel, "The Real Cost of Regulation," speech delivered Febru-
    ary 20, 2001, at Hillsdale College in Fort Myers, Florida. http://www
    .hillsdale.edu/news/imprimis/archive/issue.asp?year=2001&month
    =05.

47. Joseph Pecar, "Socialism = Permanent 'Snowstorm' Shortages," Renew
    America.com, March 16, 2010. http://www.renewamerica.com/columns/
    pecar/100316.

48. Andrew Grossman, "After MTA Cuts, Altered Routines," WSJ.com,
    July 11, 2011. http://online.wsj.com/article/SB100014240527023035
    44604576434221173854468.html.

49. Ronald Bailey, "Government Pills," Reason.com, January 25, 2011.
    http://reason.com/archives/2011/01/25/government-pills.

50. Chelsea Conaboy, "Health Care Leaders Call Drug Shortages 'Threat'
    to Patients," *Boston Globe,* February 14, 2012. http://articles.boston
    .com/2012-02-14/metro/31054263_1_drug-shortages-drugs-in
    -short-supply-doxil/2.

51. John Goodman, "Death by Regulation," National Center for

Policy Analysis, June 20, 2011. http://healthblog.ncpa.org/death-by
-regulation/.

52. John Goodman, "Rx Drug Shortages: Regulation Can Be Deadly,"
Health Affairs Blog, June 8, 2011. http://healthaffairs.org/blog/
2011/06/08/rx-drug-shortages-regulation-can-be-deadly/.

53. Rob Stein, "Critics Slam Cost of FDA-Approved Drug to Prevent
Preterm Births," *Washington Post,* March 28, 2011. http://www
.washingtonpost.com/national/fda-approval-of-drug-to-prevent
-preemies-prompts-price-jump-from-10-to-1500/2011/03/04/
AFmRo6qB_story.html.

54. Ibid.

55. Peter Loftus, "K-V Pharma Slashes Price of Drug Amid Outcry," *Wall
Street Journal,* April 1, 2011. http://online.wsj.com/article/SB100014
24052748703806304576236980798831262.html.

56. Gillian Shaw, "Hello, This Is Your Chevy Volt, You Forgot to Plug Me In,
LOL," *Vancouver Sun,* April 2, 2011. http://www.canada.com/story
_print.html?id=6343c7d8-0fea-4f17-839f-6f9b7d5a48d1&sponsor=.

57. George Gilder, "California's Destructive Green Jobs Lobby," *Wall Street
Journal,* November 16, 2010. http://online.wsj.com/article/SB1000142
405274870330540457561040211698746.html.

58. Ibid.

Chapter 4: Paychecks *or* Food Stamps?

1. Nicholas Capaldi, "The Ethical Foundations of Free Market Societies," *Journal of Private Enterprise* 20, no. 1 (Fall 2011), p. 14.

2. William Beach and Patrick Tyrrell, "The 2012 Index of Dependence
on Government," Special Report #104, The Heritage Foundation,
February 8, 2012. http://www.heritage.org/research/reports/2012/
02/2012-index-of-dependence-on-government.

3. John Stossel, "Government Creates Poverty," Reason Foundation,
April 28, 2011. http://reason.com/archives/2011/04/28/government
-creates-poverty.

4. Daniel J. Mitchell, "Exaggerating Poverty for Political Gain," International Liberty (blog), July 19, 2011. http://danieljmitchell.wordpress
.com/2011/07/19/exaggerating-poverty-for-political-gain/.

5. Michael Janofsky, "Pessimism Retains Grip on Appalachian Poor,"
New York Times, February 9, 1998. http://www.nytimes.com/1998/

02/09/us/pessimism-retains-grip-on-appalachian-poor
.html?pagewanted=all.

6. Andrew Bernstein, "Black Innovators and Entrepreneurs Under
   Capitalism," *The Freeman* 51, no. 10 (October 2001). http://www
   .thefreemanonline.org/featured/black-innovators-and-entrepreneurs
   -under-capitalism/.

7. William Beach and Patrick Tyrrell, "The 2012 Index of Dependence
   on Government."

8. Paul Krugman, "Punishing the Jobless," *New York Times*, July 4, 2010.
   http://www.nytimes.com/2010/07/05/opinion/05krugman.html?
   _r=1.

9. Liz Alderman, "Why Denmark Is Shrinking Its Social Safety Net,"
   New York Times, August 16, 2010. http://economix.blogs.nytimes
   .com/2010/08/16/why-denmark-is-shrinking-its-social-safety-net/.

10. Ibid.

11. Ibid.

12. Donald L. Luskin and Lorcan Roche Kelly, "Europe's Supply-Side
    Revolution," *Wall Street Journal*, February 17, 2012, p. A13. http://
    online.wsj.com/article/SB10001424052970204792404577225301719346924.html.

13. Paul Roderick Gregory, "American Airlines Shows the Corruption of
    Obama's GM Bailout," Forbes.com, February 6, 2012. http://www
    .forbes.com/sites/paulroderickgregory/2012/02/06/american
    -airlines-shows-the-corruption-of-obamas-gm-bailout/.

14. Ibid.

15. Ibid.

16. Ibid.

17. Michael Janofsky, "Pessimism Retains Grip on Appalachian Poor."

18. "Investor, or Pauper or Merely a Front Man?" *Tampa Bay Times*,
    April 9, 2006. http://www.sptimes.com/2006/04/09/Hillsborough/
    Investor__or_pauper_o.shtml.

19. "The Average Cost of a College Education," *U.S. News & World Re-
    port*, August 24, 2010. http://www.usnews.com/opinion/articles/
    2010/08/24/the-average-cost-of-a-us-college-education.

20. Collin Eaton, "Student-Loan Default-Rate Climbs as Economy Fal-
    ters," *The Chronicle of Higher Education*, September 12, 2011. http://
    chronicle.com/article/Student-Loan-Default-Rate/128964/.

21. Marvin Olasky, *The Tragedy of American Compassion* (Washington,
    DC: Regnery Publishing, Inc., 1992), p. 103.

22. Ibid.
23. Ibid., p. 57.
24. Ibid., p. 221.
25. Ibid., p. 189.
26. Crocker Stephenson, "Foster Care Workers Feel Overworked, Unsupported, Study Finds," *Milwaukee-Wisconsin Journal Sentinel,* May 27, 2009. http://www.jsonline.com/news/milwaukee/46266767.html.
27. John Hagedorn, *Forsaking Our Children: Bureaucracy and Reform in the Child Welfare System* (Chicago: Lake View Press, 1995), p. 49.
28. Ryan Messmore, "Proposed Decrease in Charitable Tax Deduction Crowds Out Civil Society," Heritage Foundation, April 10, 2009. http://www.heritage.org/research/reports/2009/04/proposed -decrease-in-charitable-tax-deduction-crowds-out-civil-society.
29. John Tamny, "Political Class to Prudent Americans: 'Drop Dead!'" RealClearMarkets.com, February 14, 2012. http://www.realclear markets.com/articles/2012/02/14/the_political_class_to_prudent _americans_drop_dead_99515.html.
30. Jennifer Bleyer, "Hipsters on Food Stamps," Salon.com, March 15, 2010. http://www.salon.com/2010/03/16/hipsters_food_stamps_pinched/ singleton/#comments.
31. Ibid.
32. Howard Husock, "The Housing Reform That Backfired," *City Journal,* summer 2004. http://www.city-journal.org/html/14_3_housing _reform.html.
33. Rich Lowry, "A Nation of Julias," *National Review Online,* May 4, 2012. http://www.nationalreview.com/articles/298936/nation-julias -rich-lowry.
34. Dennis Prager, "The Welfare State and the Selfish Society," DennisPrager.com, April 26, 2011. http://www.dennisprager.com/ columns.aspx?g=b45d81c0-1cd6-4c8c-89bf-a4bc49d84269.
35. Evan Newmark, "Obama Won't Say It, But Americans Are Corrupted," *Wall Street Journal,* June 17, 2011. http://blogs.wsj.com/deals/2011/ 06/17/mean-street-obama-wont-say-it-but-americans-are-corrupted/.
36. "2008 Update on U.S. Tort Costs," Towers Perrin, 2008. http://www .towersperrin.com/tp/getwebcachedoc?webc=USA/2008/200811/ 2008_tort_costs_trends.pdf.
37. "Lawsuit Over Bathroom Mirror 2 Inches Too High," Facesof LawsuitAbuse.org, U.S. Chamber Institute for Legal Reform. http://

www.facesoflawsuitabuse.org/2009/03/lawsuit-over-bathroom
-mirror-2-inches-too-high/.

38. Kathianne Boniello, "White Castle Hates Fatty's Guts," *New York Post*,
September 11, 2011. http://www.nypost.com/p/news/white_castle
_hates_fatty_gut_UQk76R1S8Mbud5aMhaxD3J.

39. "Lawsuit Seeks $15K for Rose Thorn Prick," MyFoxOrlando.com,
May 27, 2011. http://www.myfoxorlando.com/dpp/news/seminole
_news/052611-lawsuit-seeks-15k-for-rose-thorn-prick.

40. Stephen Moore, "We've Become a Nation of Takers, Not Makers," *Wall
Street Journal*, April 1, 2011. http://online.wsj.com/article/SB1000142
4052748704050204576219073867182108.html.

41. Ibid.

42. Wikipedia, "History of Quebec (British conquest 1756–1760)."
http://en.wikipedia.org/wiki/History_of_Quebec; U.S. Bureau of
the Census, *A Century of Population Growth from the First Census of
the United States to the Twelfth, 1790–1900* (1909), p. 9. http://books
.google.com/books?id=H9KwtRkiO1YC&printsec=frontcover#v
=onepage&q&f=false.

43. Alexis de Tocqueville, trans. by Arthur Goldhammer, *Tocqueville:
Democracy in America* (New York: Library of America), February 9,
2004, p. 621.

44. Steven Malanga, "Whatever Happened to the Work Ethic?" *City
Journal* 19, no. 3 (Summer 2009). http://www.city-journal.org/2009/
19_3_work-ethic.html.

45. Benjamin Franklin, *The Way to Wealth* (1758). http://www
.swarthmore.edu/SocSci/bdorsey1/41docs/52-fra.html 39.

46. Ben Franklin Tercentenary. http://www.benfranklin300.org/exhibit
.htm.

47. Handwritten note from Thomas Edison to B. C. Forbes, 1920, Forbes
Collection.

48. John Stossel and Chris Kilmer, "The Middle Class Is Doing Just
Fine, Thank You," *ABC 20/20*, March 11, 2009. http://abcnews
.go.com/2020/Stossel/story?id=7055599&page=1#.T4Hbrr9GijE.

49. John Stossel, "Government Creates Poverty," Townhall.com, April
27, 2011. http://townhall.com/columnists/johnstossel/2011/04/27/
government_creates_poverty/page/full/.

50. Katherine Dempsey, "Dr. Benjamin Carson Speaks on Perseverance, Education and Morals on MLK Day," *Daily Northwestern*,

January 17, 2012. http://www.dailynorthwestern.com/campus/dr-benjamin-carson-speaks-on-perseverance-education-and-morals-on-mlk-day-1.2685849#.T4He9b9GijE; also recounted by Ben Carson, M.D., with Candy Carson in *America the Beautiful: Rediscovering What Made This Nation Great* (Grand Rapids, MI: Zondervan, 2012).

51. Fox News, "Trailblazing Doctor's Prescription to Solve Nation's Ills," Power Player of the W interview with Ben Carson, April 1, 2012. http://video.foxnews.com/v/1542093260001/trailblazing-doctors-prescription-to-solve-nations-ills.

52. Bill Gates, *The Road Ahead* (New York: Viking, 1995), p. 35.

53. Os Hillman, *The Upside of Adversity: Rising from the Pit to Greatness* (Ventura, CA: Regal Books, 2006), p. 102.

54. Tim Harford, "Failure: It's Everywhere," Freakonomics.com, May 10, 2011. http://www.freakonomics.com/2011/05/10/why-is-failure-a-sign-of-a-healthy-economy-a-guest-post-by-tim-harford/.

55. Clifford Thies, "Work and Housing for 19th Century Poor and Paupers," *Illinois Real Estate Letter* (Summer/Fall 1993), Office of Real Estate Research, University of Illinois at Urbana-Champaign, p. 13.

56. Sharon T. Ellens, "Relationship of Philanthropy to the Industrial Revolution," LearningToGive.org, Points of Light Institute. http://learningtogive.org/papers/paper54.html.

57. Gertrude Himmelfarb, "From Victorian Virtues to Modern Values," *Law and Order* (May/June 1995), The American Enterprise. http://www.abuddhistlibrary.com/Buddhism/F-%20Miscellaneous/General%20Miscellaneous/Modern%20Values/From%20Victorian%20Virtues%20to%20Modern%20Values/article_detail.asp.htm.

58. Jason DeParle, "Abolishment of Welfare: An Idea Becomes a Cause," *New York Times*, April 22, 1994. http://www.nytimes.com/1994/04/22/us/abolishment-of-welfare-an-idea-becomes-a-cause.html?pagewanted=all&src=pm.

59. Bill Clinton, "How We Ended Welfare, Together," *New York Times*, August 22, 2006. http://www.nytimes.com/2006/08/22/opinion/22clinton.html.

60. Richard Wolf, "How Welfare Reform Changed America," *USA Today*, July 18, 2006. http://www.usatoday.com/news/nation/2006-07-17-welfare-reform-cover_x.htm.

61. Ibid.

62. Helen E. Jung, "The 'Kye' a Key to Conflict," *Seattle Times,* December 27, 1992. http://community.seattletimes.nwsource.com/archive/?date=19921227&slug=1532125.

63. Donald B. Kraybill, *The Riddle of Amish Culture* (Baltimore, MD: Johns Hopkins University Press, 2001), p. 325.

CHAPTER 5: APPLE *or* SOLYNDRA?

1. Forrest McDonald, *Alexander Hamilton: A Biography* (New York: W.W. Norton & Co., 1979), p. 4.

2. Ron Chernow, *Titan: The Life of John D. Rockefeller, Sr.* (New York: Vintage, 1999), p. 418.

3. Forrest McDonald, *Alexander Hamilton,* p. 118.

4. Jack Weatherford, *The History of Money* (New York: Three Rivers Press, 1998).

5. Leonard Read, "I, Pencil: My Family Tree as Told to Leonard E. Read," Foundation for Economic Education, Inc. (1958); available online in the Library of Economics and Liberty, www.econlib.org/library/Essays/rdPncl1.html.

6. Thomas L. Friedman, "Just Doing It," *New York Times,* April 18, 2010, p. 10. http://www.nytimes.com/2010/04/18/opinion/18friedman.html.

7. Joshua Mitnick, "Tech Diplomacy: Israeli CEO Hires Palestinian Programmers," *Christian Science Monitor,* April 22, 2011. http://www.csmonitor.com/World/Middle-East/2011/0422/Tech-diplomacy-Israeli-CEO-hires-Palestinian-programmers; Karin Kloosterman and David Shamah, "Cooperation Between Israeli and Palestinian Companies Sets the Pace for Building Peace," Israel Ministry of Foreign Affairs, July 7, 2008. http://www.mfa.gov.il/MFA/Israel+beyond+politics/Cooperation%20between%20Israeli%20and%20Palestinian%20companies%20sets%20the%20pace%20for%20building%20peace%20%207-Jul-2008.

8. Luigi Zingales, "Who Killed Horatio Alger? The Decline of the Meritocratic Ideal," *City Journal* 21, no. 4 (Autumn, 2011). http://www.city-journal.org/2011/21_4_meritocracy.html.

9. Ibid.

10. Ibid.

11. Selim Algar and Bob Fredericks, "Occupy Wall Street Kitchen

Staff Protesting Fixing Food for Freeloaders," *New York Post,* October 27, 2011. http://www.nypost.com/p/news/local/manhattan/zuccotti_hell_kitchen_i5biNyYYhpa8MSYIL9xSDL.

12. Bryan Caplan, "The Reality of Meritocracy," Library of Economics and Liberty, February 11, 2010. http://econlog.econlib.org/archives/2010/02/the_reality_of_1.html.

13. Robert Rector, "How Poor Are America's Poor? Examining the 'Plague' of Poverty in America," Heritage Foundation, August 27, 2007. http://www.heritage.org/research/reports/2007/08/how-poor-are-americas-poor-examining-the-plague-of-poverty-in-america.

14. Fredrik Bergstrom and Robert Gidehag, "EU Versus USA," *Timbro,* June 2004, p. 21. http://www.timbro.se/bokhandel/pdf/9175665646.pdf..

15. Ibid., p. 22.

16. U.S. Treasury Department report, "Income Mobility in the U.S. from 1996 to 2005," November 13, 2007. http://www.treasury.gov/resource-center/tax-policy/Documents/incomemobilitystudy03-08revise.pdf.

17. Jack Weatherford, *The History of Money,* p. 68.

18. Wikipedia.org, "House of Medici," http://en.wikipedia.org/wiki/House_of_Medici.

19. BDNews24.com/Reuters,"China Communist Elder Issues Bold Call for Democracy," September 20, 2007. http://www.bdnews24.com/details.php?id=76542.

20. Clifford Krauss, "Canada Looks for Ways to Fix Its Health Care System," *New York Times,* September 12, 2004. http://www.nytimes.com/2004/09/12/international/americas/12canada.html?_r=2&pagewanted=print&position=.

21. U.S. Department of Health and Human Services, "Multi-Employer Plans: Approved Applications for Waiver of the Annual Limits Requirements, January 6, 2012," Center for Consumer Information and Insurance Oversight, http://cciio.cms.gov/.

22. Matthew Boyle, "Nearly 20 Percent of New Obamacare Waivers Are Gourmet Restaurants, Nightclubs, Fancy Hotels in Nancy Pelosi's District," The Daily Caller, May 17, 2011. http://dailycaller.com/2011/05/17/nearly-20-percent-of-new-obamacare-waivers-are-gourmet-restaurants-nightclubs-fancy-hotels-in-nancy-pelosi%E2%80%99s-district/.

23. Michael Barone, "Obama Skirts Rule of Law to Reward Pals, Punish

Enemies," Human Events, May 26, 2011. http://www.humanevents
.com/article.php?id=43727.

24. Paul Gregory, "Kleptocrats, Oligarchs, and Billionaire Entrepreneurs,"
What Paul Gregory Is Writing About blog, March 1, 2012. http://paul
gregorysblog.blogspot.com/2012/03/kleptocrats-oligarchs-and
-billionaire.html.

25. Ibid.

26. Peter Schweizer, *Throw Them All Out* (Orlando, FL: Houghton
Mifflin Harcourt, 2011), p. xvii.

27. Ibid., p. 51.

28. *The Telegraph,* "Al Gore Could Become the World's First Carbon
Billionare," November 3, 2009. http://www.telegraph.co.uk/earth/
energy/6491195/Al-Gore-could-become-worlds-first-carbon-billionaire
.html.

29. Peter Schweizer, *Throw Them All Out,* p. xvi.

30. Matthew Kaminski, "The New Tammany Hall," *Wall Street Journal,* November 26, 2011. http://online.wsj.com/article/SB1000142
405297020371620457701609254230760.html.

31. Jonah Goldberg, *Liberal Fascism: The Secret History of the American
Left, From Mussolini to the Politics of Meaning* (New York: Doubleday,
2008), p. 305.

32. Gretchen Morgenson and Joshua Rosner, *Reckless Endangerment:
How Outsized Ambition, Greed and Corruption Led to Economic Armageddon* (New York: Times Books, 2011), p. 1.

33. Ibid., p. 4.

34. Jerry McConnell, "Assigning Blame for Fannie and Freddie," *Canada
Free Press,* October 31, 2008. http://www.canadafreepress.com/index
.php/article/5949.

35. Gretchen Morgenson and Joshua Rosner, *Reckless Endangerment.*

36. Heather Haddon, "Players Behind Land Grab: How Shady Deal
Was Done," *New York Post,* July 3, 2011. http://www.nypost.com/
p/news/local/queens/players_behind_land_grab_kcVRcK0m1iDy
AttemKYR1N.

37. Press release, "Former Comptroller Alan Hevesi Sentenced to Up to
Four Years in Prison for Role in Pay-to-Play Pension Fund Kickback
Scheme," New York State Attorney General. http://www.ag.ny.gov/
media_center/2011/apr/apr15a_11.html.

38. Sharona Coutts, "California Firm Split Fees with Figure in N.Y. Pension Scandal," *Pro Publica,* April 22, 2009. http://www.propublica

.org/article/california-firm-split-fees-with-figure-in-ny-pension
-scandal-422.

39. William M. Isaac and Robert H. Smith, "Regulations Are Burying
Small Banks Alive," AmericanBanker.com, April 4, 2011. http://www
.americanbanker.com/bankthink/regulations-are-burying-small
-banks-alive-1035395-1.html?zkPrintable=true.

40. Daniel P. Dalton, "A History of Eminent Domain," *Public Corporation Law Quarterly*, Fall 2006, no. 3. http://www.michbar.org/
publiccorp/pdfs/fall06.pdf.

41. John Feinstein, "Hostile Takeover: How a Club with Deep Pockets
Fought Off a Claim of Eminent Domain," *Golf Digest,* November
2006. http://findarticles.com/p/articles/mi_m0HFI/is_11_57/ai_
n16832692/pg_4/.

42. Randall Smith, "Teed Off: When Caddyshack Meets Wall Street,"
Wall Street Journal, February 10, 2004.

43. D. T. Armentano, "A Politically Incorrect Guide to Antitrust Policy,"
Mises Daily, September 15, 2007. http://mises.org/daily/2694.

44. Lillian Cunningham, "Google's Eric Schmidt Expounds on His
Senate Testimony," *Washington Post,* October 1, 2011. http://www
.washingtonpost.com/national/on-leadership/googles-eric-schmidt
-expounds-on-his-senate-testimony/2011/09/30/gIQAPyVgCL
_story.html.

45. Bruce Chapman, "High Taxation Correlates with High Cronyism,"
Discovery News, May 14, 2011. http://www.discoverynews.org/2011/
05/high_taxes_correlates_with_hig046601.php.

46. Alberto Alesina and George-Marios Angeletos, "Fairness and Redistribution," December 2003 draft, p. 1. http://www.najecon.org/naj/
cache/122247000000000306.pdf.

47. Alan Beattie, "Argentina: The Superpower that Never Was," *Financial Times,* May 23, 2009. http://www.ft.com/intl/cms/s/2/778193e4
-44d8-11de-82d6-00144feabdc0.html#axzz1lHE0C24T.

48. Ibid.

49. Ibid.

50. Ibid.

51. Eliana Raszewski, "No One Cries for Argentina Embracing 25% Inflation of Fernandez," Bloomberg News, May 29, 2011. http://www
.bloomberg.com/news/2011-03-29/no-one-cries-for-argentina
-embracing-25-inflation-as-fernandez-leads-boom.html.

52. Dan Mitchell, "Greetings from Argentina—An Obamaesque Land of Crony Capitalism and a Warning to America," DanielJMitchell .wordpress.com, April 19, 2011. http://danieljmitchell.wordpress.com/ 2011/04/19/greetings-from-argentina-an-obamaesque-land-of-crony -capitalism-and-a-warning-to-america/.
53. Rich Karlgaard, "What Grows an Economy?," Forbes.com, October 20, 2010. http://www.forbes.com/sites/richkarlgaard/2010/10/20/what -grows-an-economy/.

CHAPTER 6: THE SPIRIT OF REAGAN *or* OBAMA?

1. Elizabeth Mendes, "In U.S., Optimism About Future for Youth Reaches All-Time Low," Gallup.com, May 2, 2011. http://www .gallup.com/poll/147350/optimism-future-youth-reaches-time-low .aspx.
2. Joel Bakan, "The Kids Are Not All Right," *New York Times*, August 21, 2011. http://www.nytimes.com/2011/08/22/opinion/corporate-interests -threaten-childrens-welfare.html.
3. Ibid.
4. "The Top 10 Unfounded Health Scares of 2008," ACSH.org, American Council on Science and Health, December 23, 2008. http:// www.acsh.org/publications/pubID.1751/pub_detail.asp.
5. Chris Faulkner, "Shale Reserves Mean Security for U.S. and Its Oil and Gas Industry," *U.S. News & World Report*, November 29, 2011. http://www.usnews.com/debate-club/is-fracking-a-good-idea/shale -reserves-mean-security-for-us-and-its-oil-and-gas-industry.
6. "A Tale of Two Shale States," *Wall Street Journal*, July 26, 2011. http://online.wsj.com/article/SB10001424052702303678704576442053700739990.html.
7. Bob Herbert, "Nightmare Before Christmas," *New York Times*, December 22, 2007. http://www.nytimes.com/2007/12/22/opinion/ 22herbert.html.
8. Donald Boudreaux, letter, *New York Times*, December 25, 2007. http:// query.nytimes.com/gst/fullpage.html?res=9C04E3D71630F936A 15751C1A9619C8B63.
9. Bryan Caplan, *The Myth of the Rational Voter* (Princeton, NJ: Princeton University Press, 2007), p. 45.
10. Ibid., p. 44.

11. Arthur Herman, *The Idea of Decline in Western History* (New York: Simon & Schuster, 1997).

12. Donald J. Boudreaux, "Interpreting the State of the World," *The Freeman* 58, no. 5 (June 2008). http://www.thefreemanonline.org/columns/thoughts-on-freedom-interpreting-the-state-of-the-world/.

13. Quoted in Rea Hederman Jr., "Two Americas: One Rich, One Poor?" Heritage Foundation, August 24, 2004. http://www.heritage.org/research/reports/2004/08/two-americas-one-rich-one-poor-understanding-income-inequality-in-the-united-states.

14. Barack Obama, "Address by the President to a Joint Session of Congress," United States Capitol, Washington, D.C., September 8, 2011. http://www.whitehouse.gov/the-press-office/2011/09/08/address-president-joint-session-congress.

15. Ludwig von Mises, *Theory and History* (New Haven, CT: Yale University Press, 1957), p. 115.

16. Ibid., p. 118.

17. "Every Man a King," Huey Long radio address, NBC, February 23, 1934. http://www.hueylong.com/programs/share-our-wealth-speech.php.

18. Huey Long, *Every Man a King: The Autobiography of Huey P. Long* (New Orleans, LA: National Book Co., 1933), p. 291.

19. Thomas Sowell, *Dismantling America: And Other Controversial Essays* (New York: Basic Books, 2010), p. 151.

20. Ibid.

21. Milton Friedman, interview by Phil Donahue, *The Phil Donahue Show*, 1979.

22. Richard Wilkinson, "Why Inequality Is Bad for You—and Everyone Else," CNN.com, November 6, 2011. http://www.cnn.com/2011/11/06/opinion/wilkinson-inequality-harm/index.html.

23. Bruce Yandle, "Lost Trust: The Real Cause of the Financial Meltdown," *The Independent Review* 14, no. 3 (Winter 2010), p. 345. http://www.independent.org/pdf/tir/tir_14_03_02_yandle.pdf.

24. Michael Lewis, "Beware of Greeks Bearing Bonds," *Vanity Fair*, October 1, 2010. http://www.vanityfair.com/business/features/2010/10/greeks-bearing-bonds-201010.

25. Francis Fukuyama, "Social Capital and the Global Economy," *Foreign Affairs* 74, no. 5 (September/October 1995), p. 103. http://www.foreignaffairs.com/issues/1995/74/5.

26. George Gilder, *Wealth and Poverty* (San Francisco, CA: ICS Press, 1993).
27. David Brooks, "The Nation of Futurity," *New York Times*, November 16, 2009. http://www.nytimes.com/2009/11/17/opinion/17brooks .html.
28. Rodney Stark, introduction to *The Victory of Reason: How Christianity Led to Freedom, Capitalism, and Western Success* (New York: Random House, 2005), p. ix.
29. Rodney Stark, "How Christianity Led to Freedom, Capitalism, and the Success of the West," *Chronicle of Higher Education* 52, no. 15 (December 2005). http://www.independent.org/newsroom/article .asp?id=1809.
30. Bernard Baruch, "Why I Still Have Faith in the Future," reprinted in the *Tampa Bay Times*, November 25, 2010. http://www.tampabay .com/opinion/columns/why-i-still-have-faith-in-the-future/1136190.
31. Barack Obama, "2012 State of the Union Address," United States Capitol, Washington, D.C., January 25, 2011. http://www.nytimes .com/interactive/2012/01/24/us/politics/state-of-the-union-2012 -video-transcript.html.
32. Francis Fukuyama, "Social Capital and Civil Society," prepared for delivery at the IMF Conference on Second Generation Reforms, October 1, 1999. http://www.imf.org/external/pubs/ft/seminar/1999/ reforms/fukuyama.htm#figI.
33. Leonard Read, "I, Pencil: My Family Tree as Told to Leonard E. Read" (Irvington, NY: Foundation for Economic Education, 1999), retrieved from http://www.econlib.org/library/Essays/rdPnclCover .html.
34. Joseph Henrich et al., "Markets, Religion, Community Size, and the Evolution of Fairness and Punishment," *Science* 327 (March 19, 2010), p. 1,484.
35. Michael W. Macy and Yoshimichi Sato, "Trust, Cooperation, and Market Formation in the U.S. and Japan," *Proceedings of the National Academy of Sciences* 99, suppl. 3 (May 14, 2002), p. 7,214.
36. Barack Obama, "2009 Inaugural Address," United States Capitol, Washington, D.C., January 20, 2009. http://www.nytimes.com/2009/ 01/20/us/politics/20text-obama.html?pagewanted=all.
37. Ibid.
38. Ibid.

39. Ronald Reagan, "1981 Inaugural Address," United States Capitol, Washington, D.C., January 20, 1981. http://www.reagan.utexas.edu/archives/speeches/1981/12081a.htm.
40. Ibid.
41. Ibid.
42. Ibid.

Acknowledgments

THE AUTHORS wish to thank the following people for their support and encouragement.

Larry Kirshbaum's skilled representation and insights helped make this book possible. At Crown, John Mahaney's editorial vision and guidance during our second collaboration once again proved invaluable. We would also like to express our appreciation to Sean Desmond, who shepherded this project during its final phases, and to Mauro DiPreta for his patient understanding. Thanks also to Logan Balestrino and Stephanie Knapp for their efforts on our behalf. Our deepest gratitude to our excellent researchers: Nichole Hungerford for her enthusiasm and diligence, as well as Lamont Wood and Ryan Mauro. Susan Radlauer, Elizabeth Gravitt, and Scott Bistay have at numerous times handled requests for material. Jacob Laksin, Eric Odom, Mark Chapman, and Marjorie Schulman additionally provided helpful information, recommendations, and suggestions. Once again we are grateful to Audrey Wecera for her meticulousness in helping to prepare this manuscript during its various phases.

We owe a debt of gratitude to the many individuals and organizations whose ideas and research helped shape this book. George Gilder, Michael Novak, and Rich Karlgaard have powerfully articulated the moral foundation of capitalism. John Tamny and Amity Shlaes have also done much to promote today's growing appreciation of importance of a free economy. The op-ed channel for Forbes.com, which John edits, has become a critical outlet for numerous free market contributors. Many appear in this book. We would also like to thank the *Wall Street Journal*'s editorial page, whose powerful voice has played such a crucial role in the fight for free markets and free people. *Investor's Business Daily* has also consistently taken up the cudgels for the cause of capitalism. Special appreciation to Mark Skousen, founder and producer of Freedom Fest and Mallory Factor, cofounder of The Monday Meeting, for providing vital forums for many of the ideas found in this book. We are also grateful to Tom Donohue and Margaret Spellings at the U.S. Chamber of Commerce for their especially energetic support and courageous efforts as champions of free enterprise.

This book could not have been written without vital analyses from The Heritage Foundation, the Cato Institute, the American Enterprise Institute, the Manhattan Institute, the Foundation for Economic Education, the National Center for Policy Analysis, the Pacific Research Institute, the Competitive Enterprise Institute, the Reason Foundation, and the Ludwig von Mises Institute.

Steve is very grateful to Jackie DeMaria and Maureen Murray for providing assistance on this project as they have on so many others. He is thankful for Merrill Vaughan's essential help on his *Forbes* editorials. They have given rise to many of the ideas in these pages. Steve would also like to acknowledge Lewis D'Vorkin, Forbes Media's chief product officer, who each day inspires with his creativity and entrepreneurship. He is deeply appreciative to Bill Dal Col for his ever-valuable advice and counsel. And we wish to thank our families for their patience and understanding. Without them, very little is possible.

Index

About the Authors

STEVE FORBES is chairman and editor in chief of Forbes Media and an internationally respected authority in the worlds of economics, finance, and corporate leadership. He campaigned twice for the Republican nomination for the presidency. His prior books include the *Wall Street Journal* bestseller *How Capitalism Will Save Us*, the *New York Times* bestseller *Power Ambition Glory*, *Flat Tax Revolution*, and *A New Birth of Freedom*.

ELIZABETH AMES coauthored *How Capitalism Will Save Us* with Steve Forbes. She is the founder of BOLDE Communications, which advises corporate and individual clients on communications strategies. Her journalism and commentary have appeared in a wide range of publications.